Regulating Obesity?

Regulating Obesity?

GOVERNMENT, SOCIETY, AND
QUESTIONS OF HEALTH

W. A. Bogart

OXFORD
UNIVERSITY PRESS

OXFORD
UNIVERSITY PRESS

Oxford University Press is a department of the University of Oxford. It furthers the University's objective of excellence in research, scholarship, and education by publishing worldwide.

Oxford New York
Auckland Cape Town Dar es Salaam Hong Kong Karachi Kuala Lumpur Madrid
Melbourne Mexico City Nairobi New Delhi Shanghai Taipei Toronto

With offices in
Argentina Austria Brazil Chile Czech Republic France Greece Guatemala Hungary
Italy Japan Poland Portugal Singapore South Korea Switzerland Thailand
Turkey Ukraine Vietnam

Oxford is a registered trade mark of Oxford University Press in the UK and certain other countries.

Published in the United States of America by
Oxford University Press
198 Madison Avenue, New York, NY 10016

© Oxford University Press 2013

All rights reserved. No part of this publication may be reproduced, stored in a retrieval system, or transmitted, in any form or by any means, without the prior permission in writing of Oxford University Press, or as expressly permitted by law, by license, or under terms agreed with the appropriate reproduction rights organization. Inquiries concerning reproduction outside the scope of the above should be sent to the Rights Department, Oxford University Press, at the address above.

You must not circulate this work in any other form
and you must impose this same condition on any acquirer.

_____

Library of Congress Cataloging-in-Publication Data
Bogart, W. A. (William A.)
Regulating obesity? : government, society, and questions of health / W. A. Bogart.
pages cm
Includes bibliographical references and index.
ISBN 978-0-19-985620-6 ((hardback) : alk. paper)
1. Public health laws. 2. Discrimination against overweight persons—Law and legislation
3. Obesity—Government policy. 4. Overweight persons—Legal status, laws, etc.
5. Food law and legislation. I. Title.
344.03'2196398—dc23   2013011130
_____

Note to Readers

This publication is designed to provide accurate and authoritative information in regard to the subject matter covered. It is based upon sources believed to be accurate and reliable and is intended to be current as of the time it was written. It is sold with the understanding that the publisher is not engaged in rendering legal, accounting, or other professional services. If legal advice or other expert assistance is required, the services of a competent professional person should be sought. Also, to confirm that the information has not been affected or changed by recent developments, traditional legal research techniques should be used, including checking primary sources where appropriate.

(Based on the Declaration of Principles jointly adopted by a Committee of the
American Bar Association and a Committee of Publishers and Associations.)

You may order this or any other Oxford University Press publication
by visiting the Oxford University Press website at www.oup.com.

To kids—our greatest resource

"They send forth their little ones like a flock, and their children dance"
Job 21:11

{ CONTENTS }

Acknowledgments — xi

Introduction — xiii

PART I **Obesity and the Regulation of Consumption**

1. Regulating Consumption: Many Efforts—With What Effects? — 3
    I. Introduction 3
   II. The Regulatory Mix 5
  III. How Effective Is Regulation? 6
       A) Introduction 6
       B) Assessing Impact: Three Kinds of Effects 7
       C) Legal Interventions to Promote Health 10
  IV. Consumption Encounters Law: *Permit But Discourage* 13
   V. Some Ideas About Law Shaping Behavior 19
       A) Looking at the State in a Different Way: New Governance 19
       B) Ideas for New Governance: Normativity and Its Offspring 21
       C) New Governance, Normativity, and the Regulation of Consumption 26
  VI. Conclusion 28

PART II **Being Fat**

2. How Is Obesity a Problem? — 31
    I. Introduction 31
   II. What's the Problem?: Encountering Corpulence 32
  III. Obesity: A Public Health Issue? 35
       A) Increase in Weight 35
          1. Genes, Metabolism, and Antibiotics 36
          2. Chemicals: Obesogens 37
          3. Race and Ethnicity 38
          4. The Environment 38
             i. Food and Drink 38
             ii. Built Communities 39
             iii. Social Contagion 39
          5. Technology 40
          6. Depression 40
          7. Socioeconomic Status 41
       B) Consequences 42
          1. Physical Aspects 42

  2. Psychological Aspects 42
  3. Costs to Society 42
 IV. Is Being Fat Like Being Short? 43
  A) Introduction 43
  B) The Rates of Obesity Are Exaggerated 44
  C) The Physical Health Problems Related to Obesity Are Misrepresented 46
  D) Weight Loss?: What Is Shed Is Almost Always Regained 48
  E) Stigma, Shame, and Fat 49
   1. Panics, Good Norms, and Consumption 50
   2. "The Greatest Threat": Stigma, Discrimination, and the Obese 53
   3. Responses 58
    i. Fight Stigma—Battle Weight 58
    ii. Weight Is Not the Problem—It's Society That Has Issues 59
    iii. Health at Every Size (HAES) 61
 V. The Heavy Hand of The State? 63
 VI. Conclusion 69

3. Appearance Bias–Fat Rights 70
 I. Introduction 70
 II. Discrimination and Human Rights Laws 71
 III. Appearance Bias: "What is Beautiful is Good" 74
 IV. "Good Clean Wholesome Female Sexuality" and other Examples of Appearance Bias 77
 V. Resisting the Prejudice of Looks: Justifications for Invoking Law 81
 VI. Banning Appearance Bias? 85
  A) Prohibiting Prejudice against Looks 85
  B) Complexities of Banning Weight Discrimination 87
 VII. The Impact of Laws Banning Appearance Bias 90
  A) Laws against Bias, Laws Promoting Healthy Eating/Drinking and Physical Activity 90
  B) Round Up the Fat Kids! 92
 VIII. Conclusion 93

PART III Healthy Consumption, Active Living, and the Regulatory State

4. Assessing Interventions 97
 I. Introduction 97
 II. Goals of Interventions 98
 III. Perspectives on Assessment 101
 IV. Evidentiary Basis for Interventions 102
 V. What's Being Assessed? 105
 VI. Noted but not Examined 106
  A) Drugs 106
  B) Weight Loss–Diet Industry 108
  C) Bariatric Surgery 109
  D) Litigation 112
 VII. Conclusion 116

5. Just the Facts?: Educating, Mandating Information, Controlling Advertising, Restricting Marketing to Children — 117
- I. Introduction 117
- II. The Power of Advertising 119
- III. Truth in Calories: Mandatory Menu and Package Labeling 123
  - *A) Educating about Nutritious Eating and Drinking 123*
  - *B) Caloric Disclosure on Menus 126*
  - *C) Front of Package Labeling 128*
  - *D) Conclusions 130*
- IV. Marketing: The Special Case of Children 131
  - *A) Effects of Advertising 131*
  - *B) Attempts to Regulate Marketing to Children 133*
    1. Self-Regulation 133
    2. Legislative Initiatives 135
       - i. No Tax Deductions and No Toys 135
       - ii. Restricting Advertising 137
         - [one] Generally 137
         - [two] Quebec 137
           - A. The Experiment and Its Constitutional Validity 137
           - B. The Impact of the Ban 139
    3. The Challenges of the Internet and Digital Media 140
       - i. Untameable Cyberspace? 140
       - ii. Children and Advergames 142
       - iii. Conclusions 143
- V. Conclusion 144

6. Fiscal Interventions: Fat Taxes and Subsidies — 146
- I. Introduction 146
- II. Taxes and Consumption 147
  - *A) Policy Arguments 147*
  - *B) Lessons from Tobacco and Alcohol 149*
- III. Junk Food and Beverage Taxes 152
  - *A) Particular Policy Arguments 152*
  - *B) General Assessments 154*
  - *C) Experiments with SSBs (Sugar-Sweetened Beverages) 156*
    1. Why SSBs? 156
    2. Fifty Calories a Day? 157
- IV. Subsidies 160
  - *A) Introduction: The General and the Specific 160*
  - *B) Subsidies and Agricultural Policy 161*
    1. Subsidies and Obesity? 161
    2. Changing Farm Policies to Promote Healthy Eating and Drinking 164
  - *C) Targeted Subsidies through Government Support Programs 167*
    1. Poverty and the New Malnutrition 167
    2. Ban Candy—Promote Carrots: Can Government Nutrition Programs for the Poor Improve Diets? 168
    3. Soda and the City: Bloomberg's Bans #1 and #2 171

4. Promotions Piloted   173
5. Dollars, Consumption, and Norms   175
V. Conclusion   176

7. Encouraging Physical Activity: Children at Play!   178
I. Introduction   178
II. The Sedentary We: Lifestyles of The Physically Inactive   179
III. Promoting Active Lifestyles: The Range of Interventions   182
IV. While They're Young: Law's Role from The Start   183
V. Playgrounds, Schoolyards, Games, and Sports   184
   A) General Considerations: The Built Environment   184
   B) Activity and Children   188
   1. Introduction   188
   2. The First Years and Parenting   189
   3. Professional Childcare Providers   190
   4. School-Age Kids   192
      i. In Class   192
         [one] General Discussion   192
         [two] U.S. Federal and State Law   192
         [three] Measuring BMI?   194
      ii. Out of Class   197
   5. Vouchers to the Rescue?: The Canadian Children's Fitness Tax Credit   200
      i. New Governance and Vouchers   200
      ii. Vouchers as the Solution?: HLVs   201
      iii. CFTC   204
         [one] A Voucher to Get Kids Moving   204
         [two] Impact   205
         [three] More of a Good Thing   206
VI. Conclusion   207

Conclusion: Not Fat But Health—and Health Equity   209

Index   215

{ ACKNOWLEDGMENTS }

A good many people helped this book along the way, though, of course, I alone am responsible for its shortcomings.

Jennifer Gong of Oxford University Press has been an enthusiastic supporter of the book since she began to work on it. I received some very helpful comments from anonymous reviewers of the proposal, which helped get the book off to a very good start.

I would like to thank all my research assistants who have so steadfastly supported the book as it trudged along: Teri Liu, Christina Frederico, Serena Genova, Tiziana Serpa, and Michael Lippa. My administrative assistant Annette Pratt performed a multitude of tasks that moved the project along.

Many friends and colleagues discussed or read parts of or suggested sources for *Regulating Obesity?*: Sarah Atkinson, Julian Alston, Reem Bahdi, Lane Bass, Jeff Berryman, Emily Carasco, Fred Dean, Donna Eansor, Scott Fairley, Eric Gertner, Leslie Howsam, Jasminka Kalajdzic, Anna Kirkland, Ian MacKenzie, Marion Nestle, Eden Oliver, Karyn O'Neil, Susan Peterson, Suzanne Pred Bass, Gabrielle and Greg Richards, Ken Russell, Sharon and Billy Sammon, Elisabeth Scarff, Arya Sharma, John Sinclair, Jang Singh, Jean Cumming, David Sisam, Anneke Smit, Barbara von Tigerstrom, Christopher Waters, and Gerri Wong. Bruce Elman was extremely supportive of this book throughout his deanship and beyond. Research funding, gratefully acknowledged, was provided by the Ontario Law Foundation, Block Grant to the Faculty of Law, the University of Windsor, and the University of Windsor Research Grant Program.

I discussed the ideas in *Regulating Obesity?* in several places: in a seminar for lawyers of the Ministry of the Attorney General of Ontario; at "Rounds" Center for Addiction and Mental Health (CAMH), Toronto; as the Keynote Address to "Working towards Wellness" Conference, Windsor-Essex Health Unit, Windsor; as a commentator, Viscount Bennett Lecture, Justice Tom Cromwell, Supreme Court of Canada, Fredericton; in a paper for the National Law and Health Conference, Toronto; and in a paper for a meeting on "Indignation: Socio-economic Inequality and the Role of Law," held in Onati, Spain, May 2013, and which will be published in the *Onati Socio-Legal Series* Journal (http://opo.iisj.net). I thank all participants in those various meetings for their thoughtful reactions. Parts of Chapters 2, 3, 5, 6, and the Conclusion appear in an earlier form in the *Journal of Law, Medicine and Ethics*, Volume 41, no. 1, Spring 2013 and in the paper for the *Onati Journal*.

Finally, I want to thank my wife (and editor) Linda Bertoldi and my daughter (and editor) Abby Bogart. They have given me so much inspiration and support for all my books, and very much for this one.

***

As I finished *Regulating Obesity?* my thoughts were of the country. The snow, the frozen lake, and the stillness provided timeless reassurance. A source of well-being in a world filled with so many challenges to health.

W. A. Bogart
"Raspberries" Lake Kawagama
February 2013

{ INTRODUCTION }

This book is not about the regulation of obesity. The title was chosen not to mislead but to emphasize unrealistic beliefs about law and its role in addressing a complex array of issues concerning healthy eating and drinking and physical exercise. Law does have a part to play regarding these issues but it is a complicated one, the effects of which are not as straightforward or as powerful as either advocates or opponents might suggest.

We can't regulate obesity any more than we can alcoholism or drug addiction. Individuals engage in behaviors for complex reasons that lead to these various conditions. What we can do is regulate a variety of circumstances, using a range of legal interventions, in an effort to discourage harmful behaviors: intemperate use of alcohol, substance abuse, or unhealthy eating/drinking and inactive lifestyles. *How to regulate* and *with what effects* in any given situation, are big questions that are explored in these pages regarding issues of weight and of health.

Regulating Obesity? is not a work of advocacy, though the need for effective, properly directed regulation in this area is compelling. Instead, the book's starting point is a curiosity about the actual effects of law in shaping behavior and the complexities of establishing those outcomes. Law influences human action even as law is created, functions in, and is bounded by civic societies. Law does produce consequences but ascertaining what they often are gives rise to more questions than answers. Yet such complexities should only heighten our curiosity about the outcomes resulting from various forms of regulation in many different areas of human activity.

Before proceeding: a word about terminology. "Obese" is the term that has been used traditionally by health professionals and others to describe those who are significantly overweight. In contrast "fat" is employed by those who, more recently, are critiquing conventional understandings of the causes and consequences of individuals being large. These debates regarding how and the extent to which weight is an individual and societal problem are ribboned throughout the book. These pages use both terms, fat/obese, as appears appropriate, as a reflection of such controversies.

Obesity attracts much attention. The media is filled with stories often couched in terms of an "epidemic," "crisis," "panic," etc. Statistics are said to demonstrate that obesity has increased at alarming rates over the last several decades. Any number of diseases and ailments are said to be associated with significant weight gain. Ads are being run depicting fat children and warning them and their parents about the dismal life they will lead if they don't lose weight (Chapter 2).

Pharmaceutical companies offer pills, doctors are performing surgery—and on ever-younger patients—designed to alter bodies so that they just won't eat so much, the weight loss industry has innumerable diets and exercise programs that proffer wondrous responses to shed pounds and tone bodies. At the same time policy makers, stalwarts in the war against obesity, are devising a range of strategies, many with legal implications, designed to combat a culture of corpulence. Meanwhile, in the larger society, censorious messages are delivered to fat people to change their greedy, lazy, indulgent ways (Chapter 3).

There are several problems with weight loss as the goal. A main one is that it is, in many instances, unachievable. Most overweight people cannot shed pounds. Those that do cannot maintain the loss for a significant period of time. It may be that strategies can be developed to increase the success rate of weight loss efforts. But, for now, constructing the world, including the legal one, as if permanent weight loss is a realistic option often does much harm (Chapter 2).

Yet the response is not necessarily to throw up our hands and do nothing. Instead, policy makers could pay heed to a growing group of voices that urge that weight (and weight loss) be largely moved to the sidelines. Instead, the emphasis could be placed on the promotion of healthy eating/drinking and active physical lifestyles. At first glance, a reader might ask: aren't the goals of weight loss and of healthy eating/drinking and physical activity essentially one and the same? Don't people have to eat/drink well and exercise to lose weight? There is overlap between goals. The essential difference is that the former fixes on loss of pounds as the end point. The latter sets its sights on nutritious eating/drinking and physical activity as goals, in themselves, with weight loss, should it occur, as an incidental outcome. What is more, this latter approach encourages acceptance of the basic truth that people come in a variety of shapes. "One size fits all" is an ill-suited slogan for many situations. It surely misses the mark when it comes to human bodies (Chapter 3).

What would be the benefits of underscoring healthy eating/drinking and active lifestyles? First, it puts the emphasis where it belongs right from the start of human lives. Losing weight and keeping it off is extraordinarily difficult. There may be more hope in prevention: not gaining excess weight in the first place. The best chance for young people is, from the beginning, to equip them with habits of sound eating/drinking and lots of movement in play, sports, and bicycling, running, and walking in the outdoors. Whatever their weight, children who eat/drink nutritiously and who are active are more likely to be healthy kids and, then, adults (Chapter 7).

Second, this approach could result in healthier lives. Some obese people may have illnesses that are associated, directly, with significant excess weight. However, the health of many fat people would improve if they eat/drink better and were more active even if they do not lose weight. At the same time it is a fallacy to assume that if one is slim, one is necessarily fit. There are individuals who because of genetic makeup or other reasons are able to indulge in food/drink of dubious nutritional value and to be sedentary and, yet, to be thin. They could also be unhealthy by a number of measures. An approach that focuses on good consumption and active lifestyles and does not privilege thinness is more likely to deliver the right message to all individuals (Chapter 3).

Third, it paves the way for much-needed changes in norms related to body size. There is a great deal of discrimination against fat people. The obese are subject to such stigma that some suggest that the pressures these negative attitudes exert on fat people are themselves, at least partially, the cause of health problems that those who are significantly overweight can suffer. Conversely, norms that promote healthy eating/drinking and physical activity can encourage people to care about their bodies but also to accept theirs and others without regard to some fantasized ideal regarding shape and size (Chapter 3).

Fourth, it better directs evaluations of interventions, especially legal ones, in terms of assessing "effectiveness." Many such interventions are questioned because it cannot be established that they contribute to weight loss. Yet, even if individuals do not lose weight they may eat/drink better or be more active or both as a result of any such intervention. This is not to suggest that all such interventions are successful using these criteria. It is to emphasize, again, how obsession with weight may be misdirecting otherwise appropriate strategies (Chapter 4).

Fifth, it underscores the need for more public resources to promote health. Eating well and being physically active impose costs both on individuals and on society. Fresh fruits and vegetables are usually more expensive than soft drinks, fries, and burgers. Walking requires sidewalks and trails; cycling needs bike paths; sports call for equipment and athletic memberships. The extent to which any costs should be borne by individuals, on the one hand, and societies, on the other, raises critical questions about distribution and use of public and private resources. That said, more public funds will have to be available if we are to have a more fit, better-fed society (Chapter 4). If adequate financial support is not forthcoming many interventions cannot be effective.

Regulating Obesity? supports promoting healthy eating/drinking and physical activity as goals to be achieved in assessing various legal interventions. At the same time two overarching points emerge in such evaluations. First, the outcomes produced by law are complex. Effects are often not as straightforward and sometimes not nearly as effective as advocates of such interventions might hope. Establishing precisely what the impact of such laws is, itself, frequently a challenge for a number of reasons, including issues of causation and of unintended consequences (Chapter 1).

Second, these complexities concerning the effects of law promote inquiries about the relationship of law to larger social forces. In attempting to intervene in almost any area policy makers have a range of legal strategies available to them. Which ones to employ and in what combination—"mix"—are questions that, themselves, give rise to many other questions. In examining issues concerning the "regulatory mix" we'll take a look at some ideas about how to get effective results with less of the heavy hand of the state: the "new governance" (Chapter 1).

Beyond issues of the "regulatory mix" are those regarding how to achieve more effectiveness in attaining the policy goals being pursued. There are a number of such ideas but one that seems to hold particular promise in terms of consumption, generally, and issues of eating/drinking and exercise is "normativity": the relationship between law and norms. "Normativity" appears especially suited to issues relating to consumption because the everyday expression of appetites is surrounded by a variety of norms, many of which have a forceful hold on behavior. Think of unspoken rules forbidding a smoker to light up in another's home absent very clear consent. Consider the horror expressed at the idea of adults aiding and abetting underage drinking, especially if driving is involved. Or imagine the approval/envy expressed at an in-shape body confirming a three-times-a-week commitment to the gym. Yet just because consumption is encased in a multitude of norms does not mean that they necessarily produce the contemplated effect. Smoking may be frowned upon, but a significant percentage of the population still lights up. Multigrains and fresh fruit are praised even as a lot of chocolate bars and French fries are gobbled up. (Chapter 1).

Regulating Obesity? argues that the best hope of law playing an effective role lies in a codependence between appropriately targeted interventions and norms that promote healthy eating/drinking and exercise and acceptance of a variety of body shapes. Achieving such mutual reinforcement is no easy task. An idea of the challenges can be conveyed by focusing for a moment on "appropriately targeted interventions" and the relationship between law and norms (Chapter 1).

What constitutes an appropriately targeted intervention can be hugely controversial. There are a number of reasons for these debates. First, there is the general skepticism, particularly in the United States, about almost any form of regulation that interferes with market forces. Second, the food-and-drink industry is powerful and able to mount formidable challenges to any laws that it views as inimical to its interests.

Third, as discussed earlier, those focused on the interests of overweight people are, themselves, deeply divided. Some, concentrating on obesity as a medical condition and on weight loss, assess every legal intervention, actual or potential, in terms of its effectiveness in having individuals shed pounds. Others view body shape as something that can be altered, if at all, only with great difficulty. They believe that the major issue that should be addressed by law is the protection through antidiscrimination legislation of fat people from bias and oppression. Still others believe that there is a role for law in promoting healthy eating/drinking and exercise. If this focus prevents weight gain or results in weight loss, so much the better. Proponents of this view usually also support antidiscrimination protection for fat people but want these human rights laws to exist in conjunction with other interventions aimed at bolstering nutritious eating/drinking and physical activity (Chapter 3).

How to alter norms to boost any interventions and, in turn, to be supported by such strategies also gives rise to much debate. Hardly anyone suggests that the interaction between law and norms—"normativity"—is not important. The controversy begins with attempts to define that relationship. Traditional views of law have mostly treated norms as uninteresting givens: something to acknowledge as having some important yet indeterminate connection with law before quickly proceeding to the tough task of legal policy formulation. In contrast, those with high hopes for "normativity" claim that sound legal intervention must take account of, as clearly as possible, the effect of relevant norms in formulating various aspects of the "regulatory mix": "The desirability of a proposed legal rule ... does not depend only on ... competently operated legal institutions ... It also depends on the way nonlegal systems ... already address ... [the] problem and the extent to which legal intervention would interfere with those nonlegal systems"[1] (Chapter 1).

In terms of obesity there are two challenges for normativity: combating negative attitudes and actions toward fat people and promoting norms regarding healthy eating/drinking and physical exercise. Regarding the former, *Regulating Obesity?* situates protection of fat people in the larger terrain of appearance bias. The book discusses a variety of legal and other strategies to protect individuals from appearance bias and to develop more positive attitudes toward a wide variety of differences in looks. Regarding the promotion of desirable norms, the book suggests that shifting the emphasis away from weight is a fundamental place to start. Once that is done there is a much greater chance for mutually supporting laws and norms to develop. A number of concrete examples of this codependence are discussed, including what not to do (measuring students' BMI, Chapter 7) and what to do (well-designed subsidies of healthy foods, Chapter 6).

Regulating Obesity? illustrates the many challenges and controversy surrounding issues of weight by discussing in detail three sets of interventions: regulation of marketing, fiscal policy, and change to the built environment. There is overlap among the three strategies, but the first two focus on healthy eating/drinking and the last centers on exercise. The analysis of these three sets of strategies is by no means an exhaustive treatment of all interventions. But an examination of these three will provide an in-depth survey of the range of

---

[1] E. Posner, LAW AND SOCIAL NORMS 4 (2000).

issues facing policy makers, the complexities of the effects of such strategies, and the importance and difficulty of their forming a codependence with norms buttressing good eating/drinking and exercise and acceptance of diverse body shapes.

In addition, concerns for children loom large in this area: they should have a good start; they should not be unduly influenced by marketing by the food and beverage industry; the chance for their being healthy as kids and, then as adults is significantly aided by their developing good eating/drinking habits and exercise routines from the earliest years, and so forth. Thus, there is special emphasis placed on the impact these three sets of interventions and related issues may have on the lives of the youngest members of society (Chapter 4).

The first set of interventions focuses on marketing. We look at the power of advertising, generally, in postindustrial societies and with regard to promotion of food/drink of dubious nutritional value. The food-and-drink industry is formidable and fiercely opposes most efforts to curb merchandising of its products. At the same time we assess educational campaigns to promote healthy eating/drinking and physical exercise. Such efforts rest on a fundamental premise: provide people with information and they will change their behavior in light of such knowledge. Yet such promotions of healthy eating/drinking and of active lifestyles, to date, have had only minimal impact. Those backing such campaigns suggest this is because too few resources are devoted to such efforts so as to counterbalance the relentless merchandising of junk food and drinks.

We look then at two attempts to curb such marketing: mandatory labeling of food and drinks, especially regarding caloric content, and front of package labeling (Chapter 5). Menu labeling, where it has been mandated, appears to have produced limited results in terms of caloric reduction. What's more, it may send the wrong signal: counting calories, not nutritious eating/drinking, is what is important. Front of package (FOP) labeling holds more promise regarding messaging: it places much more emphasis on nutrition, not just caloric content. We discuss some interesting initiatives in respect of FOP that have the potential to make a difference with consumers.

Merchandising by the food-and-beverage industry is an enterprise to which vast resources are devoted. Those concerned about obesity and health issues advocate restrictions on such advertising. Such constraints can be effective but require great political will and a willingness to convincingly respond to claims that any such limits violate freedom of speech of corporations.

As we look at restrictions on advertising, especially to kids, we examine efforts on the part of the food-and-drink industry to self-regulate. Self-regulation has been around for a long time but has gotten a boost because of ideas about the "new governance," referred to earlier in conjunction with the discussion of the "regulatory mix." Yet self-regulation is an inadequate response to policy needs: a case in point are the efforts of the food-and-drink industry regarding policing of advertising. There are many such efforts with very few positive effects.

In contrast, strong legislative efforts can produce positive results in terms of reduction of nonnutritious food and drink. An example of forceful legislative intervention has occurred in the province of Quebec. Advertising to children under thirteen is essentially banned. This prohibition has survived a constitutional challenge, on free speech grounds, in the Canadian courts. That prohibition has produced measurable results in the reduction of consumption of nonnutritious food and drink. This decrease has been experienced only by francophone, not anglophone, children mainly because the former predominantly watch French language television programs that have no advertisements directed at them (Chapter 5).

Finally, in terms of marketing, we examine the largely unregulated Internet. The food-and-beverage industry has been quick to exploit the virtual world to market its products, especially to children. We look at one such instance: advergames. At the same time such promotions in borderless cyberspace threaten efforts in jurisdictions such as Quebec to contain the effects of such advertising (Chapter 5).

We next turn to fiscal interventions where we examine "fat" or "junk food" taxes and subsidies. Fat taxes have been much discussed and have received wide media publicity. Their purpose is to suppress consumption of nonnutritious food/drink generally but the specific target has been soda (pop, soft drinks) because of its high sugar content and level of consumption especially by children. Such taxes are not nearly as effective as some advocates suggest. For them to be effective, in many instances, the cost of the product would become prohibitive, especially for the poor. Such a hike in price raises serious issues about the equity of such policies (Chapter 6).

A better solution may be to combine some reasonable level of tax on non-nutritious food/drink with subsidies for healthy substances. This underwriting could be of two kinds. One is a generally applicable point about how some crops are subsidized and how this underwriting, it is charged, leads to cheap and unhealthy food and beverages. The other kind of subsidies are particular experiments with providing rewards to low-income individuals, on public assistance, if they purchase healthy foods. The goal here is to promote more nutritious diets among individuals who are prone to obesity and who do not have the economic wherewithal to take various preventative measures for themselves and their children.

The general point about subsidies of certain crops, particularly corn, has largely been misdirected. The charge is that such underwriting leads to an abundance of cheap commodity crops that supply ingredients that lead to inexpensive, unhealthy foods. Subsidies and overproduction of certain crops may be related but, whatever that relationship, it does not account for the price of most junk food and drinks. The cost of raw commodities is quite small compared with other costs such as processing, packaging, storing, etc. The influence on the price paid by the ultimate consumer is negligible. At the same time many healthier crops such as fruits and vegetables cost much more to grow, harvest, and transport. This is not to say that agricultural regulation could not be overhauled to encourage production of healthier foods. Some recommendations are advanced in that regard. But any such reform will be a massive undertaking, opposed by vested interests, and by no means easily achieved (Chapter 6).

There are some encouraging pilot projects regarding the subsidizing of healthy foods for low-income people on public assistance, especially regarding SNAP (Supplementary Nutrition Assistance Program, formerly food stamps). But these projects are caught up in debates about whether SNAP recipients should (at the same time or as an alternative strategy to rewards) be banned from buying unhealthy foods with funds that they receive from the program. Even more telling is that the pilots' success may lead to their own undoing. The more the pilot underwrites the cost of healthy food, the more a program costs. Any such success will likely collide with austerity measures of cash-starved governments (Chapter 6).

Finally, we examine ways to encourage physical activity. There are a number of means to do so, but a main one centers around the built environment. We need to have roads, sidewalks, parks, and so forth that encourage—not discourage—exercise. In some settings, particularly the suburbs, there will need to be fundamental changes to the infrastructure: a goal not easily accomplished. We then look at how the built environment along with various programs, in and out of schools, can be used to encourage children to be physically active from their earliest days through graduation from high school. We discuss a very controversial intervention urged by many anti-obesity advocates: schools measuring and reporting on kids' BMI. (Chapter 7)

We also look at vouchers as a policy tool to promote physical activity, especially among children. We discuss a proposal for a universal voucher to promote weight loss and suggest that, for a number of reasons, it is an idea that is highly innovative but bad. We examine a specific example of an experiment with vouchers. A Canadian effort encourages children to be physically active by underwriting the cost of activity: the Children's Fitness Tax Credit. This is a strategy that is admirable in theory, particularly because it emphasizes activity unrelated to weight. However, it has not fulfilled its promise as implemented. We discuss ways that it and related innovations might be more effective (Chapter 7).

Throughout the book the emphasis is on America. There are some strategies from other countries that are discussed: for example, the banning of advertising to children in Quebec (see above and Chapter 5), the failed Danish junk food levy (Chapter 6), and the Canadian Children's Fitness Tax Credit (see above and Chapter 7). Yet, for a number of reasons, the United States' experience is central. American society has some of the highest rates of obesity in the world even as it is obsessed with weight and with appearance. Its many institutes of policy produce excellent, if at times controversial, studies of obesity and its impacts. It is in the United States that the fat activism movement is most spirited and efforts to protect from weight and appearance bias are most concentrated. The Republic is the land of law even as efforts to employ regulation in various areas, including in terms of obesity, produce heated and seemingly endless controversy. The book is written by someone outside of America: one who admires the Republic even as he is critical of the way it often forges and implements policy.

In evaluating various interventions, mostly in the United States, we keep at the forefront two main points. First, that the primary goal should be better health; weight loss (or even prevention of excess) is a secondary consideration. Second, assessments need to take account of the ways these interventions play a role with shifting norms: away from stigmatization of fat people and toward enthusiasm for fruits and energetic walking and acceptance of people of all shapes and sizes.

The last part of the book draws conclusions about the centrality of these points. It does so by addressing them in the context of "health equity": "the fair distribution of health determinants, outcomes, and resources within and between segments of the population, regardless of social standing."[2] It also offers some observations on the role of law generally: its shaping of human action even as it, itself, is a creation of and bounded by human action. Law is a powerful but limited tool for addressing behavior.

---

[2] COMMITTEE ON CHILDHOOD OBESITY PREVENTION ACTIONS FOR LOCAL GOVERNMENTS, LOCAL GOVERNMENT ACTIONS TO PREVENT CHILDHOOD OBESITY 46 (2009) citing CENTERS FOR DISEASE CONTROL AND PREVENTION 2007 unpublished HEALTH EQUITY WORKING GROUP, CDC.

{ PART I }

Obesity and the Regulation of Consumption

{ 1 }

Regulating Consumption: Many Efforts—With What Effects?

I. Introduction

The law has long intervened in terms of different kinds of consumption: alcohol, recreational drugs, tobacco, gambling, and so forth. Such efforts have often been aimed at excess however judged. This chapter briefly discusses these attempts as an important context for the regulation of various activities to promote healthy eating/drinking and physical exercise (and to discourage consumption of nonnutritious food/beverages and sedentary ways). Many of the issues arising in promoting healthy eating/exercise have been faced in regulating other kinds of consumption. That common ground offers insights into the complexities of promoting healthy eating/exercise even as it is clear that there are ways in which such promotion is unique.

Many of the ideas discussed in this chapter have already been addressed in my earlier book, *Permit but Discourage: Regulating Excessive Consumption*.[1] As a result they are presented here in short order to provide a foundation for the detailed discussion of regulation and of obesity in subsequent chapters. More detailed treatment of the ideas in this chapter can be found in *Permit but Discourage*.

The chapter begins by looking at the many legal interventions that policy makers can use to regulate. Such intervention can range from "soft" tools, such as legislatively authorized educational initiatives, through to the most drastic tool of law, criminal sanctions, and can utilize various aspects of the administrative state. A fundamental point is that these legal strategies are, and should often be, used in combination. At the end of the day, it is usually a "mix"

---

[1] W. A. BOGART, PERMIT BUT DISCOURAGE: REGULATING EXCESSIVE CONSUMPTION chs. 2, 3, 4 (2011).

of interventions that is responsible for any success in achieving the regulatory objective.

The next section examines issues regarding the impact of law. How do we know that legal intervention has achieved the goals sought to be achieved by those who have designed and implemented the regulatory mix? This is a vital question that is too often ignored, and yet it is fundamental in terms of effective legal intervention. Ascertaining the impact of any set of laws may be very difficult, for reasons that will be discussed. However, such challenges are not an excuse for ignoring these important issues, including in terms of the regulation of consumption and particularly in terms of obesity.

We then take a brief tour of how various legal strategies have been used to regulate different kinds of consumption: alcohol, smoking, recreational drugs, and gambling. Three points emerge that we need to bear in mind in discussing efforts to use law to promote healthy eating/exercise. First, a broad theme of such regulation is *permit but discourage*. Consumption is *permitted* but harmful effects are *discouraged* though various interventions (recreational drugs are outliers). Second, these efforts at suppression have been only partially successful. Even when linked to other forms of social control, such as relevant norms, much excess continues. Third, these very regulatory efforts can, themselves, cause harm. The outcomes produced by the prohibition of alcohol, in the United States, in the early twentieth century is a classic example. Consumption did go down in some states. At the same time there were all sorts of negative consequences, including: bootlegging, smuggling, a black market, and the spread of racketeering. The potential for harming the very individuals meant to be helped is a caution for efforts to address obesity.

We then look at some important ideas of how law can shape behavior. We begin with a discussion of "new governance." There is a widely held view that, over the past few decades, there has been a paradigm shift in terms of how government is functioning. The "old" governance focused on "command and control," with legislatures and administrative bodies essentially imposing regulation in a myriad of areas and sanctioning any nonconforming behavior. The "new" governance is about more effective and efficient government open to achieving its goals in a variety of ways by using the best mix of tools to accomplish the designated objectives. The "new governance" is relevant in respect of efforts to regulate consumption. An important emphasis of *permit but discourage* is to devise ways of encouraging individuals to make healthy choices, whether in terms of smoking, alcohol, or nutritious food and physical activity, with reliance on prohibition only in the clearest of cases. There is a strong case for these open-ended efforts to promote nutritious eating/drinking and physical exercise.

A central underpinning of new governance is "normativity"—the relationship between law and norms. Normativity asserts that regulatory efforts will be more successful if relevant interventions and dominant norms work more or less in tandem. In the case of consumption, such codependence can send multiple signals about the dangers of excess, on the one hand, and the importance of moderation on the other. How to achieve such a relationship is a critical question. Answers involve much trial and error; regulatory and social experiments loom large.

II. The Regulatory Mix

Once the decision has been made to intervene legally, policy makers need to decide on the best kinds of legal intervention—"tools"—they should invoke to achieve the particular regulatory goals. Here let's have a brief, general look at the tools of legal intervention before we turn to the many aspects of regulating consumption (in general), and obesity (in particular).

There are questions with regard to which "tools" should be used. In addition, there are crucial issues about the ways in which these tools should be employed in combination—the "mix"—to enhance the likelihood of achieving various policy goals. There are many kinds of regulation, ranging from the most drastic (e.g., prohibition by criminalizing an activity) to those that are minimally interventionist (e.g., encouraging or discouraging certain behaviors through authorized programs to educate the public).[2] In between, such tools as taxation; restrictions upon advertising; self-regulation; incentives to encourage behaviors; and constraints upon how, where, and when an activity may take place can be employed to realize policy objectives.[3]

The overarching question that needs to be asked regarding legal intervention in any area is: what is the best mix of various forms of regulation that is likely to result in actually attaining the policy objective? In answering that question it is important to bear in mind that there are many forms of regulation in diverse settings. Legal regulation is but one form, albeit a very important one that is backed by the power of the state. Consider this definition of regulation that includes legal interventions while placing them in the larger context of social control techniques: "the sustained and focused attempt to alter the behavior of others according to defined standards or purposes with the intention of

---

[2] *See generally*, W. A. Bogart, Achieving Compliance: Obedience and the Limits of Deterrence (unpublished policy paper prepared for the Privy Council Office, Apr. 2006). *See generally*, REVIEW OF REGULATORY REFORM, REGULATORY REFORM IN CANADA: GOVERNMENT CAPACITY TO ACHIEVE HIGH QUALITY REGULATION (2002).

[3] THE TOOLS OF THE NEW GOVERNMENT: A GUIDE TO THE NEW GOVERNANCE (L. Salamon & O. Elliott, eds., 2002); P. Eliadis, *Foundation Paper: Instrument Choice in Global Democracies* (Policy Research Initiative, 2002); R. BALDWIN & M. CAVE, UNDERSTANDING REGULATION: THEORY, STRATEGY, AND PRACTICE (1999).

producing a broadly identified outcome or outcomes, which may involve mechanisms of standard-setting, information gathering and behavior-modification."[4]

It is this much broader conception of regulation that we will have in mind when we examine legal interventions to address obesity. We will focus on such strategies as taxes on junk food, regulations mandating caloric content information on menus, and subsidization of production and purchase of nutritious foods. How these strategies interact with other social control techniques and the overall impact that is produced are crucial issues. A main relationship that we will examine is that between law and norms: "normativity." We'll have more to say about "normativity" momentarily.[5]

III. How Effective Is Regulation?

A) INTRODUCTION

In the last six decades the role of law in industrialized societies has expanded enormously. During that period, law insinuated itself into all manner of human activity. Yet society is not some inert presence upon which law works its will. The influence of law and society goes both ways. Some insist that it is law *in* society that is crucial: how law emerges out of and is reacted to within different social relations. In any event, social change results in people viewing their environment and relationships differently. Sooner or later these altered viewpoints can lead to demands for changes in law. Such demands, more often than not in the latter part of the twentieth century, led to more—and more complex—law and, in turn, a range of reactions to it.[6]

In 2011 the Institute of Medicine (IOM) in the United States released a report on the role of law and policy in addressing various health issues.[7] The Report is important in several ways, and we will refer to it at various points in the book. For the moment what is of interest is the following assertion: "law specifically, and public policy more generally, are among the most powerful tools to improve population health."[8] This is a lofty statement, and possibly accurate in terms of many situations: laws in Canada mandating universal

---

[4] J. Black, *Regulatory Conversations*, 29 J. LAW & SOC'Y 163, 170 (Mar. 2002). *See also* J. Black, *Critical Reflections on Regulation*, 27 AUS. J. LEGAL PHILOSOPHY 1 (2002), and C. HOOD, H. ROTHSTEIN & R. BALDWIN, THE GOVERNMENT OF RISK: UNDERSTANDING RISK REGULATION REGIMES 21 (2001).

[5] *See infra* Section V(b): Ideas for New Governance: Normativity and Its Offspring.

[6] The discussion in this subsection is based on W. A. BOGART, CONSEQUENCES: THE IMPACT OF LAW AND ITS COMPLEXITY 21 (Part I: The Importance of Law *et seq.*), 51 (Part II: The Impact of Law *et seq.*) (2002).

[7] INSTITUTE OF MEDICINE, FOR THE PUBLIC'S HEALTH: REVITALIZING LAW AND POLICY TO MEET NEW CHALLENGES (2011).

[8] *Id.* at 18.

health care do improve the well-being of that country's citizens, particularly those of modest means.[9]

Nevertheless, the question in many contexts is determining the circumstances under which law will have positive impacts, and assessing the extent of such desirable outcomes.[10] One way of responding to this question is to look at efforts at evaluating the effects of any law or group of legal interventions. At its most general level impact addresses all policy-related effects of law. This wide net is meant to capture all significant outcomes relating to the presence of law in society. But that is a very wide net. Thus, within this broad framework, it is useful to think of impact as embracing three kinds of effects: law's larger pattern of influence in society, the extent to which law is complied with, and the effects of law on a particular problem sought to be addressed. Let's have a look at these three orders of impact. Then let's discuss the IOM's Report and its urging assessment of laws addressing health issues.

B) ASSESSING IMPACT: THREE KINDS OF EFFECTS

The first kind of impact suggests that the most important consequences of law reflect some larger pattern of influence in society. A number of ideas suggest that the outcomes produced by law are most clearly discerned in terms of broad contours of regulation and their interaction with larger social and economic forces.

Such ideas range from instrumental assertions about law suggesting that it can, itself, cause changes in societal conditions to claims that talking about the impact of law is, itself, mistaken: law and society are so inextricably related that one cannot coherently talk about law affecting society; rather, the focus ought to be on the way they interact with each other. In a subsequent section we will look at one such idea: "normativity"—the relationship between law and norms.[11] Normativity explains much about both the power and the limits of laws that regulate consumption.

The second kind of impact deals with the extent to which there is compliance with any law. In other words, an effect of law that is both obvious and critical is the extent to which it is obeyed. Most people comply with the law most of the time. Although not without difficulties, it is usually possible to determine, reasonably accurately, the extent to which there is compliance with a law or series of laws. However, an important element of the wider impact of law is determining how to increase compliance among those not otherwise inclined

---

[9] Canada Health Act, 1985 RSC, c. C-6; see also Government of Canada, Health Canada, Canada Health Act, Apr. 19, 2010, available at http://www.hc-sc.gc.ca/hcs-sss/medi-assur/cha-lcs/index-eng.php.

[10] C. Sunstein, *Empirically Informed Regulation* 78 U. CHI. L. REV. 1349 (2011).

[11] BOGART, *supra* note 1, at ch. 3: Excessive Consumption and Normativity.

to obedience. Enforcement can rely heavily on deterrence. Yet the effectiveness of deterrence in problem areas—where it needs to deliver its wallop—is questionable. Part of the difficulty lies with the assumptions made by those who promote theories of deterrence. Such premises are weighted heavily toward the rationality of the potential criminal.

This would-be violator weighs gains from illegal activity against the probable sanctions, if caught, and then decides to do or to refrain. Yet much criminological research stresses the range of crimes committed on impulse, the absence of calculation by offenders of the consequences, and the multitude of motivations that may not be controllable by criminal law.[12] As a result: "On the deterrent effects of legal sanctions in general it is impossible to offer confident conclusions from the results of numerous often inconsistent studies using a wide variety of methods and varying considerably in analytical sophistication."[13] In other words, sanctions do have a deterrent effect. However, the extent of that effect and how it works in any specific area can vary significantly in different contexts. We return to these issues in the next section when we discuss efforts to suppress use of recreational drugs.

The third kind of impact focuses on the extent to which a particular law or set of laws has an effect on the underlying problem sought to be addressed. To a great extent it is this meaning of impact that people refer to when they urge or oppose implementation of any law: from arguments that minimum wage laws raise the standard of compensation for people at the bottom of the economic ladder (or conversely, that they are barriers to job creation) to assertions that pornography harms women and that laws prohibiting it will buttress gender equality (or conversely, that such laws mangle free speech and/or result in the harassment of those with unconventional tastes in erotica).

Asserting that a law or set of laws has particular effects is one thing. Demonstrating that these consequences have occurred and that they have been caused by law is quite another. There are four considerations in this regard. First, there may be heated debates about the underlying issue sought to be addressed. There may be controversy concerning whether the underlying issue is a problem that needs to be addressed by the law or, indeed, at all. Those doubting that an issue gives rise to problems that should be addressed by law are likely also to be skeptical about any outcomes produced by regulation. Conversely, those insisting that law should be invoked to respond to a perceived problem are likely to be inclined to judge outcomes as positive and to attribute such results to legal intervention.

We will see such controversies played out when we turn to discuss obesity in Chapter 2. There is a growing chorus of voices arguing that obesity is not the health problem that it is made out to be by conventional wisdom. For

---

[12] BOGART, *supra* note 6, at 58–63.
[13] R. COTTERRELL, THE SOCIOLOGY OF LAW: AN INTRODUCTION 143 (2d ed. 1992).

those espousing free market principles and autonomous individualism, weight is simply a matter of personal choice. The traditional public health approach views the problem in a larger societal context. This view emphasizes the many influences that shape individuals' behaviors. Nevertheless, the issue for this approach remains excess weight: extra pounds need to be lost or better still, not gained at all. For others it is promoting healthy eating and exercise; weight should be ignored or, at least deemphasized. For still others, the problem is not that people are fat, but the censorious attitudes toward and discriminating behaviors against the overweight that oppress them, causing them all manner of psychological and physical damage.

Second, there can be a number of complications in terms of showing that a law actually caused any particular effects. At the heart of causation issues is the need to control for "plausible rival hypotheses." In other words, in order to demonstrate that a law has had a particular effect, it is necessary to demonstrate that there were no other social, political, economic, or other forces responsible for the specific result.

There are means available in specific instances to test rival hypotheses when assessing the impact of any particular law. To the extent rival hypotheses can be eliminated, conclusions can be drawn with some confidence concerning a law having caused outcomes. However, in circumstances when rival hypotheses cannot be controlled, claims about the capacity of law to achieve a determined set of outcomes are called into serious question. We will see many examples of causation debates when we look at the effects of various legal interventions to address healthier eating/drinking and exercise in subsequent chapters; these range from restrictions on advertising to children to promotion of exercise by means of tax credits.[14]

Third, laws can be linked to effects that are not contemplated or, in any event, not intended by those involved with their implementation. The phenomenon of unintended consequences has captured the attention of students of the impact of law across the political spectrum.[15] Nevertheless, those wary of activist government, at least in the economic realm, are especially inclined to invoke unintended consequences as a rallying cry in their efforts to roll back the public sector.[16] The general line of argument is that any particular law will not achieve the desired results, will create economic distortions, is philosophically bad because of the burden that government imposes, and so forth. In addition, it is contended that the law may have any number of undesirable results, even

---

[14] Part III, Chapters 5 to 7.

[15] E. Mertz, *Conclusion: A New Social Constructionism for Sociolegal Studies*, 28 LAW & SOC'Y REV. 1243, 1246–48 (1994).

[16] *See, e.g.*, THE ESSENTIAL NEO-CONSERVATIVE READER (M. Gerson ed., 1996) and, in particular, the foreword by J. Wilson.

from the perspective of the proponents of the law who would (of course) not intend them.

Unintended consequences demonstrate that law can be a more complicated instrument of policy implementation than many proponents care to acknowledge.[17] We'll look at some startling examples of unintended consequences when we discuss, in the next section, prohibition of alcohol and taxes on cigarettes in Canada. The IOM Report, referred to earlier, discussed the complexities caused by unintended consequences.[18] Two such examples are cited by the Report: the impact of agricultural laws leading to the availability of sugar-intense ingredients in many foods and drinks, and a national law intended to improve the school system that had the incidental consequence of suppressing physical education. Both these instances are related to addressing issues of obesity. We return to them in subsequent chapters.[19]

Fourth, the effects of any particular law or set of laws may be stymied by other forces. Technology often blunts the outcomes sought to be achieved through regulation. Consider cyberspace. The Internet's global and often anonymous character can challenge those seeking to enforce legal rights and obligations. A prosecutor trying to track down child pornographers using "anonymous retailers" to distribute their materials; a court attempting to provide redress to a libeled person when the defamation was perpetrated online in another, remote country; and a state striving to protect consumers that cannot determine the owner of a Web site that distributes fraudulent material are but three examples of the substantial difficulties regarding legal enforcement.[20] We return to the limits of law and the Internet when we discuss below the effort to address problem gambling in cyberspace.[21]

C) LEGAL INTERVENTIONS TO PROMOTE HEALTH

One reason the IOM Report is important is its plea for more rigorous use of evidence both in terms of the need for legal intervention and the impacts of any such regulation, if implemented, with regard to the promotion of health.[22] Let's look at its analysis with particular regard for what it tells us about the

---

[17] S. Dubner & S. Levitt, *Unintended Consequences—The Case of the Red-Cockaded Woodpecker*, N.Y. TIMES, Sunday Magazine, Jan. 20, 2008, *available at* http://www.nytimes.com/2008/01/20/magazine/20wwln-freak-t.html?pagewanted=all&_moc.semityn.www.

[18] INSTITUTE OF MEDICINE, *supra* note 7, at 2.

[19] Chapter 6: Section IV(b): Subsidies and Agricultural Policy, and Chapter 7: Encouraging Physical Activity: Children at Play!

[20] A. SHAPIRO, THE CONTROL REVOLUTION: HOW THE INTERNET IS PUTTING INDIVIDUALS IN CHARGE AND CHANGING THE WORLD WE KNOW 63–64 (1999).

[21] *Infra* Section IV: Consumption Encounters Law: *Permit but Discourage.*

[22] INSTITUTE OF MEDICINE, *supra* note 7.

complexities of the effects of law in an area of direct relevance to issues that are the focus of this book.

The Report is emphatic about the importance of taking account of the evidence concerning the need for legal intervention and assessing that evidence as a basis for invoking regulation. This need to take account of the evidence making the case for intervention and the basis for making decisions based on it is a very important point in terms of regulatory efforts to address obesity. We'll have more to say in Chapter 4 about the appropriate circumstances justifying intervention specifically in terms of promoting healthy eating/drinking and physical activity.[23]

At the same time the Report recognizes that "the best evidence may be limited." In these instances it suggests that such a qualified basis may, nevertheless, justify legal interventions when:

- health threats and potential harms from inaction are large
- opportunity costs and unintended harms from action are within acceptable limits
- the time or costs required for gathering more definitive evidence are substantial relative to the expected value of additional evidence.[24]

It also recognizes that the desirability of assessments of health impact may vary depending on such factors as the costs of these evaluations weighed against the benefits that they are likely to bestow: they may not be justified in the case of modest commercial developments, but they may be imperative where action is required to avoid damaging consequences.[25]

The Report suggests that a framework could be developed to illustrate the level of certainty and magnitude of effects that policy makers need depending on the type of decision to be made.[26] Variables in this framework could include: the level of risk presented by the legal intervention; the population impact of health risk factors being targeted; type of legal action; the potential scope of the policy, severity, and frequency of the potential health effects; availability of other options; prior experience using the intervention; and acceptability of potential risks. Such Health Impact Assessment (HIA) is a tool that "identifies the health consequences of new policies and develops practical strategies to enhance their health benefits and minimize adverse effects."[27]

It takes a similar position regarding assessments of the effects of laws once implemented. After enactment of laws an appropriate body should review the health outcomes and costs associated with implementation. That entity should

---

[23] *See* Chapter 4: Assessing Interventions.
[24] INSTITUTE OF MEDICINE, *supra* note 7, at 100.
[25] *Id.*
[26] *Id.*
[27] *Id.* at 96, *quoting* HEALTH IMPACT PROJECT, ABOUT HEALTH IMPACT ASSESSMENT, Feb. 17, 2010, *available at* http://www.iaia.org/hia2010/.

also, where appropriate, offer recommendations to the legislature and others regarding modifications that could increase positive outcomes.[28]

The Report reflects awareness of complications that can be part of evaluations. Such assessments are difficult because any effects are "often distributed across multiple segments within the population, across multiple health and social endpoints, and across long time horizons."[29] We'll talk about the built environment in Chapter 7. There is much interest in that area and its ability to either inhibit or to promote physical activity depending on a variety of relevant factors. The Report uses laws addressing the built environment as an example of complications in terms of assessing impact. Such regulation may have: (1) short-term effects—on the well-being and quality of life of users; (2) intermediate effects—on neighborhood desirability, housing prices, and air quality; and (3) longer-term effects—on chronic disease incidence and progression such as cardiovascular issues, diabetes, and asthma.

Finally, the Report underscores the need for a combination of legal strategies in order to have greater positive impact: the "regulatory mix" that was discussed earlier.[30] We'll have lots to say about "the mix" throughout the book. A number of legal interventions working, more or less, together are more likely to improve the chances of achieving any particular policy goal. That said, and as we shall see, there are still tricky questions regarding such issues as which ones to use, in what combination, and in which sequence. With such complexities, an openness to trial and error in invoking various strategies is imperative. The Report opines: "multiple, different, and ongoing interventions are sometimes necessary to achieve a substantial and sustained effect on health outcomes and health behaviors."[31]

The Report and its assertion about the power of law to transform behavior, quoted earlier, will strike some as unduly optimistic, on the one hand, and an example of regulatory imperialism, on the other.[32] In the next section we'll discuss several examples dealing with various kinds of consumption where law's effectiveness seems partial, tentative, and, at times, just misdirected. That said, the Report addresses clearly and insightfully issues regarding legal interventions to improve health. Its observations have fundamental relevance for many of the points made in these pages.

---

[28] *Id.* at 98.
[29] INSTITUTE OF MEDICINE, *supra* note 7, at 99.
[30] *Supra* Section II: The Regulatory Mix.
[31] INSTITUTE OF MEDICINE, *supra* note 7, at 99.
[32] *Supra* Section III(a): Introduction.

IV. Consumption Encounters Law: *Permit But Discourage*

Let's look at various attempts to regulate different kinds of consumption to see how complicated such efforts can be and how varied can be the results that are achieved. We'll survey alcohol, recreational drugs, tobacco, and gambling. The complexities of legal efforts to control harmful appetites in these areas are instructive in terms of campaigns to promote healthier eating/drinking and exercise and to combat prejudice based on weight, which we'll discuss in detail in subsequent chapters. This section makes two important points about the regulation of consumption: first, its effective but also limited impact, especially in respect of suppression of excess; and second, the capacity of such regulatory efforts, if misdirected, to do more harm than good.

By the end of the twentieth century an overarching theme had emerged in terms of the law and regarding prevailing norms towards consumption: permit but discourage. Attempts to prohibit various kinds of consumption had largely been abandoned. Thus, the use of the criminal law had mostly retreated (recreational drugs were, and generally remain, an exception). Instead, a variety of interventions—the regulatory "mix"—was used to discourage excessive consumption regarding alcohol, gambling, and smoking.

For centuries the law has long taken aim at alcohol and perceived immoderate ways in terms of drink.[33] In Victorian England the Society for the Study of Inebriety termed alcoholism a "disease of the will."[34] The *Habitual Inebriates Act* provided, supposedly for their own good, for the incarceration of those in the thrall of drink.[35] For some even these measures were not enough. The eradication of alcohol was the ultimate goal.

By the early twentieth century the abstinence movement had gained momentum on both sides of the Atlantic. Legislation was passed banning the manufacture, sale, and consumption of alcohol.[36] The United States led the charge with the most dramatic of legal interventions: a constitutional amendment aimed at its suppression.[37] Such efforts at suppression were largely unsuccessful while imposing unacceptable costs. Consumption may have decreased in some societies. However, efforts at prohibition, especially in the United States, gave rise to all manner of unintended, negative consequences, including smuggling, a black market, bootlegging, and, more generally, the intensification of organized crime.

---

[33] BOGART, *supra* note 1, at ch.1: Alcohol—May Attitudes, Much Law, Mixed Results. Parts of this chapter are derived from this previous work.

[34] V. Berridge, *Why Alcohol Is Legal and Other Drugs Are Not: Virginia Berridge Examines the Relevance of Past Experiences to Current Policy-Making*, 54(5) HIST. TODAY 18, 18–19 (2004).

[35] M. VALVERDE, DISEASES OF THE WILL: ALCOHOL AND THE DILEMMAS OF FREEDOM 76 *et seq.* (1998).

[36] BOGART, *supra* note 1, at 14–18.

[37] The Eighteenth Amendment took effect in 1920; it was repealed in 1932.

After the repeal of these prohibition laws, many societies evolved a complicated pattern of regulation that reflected *permit but discourage*. Along with such regulation were ambiguous attitudes and norms governing its use: "alcohol has...been considered simultaneously as socially problematic and socially acceptable in a multitude of ways."[38] Today, alcohol's capacity to impair and to addict is denounced. Its ability to relax, to enhance the pleasures of food, and even to bolster health is viewed as hugely attractive. Governments issue stern warnings regarding the hazards coming from its misuse even as they oversee its sale (in some cases as monopolistic provider) and enlarge their treasuries through the taxes they impose on it.

Meanwhile a varied mix of legal interventions is invoked to curb excess: the aforementioned taxes and educational campaigns; mandatory warnings on bottle labels etc.; restrictions upon advertising; sales to youths; and criminal sanctions for impaired driving, etc. There is also litigation seeking to compensate victims of harms caused by drunken individuals and by those who serve them in circumstances where such service should have been withheld, and to deter drinking and driving and irresponsible sale of alcohol. There has been success at containing excess.[39] Opinion has coalesced in favor of moderation, especially in terms of drinking and driving. Yet significant problems persist. Though there has been some recent evidence of further decline, the number of accidents attributable to alcohol remain too high, especially among young people.[40]

Up to the mid-twentieth century smoking was often encouraged by governments in several ways, including subsidies to farmers growing tobacco and distribution of cigarettes to soldiers during times of war.[41] Any laws on the books banning sales to children stood in stark contrast to the general availability of tobacco, including to teenagers. What's more, smoking was thought of as a glamorous activity that relaxed the individual, promoted socialization, curbed appetite, and so forth. The ubiquitous ashtray signaled widespread encouragement to light up.

Developments, especially in the United States and Canada, in the latter part of the twentieth century provide a classic example of the codependence of law and norms and the potential of the relationship to achieve policy goals. Legal intervention to suppress smoking is a story of regulation interacting with shifting norms regarding tobacco. In five decades or so smoking has gone in the minds of most of the public from a glamorous, sophisticated pastime to a filthy, dangerous addiction.[42] The changing norms have been both cause of and effect of legal intervention: as more people came to view smoking as unhealthy,

---

[38] VALVERDE, *supra* note 35, at 10.
[39] INSTITUTE OF MEDICINE, *supra* note 7, at 19.
[40] BOGART, *supra* note 1, at 31–38. *But see also Fewer Teenagers Are Driving after Drinking, Study Shows*, N.Y. TIMES, Oct. 2, 2012, at A20.
[41] *See generally* BOGART, *supra* note 6, at ch. 6: Smoking—And Waves of Cultural Antagonism.
[42] BOGART, *supra* note 1, at 58–61.

expensive, and disgusting, support grew for regulation aimed at further curtailment; as laws combating smoking intensified more people accepted, in terms of their own views and behavior, the obnoxiousness of cigarettes. Smoking was *permitted* but a web of interventions and norms clearly *discouraged* it completely.

Legal intervention to suppress smoking is also an excellent illustration of the regulatory "mix" as governments have resorted to a range of tools in order to achieve the policy goal of curtailing the use of cigarettes. The full spectrum of such interventions has been employed: from educating the public regarding the dangers of smoking to criminal prohibitions regarding the sale of cigarettes to children and smoking in public places. In addition there were legislative restrictions placed upon the advertising of cigarettes, requirements mandating ever more graphic and explicit warnings on packaging regarding the dangers of smoking, increased taxation of cigarettes, and various attempts to use litigation to compensate for the harm done by tobacco and to deter cigarette companies from peddling their poisons.

Yet not all legal strategies produced the effects hoped for. The tax hikes on tobacco imposed by the Canadian federal government in the late 1980s and 1990s essentially backfired. These increases resulted in the unintended consequence of promoting smuggling of cigarettes from U.S. states with relatively low taxes on tobacco. Estimates suggest that, at its height, black-market traffic in cigarettes constituted 20 percent of the market. After several maneuvers the Canadian government decided that it had no other choice and substantially lowered taxes to undercut sales of contraband. The percentage of those who smoke has fallen substantially over the last decades from a high of about 40 percent, but is still about 20 percent. Norms and the regulatory mix, working in tandem, have suppressed levels of smoking. Such success has been dramatic yet also limited. A significant percentage of individuals still light up.

The history of wagering has a long sweep.[43] Gambling in Regency England was everywhere: "One vast casino."[44] Laws seeking to curb gaming were largely disregarded.[45] But then things changed. Middle-class Victorians, privileging thrift and restraint, came to see gambling in the same way as an earlier characterization of it: a "dreadful vice."[46] Legal measures were taken to suppress it, and the number of gaming houses fell significantly. Norms and laws scorning

---

[43] G. REITH, THE AGE OF CHANCE: GAMBLING IN WESTERN CULTURE (2002).

[44] G. TREVELYAN, THE EARLY HISTORY OF CHARLES JAMES FOX 478 (1881), *cited in* D. MIERS, REGULATING COMMERCIAL GAMBLING: PAST, PRESENT AND FUTURE 17 (2004).

[45] BOGART, *supra* note 1, at 201–06.

[46] J. DUFF, HINTS FOR REFORM, PARTICULARLY THE GAMBLING CLUBS, BY AN MP 10 (1784), *cited in* MIERS, *supra* note 44, at 45.

gaming were more or less allied. A similar saga concerning the prohibition of gambling played out in other countries such as Canada.[47] That said, some wagering still occurred. As with other activities that are sought to be ended by the heavy hand of criminal sanctions, gambling came to have a demimonde existence. Those compelled to wager found outlets, whatever the hazards.

By the late twentieth century the legal and normative landscape for gambling had shifted yet again. Thereafter, gambling became a highly regulated and lucrative industry. But the regulation has been mostly focused on ensuring honesty regarding the various games and in promoting revenue enhancement for owners (often governments).[48] However, in the face of the mounting evidence regarding the damage caused by those with impaired control, there are increasing calls for the regulatory frameworks to take account of the damages that can result from excessive gaming.

These interventions bring *permit but discourage* to the fore in terms of gambling and problem gambling. Along the way there have been changing attitudes toward gambling. Most people think it should not be criminalized, but many remain ambivalent toward it. Again, such views and conduct are crucial in terms of legal interventions: "Attitudes towards gambling are important because they can, in aggregate, have a significant impact on laws and policies that govern public exposure to gambling and mandate measures designed to moderate negative consequences. Attitudes are also important because they more directly influence the gambling behavior of individuals who hold them as well as others within their families and wider social networks."[49]

Directing interventions toward *permit but discourage* offers possibilities for addressing those with impaired control even as the gambling industry otherwise flourishes. As with other kinds of consumption a "mix" of regulatory initiatives offers the greatest chance for effectiveness.[50] Such strategies aimed at suppressing problem gambling include: stricter enforcement of the bans on wagering by children; exclusion of problem gamblers from gaming establishments; litigation aimed at wrongful practices that contribute to problem gambling; restrictions on promotion of games of chance; and licensing of individual gamblers. Yet there are many questions regarding how effective these interventions will be even as the gambling industry may continue to expand.[51]

---

[47] S. MORTON, AT ODDS: GAMBLING AND CANADIANS 1919–1969 (2003). Other jurisdictions accepted gambling legally and attitudinally much earlier. For a discussion of Australia and Nevada in this regard, see BOGART, *supra* note 1, at 206–08.

[48] MIERS, *supra* note 44; E. MORSE & E. GOSS, GOVERNING FORTUNE: CASINO GAMBLING IN AMERICA (2007).

[49] ABBOTT ET AL., A REVIEW OF RESEARCH ON ASPECTS OF PROBLEM GAMBLING—FINAL REPORT 68 (2004).

[50] BOGART, *supra* note 1, at ch. 7: Regulating Moderation in Gambling?—Specific Interventions.

[51] ABBOTT ET AL., *supra* note 49, at 51.

What is more, the Internet poses substantial challenges for the realization of effective regulation of problem gambling. Cyberspace may trigger a fundamental shift in the enforceability of law over the next decades.[52] At the least, compliance with any regulatory framework will not easily be achieved, including regarding gambling and especially problem gambling.[53] Meanwhile some gamblers engage in out-of-control wagering in cyberspace even as the consequences of their excess are left to be addressed by the real world.[54] Responding to the burdens imposed by gambling in the real and virtual worlds is a formidable task. Yet ignoring them is not an option. Policy makers and the public struggle with the finding and effecting of a balance in terms of *permit but discourage*.

Recreational drugs are outliers. This form of excessive consumption has long been subject to criminal sanctions as a prime means of suppressing use. Drugs were generally tolerated into the nineteenth century as having a part medical, part recreational use. However, by the early twentieth century concerted efforts were mounting to ban drugs. Over the next decades these movements were successful, and criminalization of various substances became the template for addressing drugs up to the present day.[55]

Drugs as outliers in the eyes of the law is a phenomenon evident in the United States. The last decades have seen increasingly punitive measures written into law and enforced. For Provine, in her *Unequal under Law: Race in the War on Drugs*, there is an especially dark explanation for this turning to criminal sanctions. She sees racism writ large in the way that drug consumption has been and is addressed in the United States.[56] In the late nineteenth century "opium and the yellow peril" ignited the first wave of prohibition.[57] Every anti-drug initiative, thereafter, was promoted by fear of an underclass, of blacks and other minorities, and its capacity to cause turmoil.

The United States was not alone in witnessing moral entrepreneurs invoking racism to promote an agenda of drug prohibition.[58] Yet each "war" in the United States: "associated dangerous drugs with dangerous minorities bent on corrupting white, law-abiding youth."[59] Those capable of molding opinion shifted norms away from viewing drug abuse as a relatively private activity with the addict being viewed with sympathy to seeing drugs as a prime source of social disintegration and violence: "Punitive policies like the contemporary war

---

[52] J. GOLDSMITH & T. WU, WHO CONTROLS THE INTERNET?: ILLUSIONS OF A BORDERLESS WORLD (2006).

[53] J. WIEBE & M. LIPTON, AN OVERVIEW OF INTERNET GAMBLING REGULATION, REPORT PREPARED FOR THE ONTARIO PROBLEM GAMBLING RESEARCH CENTRE, GUELPH, ONTARIO, CANADA (Aug. 2008).

[54] BOGART, *supra* note 1, at 273–86.

[55] *Id.* at ch. 4: V. Recreational Drugs: The Outliers?.

[56] D. PROVINE, UNEQUAL UNDER LAW: RACE IN THE WAR ON DRUGS (2007).

[57] *Id.* at 68 *et seq*.

[58] C. Carstairs, JAILED FOR POSSESSION: ILLEGAL DRUG USE, REGULATION, AND POWER IN CANADA, 1920–1961, at 16 (2006).

[59] PROVINE, *supra* note 56, at 13.

on drugs (and its predecessor drug wars) are the typical result of moral panics. Racial minorities and those perceived to be socially deviant are typical targets for such policies and the negative media attention that accompanies them."[60]

Various countries are experimenting with alternative approaches to suppress drug use.[61] Many opinion leaders are calling for less draconian measures to encourage users to quit, to persuade even more individuals to never start, and to undercut the flourishing demimonde trade in recreational drugs: "The war on drugs has been a disaster...[T]his 100 year struggle has been illiberal, murderous, and pointless...[T]he least bad policy is to legalise drugs."[62] Much the same position was taken, in 2011, by the Global Commission on Drug Policy whose membership includes government and business leaders from several countries.[63] Still, drugs and criminal law, especially in America, remain steadfastly linked.

Two overarching points emerge from this brief survey of efforts to regulate consumption. First, such attempts, particularly in terms of suppressing excess, have, at most, been only partially successful. Despite a range of legal interventions, often aligned with other powerful techniques of social control, a significant incidence of excess remains. About 20 percent of adults in Canada and the United States still smoke. Damage to health and slaughter on the highway is ever present despite the many interventions by law and other campaigns to drive down intemperate use of alcohol. Problem gambling is a fact of life in the gaming industry even though there have been efforts to suppress it. Meanwhile a host of new challenges are being posed for regulatory efforts by the increasing ability to gamble in cyberspace. The "war on drugs" has not been won, while imposing enormous financial costs and causing great human suffering.

Second, while attempting to achieve good results, law can cause harm. A rough parallel are the iatrogenic effects of medicine. Sometimes illness is created by the very efforts to cure another disease.[64] Such harms have been a prominent hazard in attempts to regulate consumption. The Victorians wanted to imprison people just because they were alcoholics. The United States caused enormous black markets and related crime as a result of a constitutional ban on booze. Canada raised taxes in tobacco, which gave rise to a robust industry in contraband cigarettes. Efforts to regulate problem gambling pushed those with impaired control to wager in cyberspace with its loosely policed, free-wheeling ways. Substance users were stigmatized and marginalized, sometimes with disproportionate effects based on race, because of the criminalization of drugs.

---

[60] *Id.* at 8.
[61] BOGART, *supra* 1, at 164–85.
[62] *How to Stop the Drug Wars*, ECONOMIST, Mar. 7–13, 2009, at 15.
[63] WAR ON DRUGS: REPORT OF THE GLOBAL COMMISSION ON DRUG POLICY, June 2011, *available at* http://www.globalcommissionondrugs.org/wp-content/themes/gcdp_v1/pdf/Global_Commission_Report_English.pdf.
[64] BOGART, *supra* note 6, at 134.

These two observations about the qualified effects of legal efforts and the potential of such interventions to cause harm as they attempt to do good are a caution about the consequences produced by regulation. These two caveats, among others, have led to increasing skepticism about using law, at least as traditionally conceived, to reconfigure social, political, and economic arrangements. There are strong warnings about those bent on using the law to achieve a variety of ends: "[A]ctivists have been especially prone to exaggerate what [it] can accomplish."[65] We'll keep these doubts at the forefront as we examine various efforts to address obesity. In the end, law has a role—but it is a complicated one. Use it with guarded expectations and a clear eye in terms of actual outcomes produced.

V. Some Ideas About Law Shaping Behavior

Law is as much, if not more, about persuading than it is about commanding. True, wrongdoings that threaten life or property need to be sanctioned through the prohibitions of the criminal law. But beyond these matters there is increasing curiosity about how best to use the law to persuade individuals and entities to make good decisions in a range of contexts from protecting the environment to saving for retirement. Let's look at some of these ideas and then talk about their relevance for regulating consumption and, in particular, obesity. In subsequent chapters we'll return to them several times to help us to come to grips with various interventions regarding weight, health, and physical activity.

A) LOOKING AT THE STATE IN A DIFFERENT WAY: NEW GOVERNANCE

Even a casual observer senses that government does not function in the same way as it did, say, twenty-five years ago.[66] Assumptions about powerful administrative tribunals carrying out policies of big government as a realization of the public good no longer hold. Such assumptions have changed. At least some morphed into accusations that "portray[ed] government agencies as tightly structured hierarchies insulated from market forces and from effective citizen pressure and therefore free to serve the personal and institutional interests of bureaucrats instead."[67]

New means of regulation are sometimes associated with two broad developments: the crisis and transformation of the modern welfare state and the emergence and growing prominence of forms of regulation "beyond" the state: for

---

[65] R. ELLICKSON, ORDER WITHOUT LAW: HOW NEIGHBORS SETTLE DISPUTES 281 (1991).
[66] *See generally* BOGART, *supra* note 1, at 61–74.
[67] Salamon, *supra* note 3, at 1.

example, increasing delegation of rulemaking and rule-enforcing authority to private industry associations or hybrid third parties (fair trade certificates for example), and increased reliance on economic instruments such as tradable pollution permits.[68]

Traditional concepts of government and its agencies have been questioned across the political spectrum: the Right has focused on inefficiencies and government and agencies meddling in the market; the Left has focused on unresponsiveness to the needs of the disadvantaged and exclusionary practices against the historically marginalized. As a result governments and their agencies have been pushed "to be reinvented, downsized, privatized, devolved, decentralized, deregulated, delayered, subject to performance tests, and contracted out."[69]

These demands that government and the administrative state function in substantially different ways have led to analyses regarding the extent of the alterations and how such changes might be characterized. About a decade ago Salamon claimed that there is a "new governance": a shift in the paradigm of public programs.[70] The "new governance" no longer has as its centerpiece agencies or programs but, rather, the tools used to realize the various goals of the "new governance." This prominence of tools and how they should be employed has altered the very character of public management and of the administrative state:

> Instead of command and control, it must emphasize negotiation and persuasion. In place of management skills, enablement skills are increasingly required instead. Far from simplifying the task of public problem solving the proliferation of tools has importantly complicated it even while enlarging the range of options and the pool of resources potentially brought to bear.[71]

There is no assertion here that Salamon's analysis of a paradigmatic shift is exhaustive or that the transformation, whatever its exact nature, applies in just the same way to all aspects in every postindustrial society. The premises of government have been questioned in ways not fully addressed by Salamon's depiction. Such forces as globalization and fundamental alterations to the social

---

[68] Recall Hood's and others' definition of regulation cited earlier; *see* HOOD ET AL., *supra* note 4, and accompanying text. For further readings, see generally S. Wood, *Three Questions about Corporate Codes: Problematizations, Authorizations and the Public/Private Divide*, in ETHICS CODES, CORPORATIONS AND THE CHALLENGE OF GLOBALIZATION 245 (W. Cragg ed., 2005). See also S. Wood, *Green Revolution or Greenwash? Voluntary Environmental Standards, Public Law and Private Authority in Canada*, in LAW COMMISSION OF CANADA NEW PERSPECTIVES ON THE PUBLIC–PRIVATE DIVIDE 123 (2003).

[69] Salamon, *supra* note 3, at 1.

[70] A similar trend is reflected in the term "new public management." *See* J. VERSCHUUREN, THE IMPACT OF LEGISLATION: A CRITICAL ANALYSIS OF EX ANTE EVALUATION 21–22 (2009).

[71] Salamon, *supra* note 3, at 18.

safety net are only two examples of influences that have produced effects that go beyond changes in the tools of legal intervention.[72]

It may be most helpful to think not in terms of a paradigmatic shift but of a significant change in emphasis. The tools are not new; there are many examples of continuity in use. However, there is a movement away from "command and control": government and its agencies mandating the regulatory regime and its detailed implementation. Instead, there is openness to a variety of ways in which overall policy objectives can be achieved, including through active involvement on the part of those subject to regulation. This flexibility, when it occurs, is largely achieved through employment of various tools in a number of ways driven by the particular context of the regulatory initiative.

B) IDEAS FOR NEW GOVERNANCE: NORMATIVITY AND ITS OFFSPRING

The limits of law underscored by such developments as impact studies and the new governance approach cause some to cast about for ways in which to make law more effective or, at least, to better understand its constraints.[73] One such means that claims promise is "normativity": the relationship between law and norms. Excessive consumption is an important and promising context for analyzing that relationship. Consumption is universal, and a wide variety of norms surround its many forms and varieties. We can think of norms as social attitudes of approval (and disapproval), indicating desirable (and undesirable) behavior in particular situations. Many such norms are highly durable ("never eat peas with one's fingers"); but many are changeable and can shift fairly rapidly (think of attitudes toward littering of candy wrappers, beer cans and such, fifty years ago and today).

Those interested in regulating consumption and, specifically, issues related to obesity are quick to acknowledge the importance of norms. Official reports and various writers, addressing these issues, often place norms at the forefront in terms of tackling relevant questions. To refer to just a few instances, there is talk of "values, social norms, and the public view of health,"[74] of "changing social norms,"[75] and of how "social norms are powerful in determining people's actions," and that "coordinated, multi-component programs, and policies are

---

[72] Regarding globalization influence on Canadian society and government, see STREET PROTESTS AND FANTASY PARKS : GLOBALIZATION, CULTURE, AND THE STATE 1 (D. Cameron & J. Gross Stein eds., 2002). Regarding transformations in the models of the social safety net, see K. Banting, *Dis-Embedding LIberalism? The New Social Policy Paradigm in Canada*, *in* DIMENSIONS OF INEQUALITY IN CANADA 417 (D. Green & J. Kesselman eds., 2006).

[73] For efforts focused on "behavioral research," *see* THE BEHAVIORAL FOUNDATIONS OF PUBLIC POLICY (E. Shafir ed., 2013).

[74] INSTITUTE OF MEDICINE, *supra* note 7, at 23.

[75] F. SASSI, OBESITY AND THE ECONOMICS OF PREVENTION: FIT NOT FAT 225 [in association with the OECD] (2010).

necessary to effectively change social norms."[76] Wansink speaks of "consumption norms."[77] Kessler asserts that changing norms will bring about "the end of overeating": "new [ones]...will emerge and...smaller portion sizes will seem 'right' to us."[78]

The problem is that few such references specify exactly how norms relate to consumption and to the role of law in addressing relevant issues.[79] Norms are acknowledged to be important but too little is said about what role they play and how they might be harnessed to achieve policy goals, particularly when legal interventions are invoked. They are saluted but then the discussion moves on; this important form of social influence is largely ignored. So let's spend some time talking about law and norms: "normativity."

A central assertion of normativity is that legal policy makers, although acknowledging norms, have mostly treated them as uninteresting givens in terms of policy formation and implementation. By contrast, what is common among normativists is skepticism about the capacity of law to alter behavior directly. As a result, there is an emphasis in shaping conduct on the vital role of norms and their relationship to various forms of regulation.[80]

Policy goals will more likely be achieved if norms, existing or altered, support those ambitions. In this depiction, law becomes subsumed. It becomes merely a means, albeit an extremely important one, to assist in creating or changing norms. The importance of normativity is illustrated, in many ways, by efforts to suppress consumption. These examples and their implications yield a common emphasis. There is a role for law in grappling with various forms of excessive appetites and their consequences. However, addressing those issues poses huge challenges. A significant factor in any success can be the linking of law to prevailing norms. Achieving a codependence between the two can send multiple signals about, on the one hand, the dangers of excess and, on the other, the benefits of moderation.

The challenge for grappling with normativity is one of specifics: what is the relationship of law and norms regarding the achievement of any particular policy goal? The answer to that question is usually complex. Moreover any useful response is difficult to provide prospectively; it is only after legal interventions and norms have interacted that there can be a sense of their codependence in

---

[76] WHITE HOUSE TASK FORCE ON CHILDHOOD OBESITY, REPORT TO THE PRESIDENT, SOLVING THE PROBLEM OF CHILDHOOD OBESITY WITHIN A GENERATION 66–67 (May 2010).

[77] B. Wansink, *Turning Mindless Eating into Healthy Eating*, in THE BEHAVIORAL FOUNDATIONS OF PUBLIC POLICY, *supra* note 73 at 311.

[78] D. KESSLER, THE END OF OVEREATING: TAKING CONTROL OF THE INSATIABLE AMERICAN APPETITE 249 (2009).

[79] Wansink, *supra* note 77, makes an attempt. His ideas are referred to in Chapter 5, Section III(a): Educating about Nutritious Eating and Drinking?

[80] For a full discussion of normativity and its relevance for consumption: *see* BOGART, *supra* note 1, at ch. 3: Excessive Consumption and Normativity.

any specific area. Efforts to suppress smoking over the last fifty years will be used to illustrate such interaction and the effects produced. The assertion is not, by any means, that normativity is the only thing that matters in terms of the regulation of consumption. But normativity is in play, and a better understanding of it, and its relevance for addressing excessive consumption, can increase whatever chances there are for achieving policy goals.

There have been a number of interesting efforts to take core ideas of normativity and to apply them in various contexts. Let's look at two of them: Stout's "cultivating conscience" and Thaler and Sunstein's "the nudge." They are especially helpful in thinking about regulation, new governance, and, most specifically, addressing issues of healthy eating and exercise.

Lynn Stout argues that there is significant potential for prosocial behavior among humans that should be nurtured rather than mostly being ignored by legal policy makers.[81] If these unselfish elements are harnessed, societies will have more effective laws that are more in harmony with a collective moral compass. For Stout this position is not dreamy abstraction. For her, conscience is an animating force that tells us much about human interaction.

Cultivating Conscience by Stout surveys the extensive and growing body of evidence on the centrality of conscience in determining behavior. It analyzes evidence from behavioral economics, social psychology, and evolutionary biology to demonstrate that an individual's action based on conscience is widespread and subject to predictable patterns. Thus she largely rejects the tenets of many economic models that script individuals as concerned only with themselves and the pursuit of whatever course of action that will bring the most material advantage.

Stout maintains that: "Civic life in the United States is filled with…acts of courtesy, consideration, and forbearance. Unselfish, prosocial behavior is so deeply woven into the warp and woof of Western life that it often goes unnoticed."[82] Specifically, there are three cues that are especially prominent in triggering positive social behavior: instructions from authority, belief that others are being unselfish (or selfish), and perceptions about benefits to others of prosocial actions.[83] At the same time she acknowledges the evidence suggesting that ethical, unselfish behavior is declining in America.[84]

Stout gained inspiration for *Cultivating Conscience* from her years of studying the actual workings of corporate law. She found that models that gave primacy to selfish, individualistic actions did not account well for how successful corporations functioned. Instead, these entities were often characterized by a

---

[81] L. STOUT, CULTIVATING CONSCIENCE: HOW GOOD LAWS MAKE GOOD PEOPLE (2011).
[82] *Id.* at 7.
[83] *Id.* at 21.
[84] *Id.* at 18–22.

high degree of internal trust, honesty, and cooperation.[85] In the latter part of the book Stout applies her model to tort, contract, and criminal law.[86]

Stout does not comment specifically on consumption or its regulation. Her global approach to law is what is important to underscore for our purposes. Her emphasis on law as embedded in a larger version of social control techniques is a significant message for efforts to promote healthy eating and exercise. As she observes: "law must work in—and also comprise part of—our social context. To understand and use law more effectively we must take account of the many ways law changes behavior, above and beyond creating material incentives."[87]

Thaler and Sunstein reflect both the new governance and some important applications of normativity through their work on "nudges."[88] Thaler is an economist, Sunstein a prolific legal academic. Their goal in their book *Nudge* is to help people make better choices in a variety of areas without removing their right to choose. A central claim of theirs is that individuals choose more wisely when provided with a clear set of options that respond to various human idiosyncrasies. Thus they emphasize the larger contexts in which individuals make decisions; "choice architects" organize such broader circumstances.[89] Such inquiries lead them to focus on the central idea of the "nudge": "A nudge...is any aspect of the choice architecture that alters people's behavior in a predictable way without forbidding any options or significantly changing their economic incentives."[90]

Part of what prompts their message is to refute the classical economic position that "each of us thinks and chooses unfailingly well."[91] Such people Thaler and Sunstein refer to as "Econs." Instead, the authors focus their efforts on "Humans" (!) and four decades of research on how individuals actually choose. Results of such studies demonstrate that people often do not act on rational judgments, relying instead on flawed bases—idiosyncrasies—for decision making across a range of activities. Two examples of such erroneous premises are: "status quo bias," which prompts individuals to go along with the default option when they are provided with various choices; and the "planning fallacy," which is the systematic tendency toward unrealistic optimism about the time it takes to complete projects.[92]

---

[85] *Id.* at 8.
[86] *Id.* at chs. 7, 8, and 9.
[87] *Id.* at 236–37.
[88] R. THALER & C. SUNSTEIN, NUDGE: IMPROVING DECISIONS ABOUT HEALTH, WEALTH, AND HAPPINESS (2008). For a review discussing the book's relationship to "new governance," see O. Amir & O. Lobel, *Stumble, Predict, Nudge: How Behavioral Economics Informs Law and Policy*, 108 COLUMBIA L. REV. 2098, 2127 *et seq.* (Dec. 2008).
[89] THALER & SUNSTEIN, *supra* note 88, at 3.
[90] *Id.* at 6.
[91] *Id.*
[92] *Id.* at 7–8.

Thaler and Sunstein illustrate the potential of nudges in a variety of circumstances in which people make choices. The subtitle of their book is *Improving Decisions about Health, Wealth, and Happiness*, and its authors are eager to demonstrate the power of nudges in all these dimensions. They claim that *Nudge* and its ideas are animated by a particular philosophical stance: "libertarian paternalism." "The libertarian aspect...lies in the straightforward insistence that, in general, people should be free to do what they like...The paternalistic aspect lies in the claim that it is legitimate for choice architects to try to influence people's behavior in order to make their lives, longer, healthier, and better."[93]

Thaler and Sunstein are confident that the two seemingly contradictory aspects of this oxymoron are, nevertheless, compatible, and that they should be embraced across the political spectrum. Such pan-party enthusiasm will occur for several reasons, including a "central" one: "[M]any of these policies cost little or nothing; they impose no burden on the taxpayers at all." And so as to leave little doubt where they are headed the following flourish appears in italics: "*we are not for bigger government; just for better governance.*"[94]

Nudge has lots to say about consumption and how to address issues of impaired control. It has suggestions for the suppression of smoking, intemperate drinking, and problem gambling.[95] Consider one example: cigarettes and bank deposits. In one program an individual trying to stop smoking opens a bank account. For six months she deposits the amount of money she would otherwise spend on cigarettes into the account. After six months she takes a test that determines whether she has been smoking. If she hasn't she gets to keep the money in the account; if she has the account is closed and the money is donated to charity. There is evidence that participating in this bank program increases the chance of quitting by over 50 percent, giving this initiative a much higher success rate than many other cessation efforts.[96]

There are criticisms of *Nudge*. Its prescriptions for addressing some of the circumstances contributing to the 2008 economic meltdown were woefully inadequate.[97] Yet the book is an important contribution to discussions that encourage nuanced approaches to society's problems. Passing laws and throwing money at a problem is often not enough and may sometimes even do more harm than good. The British, under Prime Minister Cameron, seem particularly taken with *Nudge*. That government has established a special unit, to

---

[93] *Id.* at 5.
[94] *Id.* at 13–14.
[95] For smoking, *see id.* at 33, 47, 232. For intemperate drinking, *see id.* at 67. For problem gambling, *see id.* at 42, 233.
[96] *Id.* at 232.
[97] For this and other criticisms *see* BOGART, *supra* note 1, at 65–70.

mixed reviews, to investigate all manner of possibilities for this new technique for influencing behavior.[98]

Nudging people along is, indeed, part of a more multifaceted strategy that seeks to fashion a specific response that fits the particular problem. But the real trick is selecting the right components in the correct combination. Such challenges loom large in any attempts to regulate various issues of healthy eating and exercise.

C) NEW GOVERNANCE, NORMATIVITY, AND THE REGULATION OF CONSUMPTION

Critics accuse new governance of being window dressing for hapless policy making and, worse, allowing a variety of special interests and free marketeers to mostly have their way.[99] Some environmentalists may acknowledge that negotiation, mediation, and roundtables may be all well and good. However, at a certain point they emphasize that agencies need to be able to impose sanctions and even lay criminal charges against recalcitrant offenders.[100] This pushing back against the new governance can be replicated in a number of areas: securities regulation, human rights, and so forth.

Sunstein took many of his ideas, including those regarding the *Nudge*, to Washington to work for President Obama. He became administrator of the Office of Information and Regulatory Affairs, serving until the summer of 2012. He oversaw hundreds of rules addressing numerous and diverse issues such as those involving financial markets, the environment (e.g., higher fuel efficiency for cars and trucks, new toxic emission rules for power plants), prison safety, and many aspects of health, including the *Patient Protection and Affordable Care Act*.[101] In the present political atmosphere his role was almost bound to be controversial. At the same time those in favor of regulation may be even more critical of his term than those who were the targets of various interventions: "[H]e is departing with a record that left many business interests disappointed and environmental, health and consumer advocates even more unhappy."[102]

---

[98] E. Day, *Julia Neuberger: "A Nudge in the Right Direction Won't Run the Big Society,"* GUARDIAN, July 17, 2011, available at http://www.guardian.co.uk/society/2011/jul/17/julia-neuberger-nudge-big-society; *The Nudge Saving UK Taxpayers Millions,* NEWS.COM.AU, Feb. 3, 2013, available at http://www.news.com.au/world/the-nudge-saving-uk-taxpayers-millions/story-fndir2ev-1226568163694.

[99] J. FREEMAN & M. MINOW, GOVERNMENT BY CONTRACT: OUTSOURCING AND AMERICAN DEMOCRACY (2009).

[100] H. BENEVIDES, PROTECTION AND PRECAUTION: CANADIAN PRIORITIES FOR FEDERAL REGULATORY POLICY (2005); P. Webster & J. Cuthro, *HANDS OFF—Is Smart Regulation Dumb for Canada's Wilderness Areas?* WALRUS 40, Special Arctic Issue, Nov. 2007.

[101] Patient Protection and Affordable Care Act, 2010, H.R. 3590.

[102] J. Broder, *Powerful Shaper of U.S. Rules Quits, Leaving Critics in Wake,* N.Y. TIMES, Aug. 4, 2012, at A1, A9.

These criticisms should be kept in mind. The mixed reviews of Sunstein's track record also give pause. Still new governance may be, generally, well-suited to the regulation of excessive consumption. As we observed earlier, an overall theme that has emerged about such regulation is *permit but discourage*. Legal intervention is mostly not about prohibition of consumption and its excessive aspects; command and control, top-down initiatives, and administrative fiat are used comparatively sparingly. Instead, educational efforts, incentives, the tax system, and other tools are being employed to encourage healthy levels of consumption with regard to alcohol, nonnutritious foods, etc. These strategies try to counterbalance industry forces that are all too willing to supply harmful amounts of products and services in terms of smoking, gambling, and so forth.

This is not to say that the new governance approach has always dominated. There are historical examples where a particular view of consumption was dictated through law: the constitutional prohibition regarding alcohol is probably the most famous and drastic one.[103] Even now prohibition is used in a limited number of instances; for example, regarding consumption by children in terms of tobacco and alcohol because of widespread acceptance that children, just because they are children, are incapable of making autonomous decisions regarding consumption. Illicit drugs are criminalized. These are outliers that do not fit the *permit but discourage* paradigm.[104]

Otherwise, new governance has found receptive ground in terms of regulating consumption and especially its immoderate aspects. Policy makers search for ways to educate, offer incentives to moderation (and disincentives against excess), shape advertising, and encourage healthy decisions. Various industries (food, soda, alcohol, and gambling) when faced with pressures for intervention often claim the right to self-regulate in order to stave off the heavy hand of government.

New governance is also in evidence in terms of obesity. There are lots of efforts directed to having people eat/drink more healthily and to provide environments conducive to people choosing to be physically active; these employ education, provide various kinds of incentives, allow for self-regulation, and so forth. We'll see these approaches in evidence when we look at various interventions to address healthier eating/drinking and exercise in Part III. At the same time the coercive power of the state waits in the wings to be called upon when it is judged necessary. A case in point: passing laws prohibiting discrimination against fat people. Another: the banning of advertising to children under thirteen in the province of Quebec, Canada. These are controversial interventions that we'll discuss in detail in subsequent chapters.[105]

---

[103] BOGART, *supra* note 1, at ch. 1: IV. Prohibition: Unintended Consequences.
[104] *Id.* at ch. 4: V. Recreational Drugs: The Outliers?.
[105] Regarding laws prohibiting discrimination, *see* Chapter 3; regarding banning advertising to children in Quebec, *see* Chapter 5, Section IV(b)2(ii) [two]: Quebec.

Normativity and the regulation of consumption are also closely entwined. How we actually establish norms that promote healthy consumption and harness them to interact with legal interventions is the big question. Contemporary attempts to promote good choices and minimize harm would do well to bear in mind the importance of establishing and buttressing norms that support such regulatory goals. Norms can pave the way for regulatory intervention. Sound intervention can bolster such norms. Strengthened norms can support even more effective regulatory efforts.

At a basic level normativity is effective in terms of consumption. The regulatory mix in conjunction with prevailing norms achieves the sought-after goals: most individuals do not smoke, drink to excess (at least on any regular basis), are not obese, and are not problem or even at-risk gamblers. Criminalization of drugs, despite the suffering it causes, is effective to the extent that most people do not use illicit substances. All that said, the percentage of individuals who are in the thrall of excess can impose significant costs on themselves, their families, friends, employers, and communities. Efforts to bring down these percentages, largely through prevention strategies, is a real test for the laws and norms that are in play. There is still much excess and the costs, gauged in a number of ways, it imposes is still very high. Much remains to be done.

VI. Conclusion

This brief tour of regulation tells us how complicated an enterprise it is, from selection of tools to implementing legal interventions to the outcomes that are produced by any such efforts. Attempts to control consumption, especially excessive aspects, reflect such complexities.

Law can be a powerful force for achieving policy goals. But its effects can also be partial, sometimes unintended, and, at times, misdirected. Law's limits are underscored in an era of suspicion of government and its heavy-handed ways. Enter new governance and normativity as different ideas to look at regulation and the outcomes it produces. These limits, suspicions, and different ideas figure prominently in efforts to address obesity. Can we shift norms (and thus behavior) away from the stigmatization of fat people to an embrace of lettuce and brisk walking and acceptance of bodies of various shapes and sizes?

{ PART II }

Being Fat

{ 2 }

How Is Obesity a Problem?

I. Introduction

> Ad from Children's Health care of Atlanta showing a young fat girl with her eyes downcast with the tagline "it's hard to be a little girl if you're not"
>
> —One of several and similar anti-obesity ads in 2012 from that institution.[1]

> "[T]he human body continues to fight against weight loss long after dieting has stopped ... [O]nce we become fat, most of us, despite our best efforts, will probably stay fat."
>
> —Tara Parker-Pope, 2012, in the *New York Times Magazine*.[2]

The foregoing, both appearing in early 2012, represent very different understandings about the significance of being overweight and possible responses. The first focuses on being fat as the problem. The solution is weight loss or, better still, prevention of weight gain. Of particular note is the plight of obese children and their physical ailments and psychological stresses because of the bullying by other kids and embarrassment in the wider society. The second underscores the enormous difficulty of losing weight and, even more so, maintaining any such reduction. Being fat may give rise to problems. But the greatest difficulty may be in not accepting that most people who become fat remain fat. That denial stymies efforts to foster the healthiest state possible for all individuals, including the obese.

---

[1] Meghan Keneally, *Mom, Why Am I Fat?: Controversy over Shock Anti-Obesity Ads Featuring Overweight Children*, DAILY MAIL, Jan. 2, 2012, *available at* http://www.dailymail.co.uk/news/article-2081328/Weighty-debate-anti-obesity-ads-featuring-fat-kids-causes-criticism-health-advocates-shock-tactics.html.

[2] T. Parker-Pope, *The Fat Trap*, N.Y. TIMES MAG., Jan. 1, 2012, *available at* http://www.nytimes.com/2012/01/01/magazine/tara-parker-pope-fat-trap.html?pagewanted=all.

We will return to the implications of both the Parker-Pope article and the Children's Health care of Atlanta's campaign later in the chapter.[3] They illustrate two of several very different perspectives on the extent to which being large is a problem and the best way to address issues of excess weight, including through law.

Discussion of obesity and its potential regulation triggers significantly different views of how being fat is a problem and about the nature of any appropriate responses. There are fiery debates about the extent to which obesity is a problem at all, let alone one that should become the focus of legal scrutiny. We can assess these controversies from a number of perspectives. First, we'll look generally at the quandaries of determining whether a problem should be the focus of legal redress. Then we'll examine debates about obesity and how it is viewed as a problem. Finally, we'll see how such conflicts spill over into debates about how, if at all, law should be employed to address issues of excess weight.

II. What's the Problem?: Encountering Corpulence

To provide good solutions, those charged with responding must first, more or less, agree concerning the nature of the problem. Yet policy making is replete with examples where achieving common understanding of the issues to be addressed has proven daunting. The debates around outcomes can start before any law comes into play. If one does not believe the phenomenon in question is a problem at all or, at any rate, one that the law should solve, then one is more likely to be skeptical about the effects produced by any law that is invoked as a solution. Such skepticism may include predictions that undesirable results will occur that are at odds with the effects sought to be achieved. Conversely, those urging a legal response to a claimed problem may be inclined to view outcomes as positive, ignore any warnings about undesirable consequences, and conclude that any good effects (as judged by the proponents of the law) are the result of the law, or series of laws meant to respond to the ill sought to be remedied.[4]

The saga of laws in the United States requiring wearing a helmet while on a motorcycle is a case in point.[5] The *Highway Safety Act* of 1966 stipulated that states enact and enforce motorcycle helmet laws in order to receive certain federal funding. By 1975, forty-seven states and the District of Columbia

---

[3] For Parker-Pope, *see infra* Section IV(d) *Weight Loss?: What Is Shed Is Almost Always Regained*; for the Atlanta campaign *see infra* Section IV(e)(2): "The Greatest Threat": Stigma, Discrimination, and the Obese.

[4] W. A. BOGART, CONSEQUENCES: THE IMPACT OF LAW AND ITS COMPLEXITY 84–87 (2002); *see also* discussion in Chapter 1, Section III: How Effective Is Regulation?

[5] INSTITUTE OF MEDICINE, FOR THE PUBLIC'S HEALTH: REVITALIZING LAW AND POLICY TO MEET NEW CHALLENGES 59–61 (2011). This is the report discussed at length in Chapter 1, Section III(c): Legal Interventions to Promote Health.

had done so. Yet by 2007 the situation was dramatically reversed: only twenty states and the District of Columbia required all riders to wear helmets. Most of the laws on the books in 1975 had either been repealed outright or, at the least, drastically amended to dilute such requirements. Three states have no such laws at all, and the other twenty-seven had drastically modified ones, mostly focused on requiring young and inexperienced riders to wear helmets.[6] What happened?

Significant disagreement about what the problem was played a major role in the legislative tussles. Proponents of the laws made three arguments: (1) the costs incurred by society because of such accidents; (2) the effectiveness of helmets in preventing deaths and injuries; and (3) the concept that governments should protect citizens from inflicting injuries on themselves with the accompanying costs to themselves, families etc.[7] Moreover, proponents had sound empirical evidence to support their positions. One study estimated that hospital treatment for riders not wearing a helmet exceeded costs for those wearing one by over $250,000,000 in an applicable period.[8]

But such arguments and evidence were unavailing against those asserting individual freedom to choose whether to don such protections. "Choice" is a forceful rallying cry, particularly in America.[9] The motorcyclist as a freewheeling rebel defying anyone with a whiff of authority may be romantic fantasy. It appears also to be a dangerous one. Nonetheless, after initial setbacks, anti-helmet forces were hugely successful in narrating the problem as one of preservation of choice and personal freedom. Sober arguments (and evidence) regarding lives saved and costs averted, over time, came to have less force and were, ultimately, overridden.

At the same time Thaler and Sunstein, proponents of "the nudge," discussed in Chapter 1 have weighed in.[10] They believe that relevant issues can be addressed by not requiring helmets but, instead, mandating an extra driving course and that drivers be covered by health insurance.[11] The concept of the "nudge" and its approach to regulation is attractive in the way it can promote good choices with minimal restrictions of freedom. But the proposal here is questionable. Shouldn't motorcycle drivers be insured in any event and for a sum that can cover the horrific damages they may suffer? How's "an extra driving course" an

---

[6] R. Moulton et al., *Perspective: Law and Great Public Health Achievements*, in LAW IN PUBLIC HEALTH PRACTICE 3–24 (R. Goodman et al. eds., 2007).

[7] L. O Gostin & K. G Gostin, *A Broader Liberty: J. S. Mill, Paternalism and the Public's Health*, 123 PUB. HEALTH 214 (Mar. 2009).

[8] B. Eastridge, *Economic Impact of Motorcycle Helmets: From Impact to Discharge*, 60 J. TRAUMA 978 (May 2006).

[9] L. FRIEDMAN, THE REPUBLIC OF CHOICE: LAW, AUTHORITY, AND CULTURE (1990).

[10] R. THALER & C. SUNSTEIN, NUDGE: IMPROVING DECISIONS ABOUT HEALTH, WEALTH, AND HAPPINESS (2008); *see* Chapter 1, Section V(b): Ideas for New Governance: Normativity and Its Offspring

[11] THALER & SUNSTEIN, *supra* note 10, at 232–33.

answer? Accidents still happen to very careful drivers, including because of the negligence of someone else.

Some see a fact of daily life and view it as a problem crying out for regulatory intervention—the costs, however measured, are sure to be dwarfed by the benefits. Others cast their gaze on the same happenings and are certain that a legal solution will impose more harm than good, or they prefer a "nudge" that risks being so-so libertarianism and ineffective paternalism.[12] Ruminations on obesity clearly illustrate a number of very different ideas about the issues that are at stake and competing views about "What's the problem?"

Reports in the media suggest that obesity is a clear and growing danger. Too many people weigh too much and the numbers of such individuals have increased substantially over the last decades. Such excess weight is associated with a variety of diseases and other negative consequences, ranging from high blood pressure to inability to fit into an airline seat, from diabetes to coffins that are too small for obese deceased.

Such narratives of obesity are increasingly challenged. Critics allege that the incidence of obesity has been exaggerated. At the same time they point to evidence suggesting that rates have leveled off and may even be declining. They also question the extent that obesity causes or is even associated with various diseases. They point to the dismal statistics regarding weight loss: some can lose pounds but very few can keep them off over a five-year period. As a result critics insist that weight should not be, in and of itself, the issue. By harping on people's size, the health professions and the media create a climate of stigmatization that, in itself, creates enormous stress for, and discrimination against, fat people.

These debates are the result of genuine policy differences and scientific and medical uncertainties that may or may not be clarified over time. However, there are also strong financial interests in play. The food-and-drink industry and others have powerful economic motivations to downplay and, in any event, distance themselves from concerns about excess weight. Conversely, the pharmaceutical and weight loss industries and health professionals associated with bariatric surgery and other interventions have significant monetary incentives to fuel anxieties about obesity and its consequences. These various and contending interests dedicate substantial resources to publicity campaigns, lobbying efforts, and research to advance whatever may be their positions in the intense and shifting debates in this area.

Even more fundamentally, fat provokes thoughts and emotions that hinge on basic worldviews about the social order and the individual. Personal responsibility, the interplay of the market and consumption, and the extent to which

---

[12] A play on Thaler and Sunstein's "libertarian paternalism": *id.* at 4–6.

law and politics can and should engage obesity in this divisive age are all in play. Fat invites conversations, sometimes very loud ones, about society and the self.

III. Obesity: A Public Health Issue?

Traditional responses to excessive weight characterize people as "obese." They focus on the increase in the incidence of obesity in recent decades, the explanations for that rise, the consequences for the individual and society, and the way to get people to shed pounds or, better still, not gain them in the first place. Global assessments of weight status are reflected in an individual's Body Mass Index (BMI); a figure derived from a person's height and weight (weight in kilograms divided by the square of the height in meters). Individuals who have a BMI of over 25 are considered overweight; over 30 are considered obese; over 40 morbidly so.

Obesity is considered a public health issue in a number of ways. First, that characterization conveys that there are consequences of obesity for not only fat people themselves but also the larger society. Second, addressing obesity is not only a matter of individual responsibility. Why people eat excessively and are not physically active also raises larger questions of society's role, the market and consumption, and appropriate responses from the health care and other professions. Third, legal interventions to foster weight loss are justified because of this shared responsibility of individuals and society for conditions leading to the elevated incidence of obesity in the last decades.

The following section presents details concerning the increase in the incidence of obesity and its associated costs. Characterizations and statistics are taken from literature that mostly focuses on the need for weight loss (and prevention of gain) as the correct response to the obesity epidemic. We'll come to critiques of these characterizations, statistics, and that response momentarily.

A) INCREASE IN WEIGHT

The conventional account of obesity as a problem emphasizes its incidence, its rapid increase, and the particular challenges faced by seriously overweight children.[13] As this out-of-control growth in pounds occurs, all manner of personal and systemic heath issues are intensifying. The primary response to all of this is for people to lose weight (or not gain excess pounds in the first place). As a result there is a constant search for explanations of the causes of weight gain and effective ways to lose excess pounds and to maintain that lighter weight.

---

[13] INSTITUTE OF MEDICINE, ACCELERATING PROGRESS IN OBESITY PREVENTION: SOLVING THE WEIGHT OF THE NATION (2012).

In 1978 Americans took in 1,826 calories a day; by 2011 it was 2,157. The average American woman weighed 142 pounds in the 1960s; by 2011 that figure was 152. In 1981 a forty-five–year-old Canadian male who was 5' 8" weighed approximately 171 pounds; in 2008 the figure was 191 pounds. During the same period Canadian females of the same age, standing 5'4" weighed 139 pounds. That figure increased to 151 pounds.[14] Globally, WHO estimates that in 2011 one billion individuals were overweight and 300 million were obese.[15] In 2011 it was projected that if present trends continued every American would be overweight in forty years.[16]

Children are of special concern.[17] Problems with weight can start very early. In 2011 approximately 21 percent of U.S. children, ages two to five, were either overweight or obese.[18] Worse, over about three decades the percentage of young people in the United States that are overweight tripled from 5.2 percent in 1971 to 17.3 by 2004.[19] Once overweight or obese, children rarely return to a regular size.[20] Thus, there is special emphasis placed on prevention of excess weight gain even from the first stages of life.

There is much discussion of the causes of all this excess poundage. At its simplest, weight gain can be caused by individuals taking in more calories than they expend. But why this excess consumption generally, and for various individuals, particularly? Are there still other explanations? Researchers cite a number of factors. The following are basic points regarding some of the main ones.

1. Genes, Metabolism, and Antibiotics

Few make the case that genes are the single influence regarding obesity. There is much more to discover regarding genetic factors and weight.[21] Genes may contribute to excess poundage in several ways, including by affecting appetite, creating a sense of fullness, affecting body fat distribution, and coping with stress. Their precise role has not been determined. Studies suggest that genetic

---

[14] N. SEEMAN & P. LUCIANI, XXL: OBESITY AND THE LIMITS OF SHAME 28 (2011).

[15] Press Release, World Health Organization, The World Health Organization Warns of the Rising Threat of Heart Disease and Stroke as Overweight and Obesity Rapidly Increase (Sept. 22, 2005), *available at* http://www.who.int/mediacentre/news/releases/2005/pr44/en/.

[16] A. Norton, *All U.S. Adults Could Be Overweight in 40 Years*, Aug. 6, 2008, *available at* http://www.reuters.com/article/2008/08/06/us-overweight-idUSCOL66909620080806.

[17] WHITE HOUSE TASK FORCE ON CHILDHOOD OBESITY REPORT TO THE PRESIDENT, SOLVING THE PROBLEM OF CHILDHOOD OBESITY WITHIN A GENERATION (2010).

[18] COMMITTEE ON OBESITY PREVENTION POLICIES FOR YOUNG CHILDREN, EARLY CHILDHOOD OBESITY PREVENTION POLICIES 19 (2011).

[19] SEEMAN & LUCIANI, *supra* note 14, at 24.

[20] COMMITTEE ON OBESITY PREVENTION POLICIES, *supra* note 18, at 19.

[21] C. Abraham, *Goodbye, Thrifty Gene, and Hello to a New Prime Suspect behind the Global Upsurge in Obesity and Diabetes: the Womb*, GLOBE & MAIL, Mar. 5, 2011, at F6, F7.

influences can vary from 25 to as high as 80 percent regarding weight gain in various individuals.[22] An additional complication may be maternal age at birth.[23]

Another idea holds that obese people have less brown fat than thin people. Brown fat is related to the body's metabolism. Fat of that color burns calories at a very high rate. If, somehow, overweight people can produce more brown fat they could become considerably thinner.[24]

Still other contentions maintain that certain antibiotics interrupt gut bacteria, leading to weight gain.[25] They may have particular impact on infants. One study has found that infants given antibiotics within six months of birth were 22 percent more likely to be overweight at age three compared with those who were not given those drugs in the same period.[26]

2. Chemicals: Obesogens

Chemicals in the environment can play a role in some individuals, causing them to put on excess pounds.[27] Exposure to endocrine disrupting chemicals (EDC) may be a factor in the development of some diseases, such as diabetes, and of obesity. Scientists also refer to such chemicals as obesogens.

These substances may promote obesity in several ways, including increasing the number of fat cells, altering the amount of calories utilized while an individual is at rest, altering the energy balance, and modifying the body's mechanisms for appetite and satiety. The White House Task Force on Childhood Obesity warned in 2010 that if a child is exposed to EDCs during fetal and infant development, the consequences may persist throughout that person's life. Such exposure may occur in dangerously easy ways: baby bottles and plastic containers should not be microwaved unless explicitly labeled as safe for that purpose.[28] Various obesogens may also be in the food supply, including through the production of meat and crops.[29] As Guthman puts it: "[A] food system perspective must include a hard look at the chemicals used in food production and distribution, alongside the calories."[30] Kristof sounds this dire warning: "[E]ndocrine disruptions may be the tobacco of our time."[31]

---

[22] SEEMAN & LUCIANI, *supra* note 14, at 41.

[23] A. Ali & N. Crowther, *Factors Predisposing to Obesity: A Review of the Literature*, 14 J. ENDOCRINOLOGY, METABOLISM & DIABETES OF SOUTH AFRICA 81, at 83 (2009).

[24] G. Kolata, *Brown Fat, Triggered by Cold or Exercise, May Yield a Key to Weight Control*, N.Y. TIMES, Jan. 25, 2012, at A21.

[25] A. Barton, *Are Chemicals, Not Calories, Making Us Fat?*, GLOBE & MAIL, Jan. 11, 2012, at L5.

[26] N. Bakalar, *Risks: Weight Implications for Infant Antibiotics*, N.Y. TIMES, Aug. 28, 2012, at D6; see also D. Grady, *Bacteria in the Intestines May Help Tip the Bathroom Scale*, N.Y. TIMES, Mar. 28, 2013, at A18.

[27] Barton, *supra* note 25.

[28] WHITE HOUSE TASK FORCE, *supra* note 17, at 17.

[29] J. GUTHMAN, WEIGHING IN: OBESITY, FOOD JUSTICE, AND THE LIMITS OF CAPITALISM 100 *et seq.* (2011).

[30] *Id.* at 111.

[31] N. Kristof, *Warnings from a Flabby Mouse*, N.Y. TIMES SUN. REV., Jan 20, 2013, at 11.

3. Race and Ethnicity

Studies suggest that some groups may have a predisposition to obesity. Data from the Centers for Disease Control and Prevention indicate that Hispanic males and African American females have a higher prevalence of obesity than other groups, particularly in the teenage years.[32]

4. The Environment

The environment plays a significant role in influencing people's weight. The role of chemical obesogens, mentioned above, is one such possibility. More generally, it's helpful to think of its influence in at least three ways: food and drink, built communities, and social contagion.

i. Food and Drink

The conditions of day-to-day living promote weight gain by both encouraging consumption of excess calories and by discouraging physical activity. Such circumstances over time create an environment that many individuals cannot resist in terms of controlling their weight.

The easy availability of relatively cheap, calorically dense foods, aggressively merchandised, is viewed as a predominant factor leading to consumption of too many calories. Mass food chains targeting children is an especially objectionable practice. Whether regarding fast food, candy, soft drinks, or other "junk" foods, the industry's answer is almost always the same: we give them what they want. However, those advocating sound nutrition say otherwise. They charge that the food-and-drink industry is creating an "obesogenic" environment.

Prominent among these critics of the food industry is Marion Nestle. Her *Food Politics* documents the many ways that the industry manipulates consumers and governments in the name of selling ever more food, especially of the junk variety: "[M]any of the nutritional problems of Americans—not least of them obesity—can be traced to the food industry's imperative to encourage people to *eat more* in order to generate sales and increase income in a highly competitive marketplace."[33] Foods are engineered to be high in fat, salt, and sugar, designed to promote cravings. At the same time, their promotion has blended "eatertainment": consumption as a pastime.[34]

In addition, there is confusion—often contributed to by food suppliers—regarding the caloric content of food and drinks. For example, there is evidence

---

[32] Centers for Disease Control and Prevention, *CDC Grand Rounds: Childhood Obesity in the United States*, 60 MORBIDITY & MORTALITY WEEKLY REPORT 2, 42–46 (2011).

[33] M. NESTLE, FOOD POLITICS: HOW THE FOOD INDUSTRY INFLUENCES NUTRITION AND HEALTH 4 (emphasis in the original) (2007).

[34] E. Kolbert, *XXXL—Why Are We So Fat?*, NEW YORKER, July 20, 2009, *available at* http://www.newyorker.com/arts/critics/books/2009/07/20/090720crbo_books_kolbert; E. ABBOTT, SUGAR: A BITTERSWEET HISTORY (2008).

that the fat content of our diets has decreased over the last several years. But many low-fat foods are, nonetheless, high in calories because of the amounts of sugar they contain. The food-and-drink industry argues that nearly all its products have some nutritional value so there should not be a threshold established by regulation to determine what constitutes good food.[35]

ii. Built Communities

Environmental conditions that do not do enough to encourage physical activity are also viewed as important factors in gaining excessive weight. Cities built to facilitate cars, inadequate public parks, and schools that shorten or even eliminate recess and lunch hour play are just some elements that can contribute to individuals, especially children, being too sedentary.[36] Conversely, bicycle paths, safe sidewalks, school and recreational facilities and programs, and planning that encourage walking to do food and other shopping are some aspects of environmental conditions that encourage people to be physically active.[37] We'll have lots more to say about such matters in Part III.[38]

iii. Social Contagion

"Social contagion" asserts that as people are connected so, too, is their health. Christakis and Fowler examined data from the Framingham Heart Study, an ambitious longitudinal project begun in 1948 that follows over fifteen thousand individuals by examining them with a comprehensive physical, on average, every four years. Its rich database is being used for several purposes beyond the original examination of heart disease.[39]

The accuracy of some of their findings has been doubted.[40] Nevertheless, their analysis suggests that good behaviors—such as quitting smoking or being physically active—passed from friend to friend in a manner akin to a contagious virus. The converse also holds: negative conditions are also "catching." When an individual in the Framingham Study became obese, his or her friends were 57 percent more likely to become fat.[41]

---

[35] E. OLIVER, FAT POLITICS: THE REAL STORY BEHIND AMERICA'S OBESITY EPIDEMIC 169 (2006).

[36] L. FRANK ET AL., HEALTH AND COMMUNITY DESIGN: THE IMPACT OF THE BUILT ENVIRONMENT ON PHYSICAL ACTIVITY (2003); COMMITTEE ON CHILDHOOD OBESITY PREVENTION ACTIONS FOR LOCAL GOVERNMENTS, LOCAL GOVERNMENT ACTIONS TO PREVENT CHILDHOOD OBESITY (2009).

[37] FRANK ET AL., supra note 36; COMMITTEE ON CHILDHOOD OBESITY, supra note 36.

[38] Chapter 7: Encouraging Physical Activity: Children at Play!.

[39] N. CHRISTAKIS & J. FOWLER, CONNECTED: THE SURPRISING POWER OF OUR SOCIAL NETWORKS AND HOW THEY SHAPE OUR LIVES (2009).

[40] G. Kolata, Catching Obesity from Friends May Not Be So Easy, N.Y. TIMES, Aug. 9, 2011, at D5.

[41] N. Christakis & J. Fowler, The Spread of Obesity in a Large Social Network over 32 Years, 357 NEW ENGLAND J. MED. 370, 370 and especially at 376 (2007); C. Thompson, Are Your Friends Making You Fat?, N.Y. TIMES MAG., Sept. 13, 2009, at MM28.

5. Technology

Technology can contribute to obesity in a number of ways. The most obvious are television and, in more recent decades, the Internet. Children watching too much TV and spending too much time on the Net can have several consequences. Physical inactivity may be a prominent outcome. Lack of sleep may be another.[42] What is more, television is a medium of advertising that can shape young peoples' preferences, suggesting that burgers, fries, cookies, and pop are much cooler than fruit, fish, and whole grains.

Technology is associated with obesity in other ways. It has helped produce all sorts of convenience foods that are full of questionable ingredients both in terms of calories and nutrition.[43] More efficient forms of food production have brought down the actual cost of foods, especially those of dubious quality. One study suggests that the real price of fats and oils declined by 16 percent, and that of sugar-laden soft drinks by 20 percent. As consumption is related to cost, lower prices can mean higher rates of consumption of those foods.[44]

6. Depression

There is a complicated association between being overweight and mental health issues, especially depression. Both the jolly fat person and the so-happy individual who has shed pounds are, in many cases, pernicious stereotypes. A BMI in excess of 30 among women is linked to about a 50 percent increase in depression over a lifetime. The situation is more complicated with men but, again, there are associations between being overweight and being depressed.[45] There are also complexities in terms of what is responsible for what: are obese people depressed because they are substantially overweight, are they obese because they are depressed, or do the two conditions interact in still other problematic ways?[46] A further complication may be that a number of drugs, including antidepressants, can lead to increased weight gain.[47]

Weight *loss* can also be associated with mental health issues. Suicide occurs more frequently among those who have shed significant amounts of weight. In circumstances where individuals are successful in losing pounds, their mental state may need to be monitored.[48]

---

[42] Ali & Crowther, *supra* note 23, at 83; T. Parker-Pope, *Lost Sleep Can Lead to Weight Gain*, N.Y. TIMES, Mar. 19, 2013, at D4.
[43] Kolbert, *supra* note 34.
[44] SEEMAN & LUCIANI, *supra* note 14, at 45.
[45] *Id.* at 46–47.
[46] D. RHODE, THE BEAUTY BIAS: THE INJUSTICE OF APPEARANCE IN LIFE AND LAW 39–40 (2010).
[47] Ali & Crowther, *supra* note 23, at 83.
[48] SEEMAN & LUCIANI, *supra* note 14, at 47.

7. Socioeconomic Status

Poverty does not cause obesity but it is associated with being overweight.[49] Eating fresh fruit and vegetables can cost more than calorically dense foods. Poor people may live in neighborhoods where access to nutritious food and drink is difficult because of the selection carried by local stores ("food deserts").[50] The poor may not have knowledge of what constitutes a balanced diet and the ways to prepare food so that it is nutritious and not highly caloric. People who are below the poverty line are nearly 15 percent more likely to be obese than the general population.[51]

We'll have more to say, later, about the many and complicated causes of obesity. For the moment, let's note that some of the explanations challenge straightforward explanations concerning caloric balance. If more calories are consumed than expended the individual gains weight: if people eat and drink too much, for whatever reason, they become fat. But explanations, just discussed, involving genes, metabolism, antibiotics, and obesogens (or EDCs) and so forth suggest that some individuals are obese for reasons that go beyond "calories in/calories out."[52] Such explanations may be linked to fetal and infant development producing consequences that can last that individual's lifetime. As the White House Task Force observed in its discussion of EDCs: "Research on such chemicals suggests that the origins of obesity may lie not only in well established risk factors such as diet and exercise, but also in the interplay between genes and the fetal and early postnatal environment."[53]

This is not to suggest that diet and exercise are irrelevant. Healthier eating/drinking and physical activity are important in terms of weight, perhaps particularly in terms of preventing excess weight gain in some individuals. However—and this is a crucial point made throughout this book—"calories in/calories out" may not be the key for either prevention or for weight loss and maintenance for others. At the same time, good eating/drinking and an active lifestyle can bestow significant health benefits regardless of the individual's weight. It is this last point that will be emphasized when we come to examine particular legal interventions in Part III.

---

[49] P. Ernsberger, *Does Social Class Explain the Connection between Weight and Health?*, in THE FAT STUDIES READER 25 (E. Rothblum & S. Solovay eds., 2009).

[50] COMMITTEE ON OBESITY PREVENTION POLICIES, *supra* note 18, at 101–07; RHODE, *supra* note 46, at 42–43 and cited sources.

[51] COMMITTEE ON OBESITY PREVENTION POLICIES, *supra* note 18

[52] K. Wartman, *What's Really Making Us Fat?*, ATLANTIC, Mar. 8, 2012, *available at* http://www.theatlantic.com/health/archive/2012/03/whats-really-making-us-fat/254087/.

[53] WHITE HOUSE TASK FORCE, *supra* note 17, at 17.

B) CONSEQUENCES

Traditional characterizations of those who are overweight as being obese also emphasize the negative consequences that flow from individuals being very heavy. It is contended that obesity imposes substantial costs not only for overweight people themselves but also for society at large. Such effects for individuals involve physical and psychological costs and impose burdens on society, especially on health care systems.[54]

1. Physical Aspects

Obesity has been linked to a variety of physical ailments such as: complications in pregnancy, certain types of cancer, diabetes, hypertension, and stroke, knee and hip pain, and urinary incontinence. Obesity is an independent risk factor for heart disease: it can predispose an individual to such problems even if that person has no other risk factors. Obesity threatens the heart by raising blood pressure, increasing inflammation, and making the blood more likely to clot. It is associated with heart disease and heart failure.[55]

2. Psychological Aspects

The complicated relationship between obesity and psychological conditions has been discussed earlier.[56] Whether cause or effect or both, being significantly overweight is associated with depression and mood disorders. Obesity has been found to increase disability claims on the grounds of psychiatric impairment, thus creating difficult situations for both employees and employers.[57]

3. Costs to Society

There are a number of negative consequences to society as a whole associated with obesity. Two main ones are productivity and health costs. In 2011 it was estimated that the loss to U.S. business from individuals who were significantly overweight was $12.8 billion in absenteeism and $30 billion due to reduced productivity on the job. In addition, something like $35 billion was spent on weight-loss products and services.[58] Such services mostly deliver disappointing results.

Between 1998 and 2006 annual expenditures attributed to obesity rose from 6.5 to 9.1 percent of yearly medical spending in the United States. During that same period per capita spending on medical services for obese persons was in excess of 40 percent of that for individuals of healthy weight.[59] About

---

[54] *See, generally,* INSTITUTE OF MEDICINE, *supra* note 13, at ch. 2: "Assessing the Current Situation."

[55] SEEMAN & LUCIANI, *supra* note 14, at 9–15; *Obesity and Prostate Cancer*, N.Y. TIMES, Apr. 30, 2013, at D4.

[56] *See supra* notes 45–48 and accompanying text.

[57] SEEMAN & LUCIANI, *supra* note 14, at 15–16.

[58] *Id.* at 16–17.

[59] E. Finkelstein et al., *Annual Medical Spending Attributable to Obesity: Payer- and Service-Specific Estimates*, 27 HEALTH AFFAIRS (Millwood) w822 (2009).

90 percent of hip and knee replacements in Canada, the United States, and Britain are performed on overweight and obese persons. In 2005, and for just the United States, knee replacements cost $11 billion.[60]

A 2009 study reported on the rising costs for hospitals attributed to very overweight children. Between 1999 and 2005 the number of hospital stays for kids age two to nineteen nearly doubled. The costs for these hospitalizations increased from about $126 million in 2001 to $238 million in 2005.[61] In 2005 a study contended that the steady rise in life expectancy in many countries might soon level off or even decline because of the health consequences associated with obesity.[62]

IV. Is Being Fat Like Being Short?

A) INTRODUCTION

By the turn of this century there had developed strong reactions to the so-called obesity epidemic. Books such as Oliver's *Fat Politics*, Kirkland's *Fat Rights*, Rhode's *The Beauty Bias*, Farrell's *Fat Shame*, Guthman's *Weighing In*, and Saguy's *What's Wrong with Fat?* appeared in short order, challenging, in various ways, weight as the problem, and weight loss as the solution.[63] These critiques were fueled by divergent perspectives and differed in terms of any action to be taken. They share much common ground in their assertions that the dangers coming from obesity are overstated. There are three main aspects to these assertions: the rates of obesity are exaggerated; the health problems related to being fat are misrepresented; and significant excess weight is very difficult to lose and, if lost, not to regain. They also share much common ground in the charge that such exaggeration and misrepresentations are contributing to the stigmatization of the obese and discrimination toward them.

In reacting to such misrepresentations, stigmatization, and acts of prejudice these critiques reach different conclusions about what should (or should not) be done about people's weight and such negative norms and biased behavior in the rest of society. One view opposes these harmful attitudes and acts while still focusing on weight loss. A second places blame squarely on society and its discrimination against fat people. The main response should be to protect

---

[60] SEEMAN & LUCIANI, *supra* note 14, at 23.
[61] *Id.* at 19–20.
[62] S. Olshansky, *A Potential Decline in Life Expectancy in the United States in the 21st Century*, 352 NEW ENGLAND J. MED. 1138 (2005).
[63] OLIVER, *supra* note 35; A. KIRKLAND, FAT RIGHTS: DILEMMAS OF DIFFERENCE AND PERSONHOOD (2008); RHODE, *supra* note 46; ROTHBLUM & SOLOVAY, *supra* note 49; AGAINST HEALTH: HOW HEALTH BECAME THE NEW MORALITY (J. Metzl & A. Kirkland eds., 2010); A. FARRELL, FAT SHAME STIGMA AND THE FAT BODY IN AMERICAN CULTURE (2011); GUTHMAN, *supra* note 29; A. SAGUY, WHAT'S WRONG WITH FAT? (2012) published as this book was being prepared for publication.

victims through laws addressing fat prejudice. A third joins the fight against stigmatization and bias. It also promotes "HAES": Health at Every Size. The HAES movement focuses on social support, good nutrition, physical activity, and other positive factors—whether or not the person loses weight.

Some aspects of these reactions may be misdirected and exaggerated. Yet, these critiques, taken together, sound a strong note of caution both in terms of what constitutes the problem and the nature of any solutions. Interventions focused on weight loss are likely to encounter strong opposition and not just from expected quarters such as the food-and-drink industry. Likewise, using only pounds shed can be a narrow and objectionable criterion for evaluating any interventions. Improvements in healthy eating and exercise and to overall health status are the more appropriate criteria for assessing such regulatory activity. Finally, we need to shift norms dramatically away from stigmatization of fat people and toward the promotion of healthy lifestyles, whatever the shape and size of individuals. One step in this direction will be to use human rights laws to protect fat people from bias.

B) THE RATES OF OBESITY ARE EXAGGERATED

This criticism takes issue with the claims regarding the extent of the "problem." Simply put, it asserts that there are fewer fat people than the numbers weight-loss advocates bandy about, and that there has been an overreaction about just how many people are, in fact, obese. There are two main aspects to these assertions: Body Mass Index (BMI) as a measure of excess weight is flawed, and the rates of obesity are leveling off or even declining.

In terms of the first aspect, the criticisms of BMI are twofold: it is a flawed measure of excess weight and, in any event, those measures have been manipulated to make the population seem fatter independently of any weight that may have been gained. An individual's BMI is basically a ratio of height to weight. By conventional standards people who have a BMI over 25 are overweight; those with a BMI of 30 are obese; those with a BMI of 40 are morbidly obese. Critics contend that such categorization is simplistic.[64]

Because muscle weighs more than fat, people in good physical shape may have a BMI in excess of 25 (because their body has a lot of the former, especially for their height). As a result there is a percentage of the population that has a BMI in excess of 25 or even 30 who are not overweight or at least not obese. In any event, the relevance of BMI to health status has been questioned. A 2008 study concluded that BMI measurements were of only limited use in predicting risks of death. A big waistline is a better indicator: men with waistlines in excess of 40" and women with waists over 35" were most at risk. Obese

---

[64] GUTHMAN, *supra* note 29, at 26–32.

people can have such waistlines but so can many individuals with "normal" BMIs.[65] What is more, whatever weight gain there may have been, its significance in wider historical sweep, in terms of standard of living, longevity, and other indicators of well-being, has been doubted.[66]

Moreover, critics also point to the fact that standards for BMI indicating individuals who are overweight were adjusted downward in the late 1990s. Such adjustments immediately caused many more people to be considered overweight without their having gained anything.[67] Between 1980 and 2000 the U.S. Dieting Guidelines defined overweight at various BMI levels ranging from 24.9 to 27.1. In 1985 the U.S. National Institute of Health (NIH) recommended that the category of overweight be set at a BMI of 27.5 for men and 27.3 for women. However, in the 1990s, WHO recommended that a BMI of 25 should be considered overweight.[68] As a result the NIH in 1998 concluded that a BMI of 25 should be the dividing line for being overweight.[69]

The basis of such shifts has been questioned, a matter we return to in the next section. In any event, as Oliver points out: "[O]vernight, more than 37 million Americans suddenly became 'overweight,' even though they had not gained an ounce."[70] Or, as Kirkland puts it: "A person with a BMI of 25 (a five foot five inch woman weighing 150 pounds, for example) would look very out of place among fashion models, but would look perfectly acceptable to the vast majority of ordinary Americans."[71]

In terms of the second aspect, challenging the incidence of obesity, critics point to studies that began to report leveling off or even declines in the rates as assessed by (flawed) BMI standards. For example, a 2006 study by the Centres for Disease Control suggested that the rates of obesity for children in the United States had leveled off.[72] National health surveys in the United States indicate that from 1999 to 2004 the prevalence of obesity increased in men but there were no overall increases for women.[73]

---

[65] SEEMAN & LUCIANI, *supra* note 14, at 8; T. Pischon et al., *General and Abdominal Adiposity and Risk of Death in Europe*, 359 NEW ENGLAND J MED 2105–20 (2008).

[66] J. Groopman, *The Body and Human Progress*, N.Y. REVIEW BOOKS, Oct. 27, 2011, at 76–81 (reviewing R. FLOUD ET AL., THE CHANGING BODY: HEALTH, NUTRITION, AND HUMAN DEVELOPMENT IN THE WESTERN WORLD SINCE 1700 (2011).

[67] KIRKLAND, *supra* note 63, at 112–113; OLIVER, *supra* note 35, at 21–28.

[68] WORLD HEALTH ORGANIZATION, OBESITY: PREVENTING AND MANAGING THE GLOBAL EPIDEMIC: REPORT OF WHO CONSULTATION (1997).

[69] National Institute of Health, *Clinical Guidelines on the Identification, Evaluation, and Treatment of Overweight and Obesity in Adults: The Evidence Report* (NIH Publication No. 98-4083, 1998).

[70] OLIVER, *supra* note 35, at 22.

[71] KIRKLAND, *supra* note 63, at 113.

[72] T. Parker-Pope, *Hint of Hope as Child Obesity Rate Hits Plateau*, N.Y. TIMES, May 28, 2008, *available at* http://www.nytimes.com/2008/05/28/health/research/28obesity.html.

[73] G. Gaesser, *Is "Permanent Weight Loss" an Oxymoron?—The Statistics on Weight Loss and the National Weight Control Registry, in* ROTHBLUM & SOLOVAY, *supra* note 49, at 37.

Then, in 2012, it was reported that obesity rates (using BMI in excess of 30) in the United States had remained largely unchanged for the previous twelve years.[74] Another study that year indicated there may have been slight declines in rates among very young low-income children.[75] In other countries rates have also plateaued or may have even declined somewhat.[76] Where rates will go over the next decade remains to be seen. A newspaper report of the twelve-year statistics commented: "[N]ational efforts at promoting healthful eating and exercise are having little effect on the overweight."[77] Critics of BMI and obesity rates might react to this statement by suggesting "little effect" is a rush to judgment. The rates have at least leveled off. What is more, it could be that people who are obese are healthier because they are exercising more and eating better. Shouldn't that latter possibility be investigated as an effect of such campaigns? Why such a preoccupation with BMI ratings?

C) THE PHYSICAL HEALTH PROBLEMS RELATED TO OBESITY ARE MISREPRESENTED

Whatever the rates of obesity may be, it is has been asserted that the physical dangers of being overweight, and even obese, are blown out of proportion. There are a number of aspects to this criticism: studies indicate that being overweight is associated with lower death rates for people as they age; the number of deaths related to obesity has been erroneously reported; the association between being fat and many ailments is much weaker than conventional assessment of obesity contends. At the same time many thin people are in poor physical shape but society's obsessions with fat keeps the focus on large individuals.

A much-cited example of overstated dangers of obesity comes from a study on obesity-related deaths and reactions to it. In 1993 a report was published that indicated that "dietary factors and activity patterns that are too sedentary are associated with 300k [300,000] deaths per year."[78] Despite these findings being questioned by reputable researchers the 300,000 deaths per year attributable to obesity became widely used in various campaigns to raise public awareness and to encourage governmental action.

---

[74] T. Parker-Pope, *Obesity Rates Stall in the US but Stay Stubbornly High*, N.Y. TIMES, Jan. 18, 2012, at A11; *see also* INSTITUTE OF MEDICINE, *supra* note 13, at 64–68.
[75] S. Tavernise, *Obesity Declines among Low-Income Preschoolers*, GLOBE & MAIL, Dec. 27, 2012, at L8 (reporting on studies done in the United States).
[76] *Id.*
[77] *Id.*
[78] J. McGinnis & W. Foege, *Actual Causes of Death in the United States*, 270(18) J. AM. MED. ASS'N 2207–12 (1993).

In 2005 a paper published by Flegal and others from Centers for Disease Control and the National Cancer Institute challenged the 300,000 deaths figure. That paper pointed out methodological flaws in the 1993 study. It suggested that the figure was more like 112,000, and even then only for those with BMIs in excess of 35. Even more startling for the accepted wisdom that any excess weight is dangerous was the finding that slightly overweight individuals had lower mortality rates and underweight people had higher ones.[79] Another study by Flegal and others published in 2013 drew similar conclusions as the one in 2005.[80] These studies have been criticized for their own methodological complications even as Flegal stands by her conclusions.[81]

The contention that obesity is associated with many specific ailments—diabetes, high blood pressure, and so forth—has also not gone unchallenged. It is asserted that such associations, where they exist, are less clear than conventional wisdom would suggest. It is argued that the link between obesity and various health concerns—hypertension, diabetes, and cardiovascular disorders, etc.—is much weaker than weight-loss advocates might suggest. Many of the studies addressing such associations do not take account of other factors that could contribute to the diseases under examination such as smoking, access to medical care, family history, exercise, and diet.[82] It has been asserted that the correlations between health problems and BMI explain only about 9 percent of such outcomes; 91 percent of the determinants of health issues (such as smoking and exercise) have nothing to do with BMI.[83]

Conversely, it is emphasized that thinness is not always associated with good health. Anorexia is an extreme example where excessive thinness is related to many physical and psychological disturbances. Similarly, a U.S. study found that 51 percent of overweight and almost one-third of obese individuals had mostly normal levels of blood pressure, cholesterol, blood fats, and sugar. In contrast, about one-quarter of individuals with recommended weight had unhealthy levels of at least two of these measures.[84]

---

[79] K. Flegal et al., *Excess Deaths Associated with Underweight, Overweight, and Obesity*, 293(15) J. AM. MED. ASS'N 1861–67 (Apr. 2005).

[80] K. Flegal et al., *Association of All-Cause Mortality with Overweight and Obesity Using Standard Body Mass Index Categories: A Systematic Review and Meta-analysis*, 309(1) J. AM. MED. ASS'N 71–82 (2013).

[81] M. Stobbe, *Study That Plays Down Obesity Risk Called "Rubbish,"* GLOBE & MAIL, Jan. 3, 2013, at L6; *see also* P. Taylor, *Fat and Fit? Think Again. Extra Pounds Can Be Deadly*, GLOBE & MAIL, Dec. 3, 2010, at L6.

[82] OLIVER, *supra* note 35, at 27.

[83] D. Burgard, *What Is "Health at Every Size?,"* in ROTHBLUM & SOLOVAY, *supra* note 49, at 42, 43.

[84] R. Wildman, *The Obese without Cardiometabolic Risk Factor Clustering and the Normal Weight with Cardiometabolic Risk Factor Clustering*, 168 ARCHIVES INTERNAL MED. 1617 (2008).

D) WEIGHT LOSS?: WHAT IS SHED IS ALMOST ALWAYS REGAINED

> ...[U]nderstanding the science of weight loss has helped make sense of my own struggles to lose weight, as well as my mother's endless cycle of dieting, weight gain and despair. I wish she were still here so I could persuade her to finally forgive herself for her dieting failures.[85]

The foregoing is another quote from the Parker-Pope article that we referred to in the introduction of this chapter. In it Parker-Pope, who also struggles with her weight, describes the efforts of fat people as they strive to lose pounds and the anguish and frustration of the vast majority of those who do so because they gain it back (and sometimes even more). Critics of the public health model that focuses on weight loss accuse its proponents of being in denial regarding a simple but damning fact: of the obese individuals who do manage to shed weight, almost all gain it back within five years of the loss.[86]

The precise statistics regarding long-term weight loss are not completely clear but, overwhelmingly, they suggest that the vast majority of obese people who are able to lose weight cannot maintain their thinner selves for more than a few years. Some commentators assert that as many as 95 percent of obese people, of those who are able to lose weight, gain it all back within five years.[87] That figure appears to be derived from a decades-old report, and there have been many innovations since then.[88] That said, in 1993 an expert report of the National Institutes of Health concluded, in terms of efforts to shed pounds, that "[O]ne third to two thirds of the weight is regained within 1 year [after weight loss], and almost all is regained within 5 years."[89] In 2011, Bacon and Aphramor, reviewing the evidence to date, stated: "Long-term follow-up studies document that the majority of individuals regain virtually all of the weight that was lost during treatment, regardless of whether they maintain their diet or exercise program."[90]

In an attempt to learn more about fat people who lose weight and who maintain the loss over a period of time the National Weight Control Registry tracks 10,000 people who have shed pounds and kept them off.[91] The registry

---

[85] Parker-Pope, *supra* note 2.

[86] L. Bacon & L. Aphramor, *Weight Science: Evaluating the Evidence for a Paradigm Shift*, 10 NUTRITION J. 69 (2011).

[87] RHODE, *supra* note 46, at 6.

[88] Gaesser, *supra* note 73 at 37, 39. Gaesser points out the difficulties with the 95 percent rate but, nevertheless, concludes it may be accurate.

[89] NIH Technology Assessment Conference Panel, *Methods for Voluntary Weight Loss and Control*, 119(7) ANNALS MED. 764, 764 (1993); *see also* R. Puhl & C. Heuer, *Obesity Stigma: Important Considerations for Public Health*, 100(6) AM. J. PUB. HEALTH 1019, 1021 (June 2010).

[90] Bacon & Aphramor, *supra* note 86, at 5.

[91] Gaesser, *supra* note 73.

is a source of useful information regarding the heroics of those who strive to lose weight and then struggle to maintain the loss. Yet these 10,000 individuals are a very small percentage of the millions of individuals in the United States alone who have tried and not been able to lose weight or, having shed it, rapidly regain it. Or, as Kelly Brownell, Director of the Yale University Rudd Centre for Food Policy and Obesity, in speaking of the Registry puts it: "All it means is that there are rare individuals who do manage to keep [weight] off."[92]

Why individuals regain weight despite their struggles not to do so is unclear. Some of the reactions to the Parker-Pope article insisted that their special diet held the key to permanent weight loss and maintenance.[93] This is a questionable claim given that there have been decades of experiments with all manner of diets and exercise programs with nearly always the same dismal, weight-loss–regain results.[94] Parker-Pope favors explanations focused on fat bodies having a set weight level. When pounds are shed the body struggles against itself to return to, more or less, the same weight.[95]

Whatever the reason, the inability of the vast majority of obese people to lose weight and keep it off appears to be a central fact that must be countenanced. It is repeatedly pointed to in making the case that public health campaigns aimed at having fat people lose weight are misdirected and are contributing to the censorious attitude toward overweight people that makes their lives miserable. More recently, those who insist that the obesity rate must be lowered have shifted their emphasis to focus on prevention.[96] Problems with fat will be avoided if people just don't gain excess weight at all. There is an increasing focus on children and avoiding weight gain from the earliest years. What such campaigns might look like and how successful they might be raises a number of interesting issues. We will tackle these questions, in detail, in Part III.

E) STIGMA, SHAME, AND FAT

One of the strongest criticisms of anti-obesity campaigns is that they do more harm than good by contributing to the stigmatization of fat people and discrimination against them. These negative norms and behaviors lead to an immense sense of shame and related problems for those who are significantly overweight. In a pronounced form this reaction asserts that the problem is not that individuals are fat. Rather, the problem is the stress that overweight

---

[92] Parker-Pope, *supra* note 2.
[93] Letter from G. Taubes signed by 250 medical experts, N.Y. TIMES MAG., Jan. 22, 2012, *available at* http://www.nytimes.com/2012/01/22/magazine/reply-all-fat-trap.html, and http://www.ipetitions.com/petition/response-to-nytimes-the-fat-trap/.
[94] A. Picard, *Most Canadian Dieters Can't Keep Pounds Off, Poll Finds*, GLOBE & MAIL, Apr. 1, 2010, at L4.
[95] Parker-Pope, *supra* note 2.
[96] INSTITUTE OF MEDICINE, *supra* note 13.

individuals are caused due to acts of prejudice, hostile attitudes, and questionable "cures" that are forced upon them. We'll refer, generally, to such ideas as the *fat shame critique*.[97]

For those holding such views there are a number of differing implications. One decries such stigmatization but contends that the solution is to provide novel strategies for addressing excess weight. A second asserts that fat people do not need to do much of anything—it is society with its toxic actions and beliefs that needs reform. At the same time law has a role: fat rights protections should be enacted and enforced. A third contends that all people should be accepted regardless of their size. Strategies that do not focus on weight but rather nutritious eating, physical activity, and acceptance of various body shapes and sizes need to be encouraged.

We begin our discussion of these points by quickly surveying society's reactions over time to other forms of consumption when a sense of excess took hold. History suggests that the fat shame critique has some justification.

1. Panics, Good Norms, and Consumption

Those decrying societies' attitudes toward the obese can point to other forms of consumption and the ways in which communities have overreacted in terms of moralizing about various guilty pleasures. There is a body of literature on "moral panics."[98] Essentially the assertion is that excessive reaction to what is considered a threat to the "good morals" of a society can set off hysteria that can lead to abuse of the objects of such upset. Historical examples include the "red scare" in 1950s' America,[99] and the oppression of lesbian, gay, bisexual, and transgendered communities in many societies, during many periods.[100]

Whether reactions to perceived excessive consumption can be characterized as "moral panics" may be debatable. We can certainly point to examples of disproportionate reaction. Such immoderate actions were often the product of drastic shifts in attitudes and norms: from acceptance, even embrace, to denunciation. We encountered some of these examples in Chapter 1.[101]

In Regency England gambling was ubiquitous: "one vast casino."[102] But the Victorians seized upon it as a "dreadful vice."[103] They criminalized it, drove

---

[97] "Fat Shame" is the title of a prominent work addressing many of the issues discussed in this subsection: FARRELL, *supra* note 63.

[98] E. GOODE & N. BEN-YEHUDA, MORAL PANICS: THE SOCIAL CONSTRUCTION OF DEVIANCE (2d ed. 2009); R. LANCASTER, SEX PANIC AND THE PUNITIVE STATE (2011).

[99] A. FRIED, MCCARTHYISM: THE GREAT AMERICAN RED SCARE: A DOCUMENTARY HISTORY (1997).

[100] F. FEJES, GAY RIGHTS AND MORAL PANIC: THE ORIGINS OF AMERICA'S DEBATE ON HOMOSEXUALITY (2010).

[101] Chapter 1, Section IV: Consumption Encounters Law: *Permit but Discourage*.

[102] G. TREVELYAN, THE EARLY HISTORY OF CHARLES JAMES FOX 88–89 (New York: Harper and Brothers 1881), *cited in* DAVID MIERS, REGULATING COMMERCIAL GAMBLING: PAST, PRESENT AND FUTURE 18 (2004).

[103] J. DUFF, HINTS FOR REFORM, PARTICULARLY THE GAMBLING CLUBS, BY AN MP 10 (1764), *cited in* MIERS, *supra* note 102, at 45.

it underground, and hounded those who lived a demimonde existence when it came to wagering. Yet by the end of the twentieth century gambling had returned as a highly regulated, big-money industry with a large share of the earnings taken by governments and often used to fund commendable public projects.[104]

Drugs were widely tolerated in the nineteenth century: opium was given to babies to soothe them. But by the early twentieth century, campaigns to eradicate recreational drugs were in high gear. A significant reason for such "wars" was racism. Opium and "the yellow peril" were especially feared: lascivious Chinese men luring young white women into a life of sex and drug trafficking. Thereafter, other antidrug initiatives were fueled by similar irrational fears of the underclass, blacks, and other minorities and what would become of decent society.

Abhorrence of alcohol intensified in the early twentieth century. Such hatred was widespread, pushed along by a grab bag of moral entrepreneurs dedicated to awakening society to the evil of spirits and the moral decay that they caused. It reached a zenith in the United States where the foes of alcohol were successful in having a constitutional amendment prohibiting alcohol and permitting the hounding of anyone who wanted to have even the occasional drink.

Smoking may never have been subject to a "panic" but attitudes toward it have dramatically shifted within a relatively short period. Seventy years ago troops were sent cigarettes as a treat and to bolster their spirits while civilians lit up so as to engage in a sophisticated pastime. Six decades later use of tobacco is considered a dirty and expensive habit. Regulations to ban smoking even outdoors are proceeding apace.[105]

These examples of overreaction in the name of suppressing what is taken as excessive consumption suggest why fat shame critiques have developed so strongly. Intemperate reactions to various forms of consumption dot the landscape of the last hundred years or so of several Western societies. Such reactions have resulted in decidedly negative consequences for those who have been the objects of such disproportionate responses. Yet there is another aspect of reactions to consumption of which we should also take note.

We saw in Chapter 1 that the overarching theme, in the eyes of the law, regarding consumption in the last century has been *permit but discourage*.[106] Various forms of consumption are permitted, freed from criminal restrictions, but excess is discouraged through various kinds of regulation ranging from education policies to taxes on consumables. In addition—this is critical—social norms and the regulatory initiatives interact in mutually supporting ways to suppress intemperate behavior. Recreational drugs remain a conspicuous

---

[104] W. A. BOGART, PERMIT BUT DISCOURAGE: REGULATING EXCESSIVE CONSUMPTION ch. 6 (2011).
[105] Letters to the Editor, *Coming Soon: Smoke-Free in the Park*, N.Y. TIMES, May 12, 2011, at A22.
[106] Chapter 1, Section IV: Consumption Encounters Law: *Permit but Discourage*.

exception: their use is still subject to criminal sanctions. Yet even with them there is a growing body of opinion that they should mostly be decriminalized and regulated.

For norms to play a role in bringing down rates of consumption there have to be strong attitudes, widely shared, on the part of the public against excess. Such attitudes may not reach the level of stigmatization of the frowned-upon activity but they certainly carry with them strong elements of disapproval. Think about smoking. Those who use tobacco are now regarded with a mixture of pity and derision. It is the age of rights. But smokers who assert any are turned away: by the media, the courts, the legislatures, and dominant public opinion. Even the movement to ban smoking outdoors is gaining momentum. Those who persist in indulging are to do so as inconspicuously as possible and without complaint about the few places in which they can light up.

Consider the drinking of alcohol. Public education campaigns aimed at drinking and driving carry with them the condemnation of those who imbibe and then get behind the wheel. A pregnant woman seen drinking brings reactions of horror from those who fear she will damage the fetus. Focus for a moment on gaming. A line is drawn between recreational gamblers and those with impaired control. Problem gamblers are viewed as out-of-control individuals prone to damage themselves and their families because of their incapacity to exercise restraint when they wager. No matter their compulsion, gamblers are admonished to "Know your limit. Play within it."[107]

All of this is to say that it is not only the obese who are subject to scornful treatment. In the case of alcohol, tobacco, gambling, and drugs, censorious attitudes are widely viewed as part of the campaigns against what is judged to be harmful excess. This is not to suggest that there is some rough equivalence between being fat and drunk driving: that because we should be scornful of those who get behind the wheel after three martinis it is all right to gasp and raise eyebrows as that obese administrative assistant gets in the elevator.

Negative views of excess are an intricate part of normative orderings against many forms of excess. Such views have spilled over into attitudes against fat people as judgments against overindulgence. But being fat is far more complicated. As we saw earlier in this chapter there are many causes of obesity. Overindulgence is only one aspect, and may be irrelevant for many fat people. Our norms regarding weight tilt more in the direction of a panic toward the fat rather than toward constructive habits of nutritious eating/drinking and active lifestyles. Meanwhile such scornful attitudes have led to prejudice against and much stress for those who are large.

---

[107] Phrase used by the Ontario Lottery and Gaming Corporation (OLG) in association with its responsible gambling practices, *available at* http://www.knowyourlimit.ca/.

2. "The Greatest Threat": Stigma, Discrimination, and the Obese

> For the long term the greatest threat to our society is not al-Qaeda and it is not North Korea and it is not Iraq. It is the way we choose to sit, how much we choose to eat.[108]

Perceiving obesity as a lack of self-control and of overindulgence paves the way for stigmatizing fat people. A widespread belief that obesity is killing people, causing all manner of ailments, and significantly contributing to health costs seems to justify extreme measures.[109] Any distress to fat people is seen as a necessary side effect. Indeed, shaming overweight people may even be seen as desirable, spurring them on to lose weight so as to bask in caloric redemption.

We have seen that attitudes and norms concerning various forms of consumption have shifted as judgments about them and their role in society have changed. The same is true concerning weight.[110] Weight has been used in many societies over time to signal status. Generally, where food has been scarce plumpness has been viewed as a signifier of wealth and of plenty. An ample body in women has also been taken as a sign of capacity for childbearing—with some justification as low weight is associated with reproductive dysfunction. Yet when food is relatively plentiful, as is the case in postindustrial societies, attitudes shift toward privileging thinness.[111] Indeed, a svelte figure, especially for women, came to be associated with a confluence of forces in changing societies: "[A] cultural obsession with weight became firmly established ... when several disparate factors that favoured a desire for thinness—economic status symbols, morality, medicine, modernity, changing women's roles, and consumerism—all collided at once."[112]

Official norms have been harnessed in this battle against the bulge. Consider, as only examples, this litany of efforts to target the fat:

- A senior British government official wants an emergency telephone number for distress calls to be placed on XXL (extra extra large) clothing
- A video by the European Union depicts the obese as miserable and helpless
- The Australian education system routinely weighs and measures children and talks to them about their diet

---

[108] Frank Deford, journalist, quoted in FARRELL, *supra* note 63, at 9.
[109] P. Campos, A. Saguy, P. Ernsberger, E. Oliver & G. Gaesser, *The Epidemiology of Overweight and Obesity: Public Health Crisis or Moral Panic?*, 35(1) INT'L J. EPIDEMIOLOGY 55–60 (2006).
[110] FARRELL, *supra* note 63.
[111] RHODE, *supra* note 46, at 7–8.
[112] L. Fraser, *The Inner Corset: A Brief History of Fat in the United States, in* ROTHBLUM & SOLOVAY, *supra* note 49, at 11, 13.

- Lincoln University in the United States required students with a BMI in excess of 30 to take fitness classes three times a week
- The City of Boston conducted a public advertising campaign. One ad showed an overweight child on a scale with the caption "Fat Chance."[113]

Or consider the way of the Japanese. In that country there are state-prescribed limits on waistlines, forced measurements of individuals, and penalties imposed on companies and local governments if individuals under their authority do not meet weight targets.[114] Quite apart from civil liberties concerns that such measures raise, critics suggest that the limits are so strict that, based on them, over half of Japanese men will be considered overweight when such is not the case.

In the wider society cracks about, and jabs at, the obese are all too familiar. YouTube is full of videos that mock fat people.[115] A media star has referred to the obese as "lazy f—...pigs."[116] Meanwhile television reinforces the image of fat people as unhealthy and in desperate need of losing weight. Their struggles are seen as a source of entertainment: "[S]hows like *Bulging Brides, Celebrity Fit Club, Honey, We're Killing the Kids*, and *The Biggest Loser* encourage viewers to peer and gawk at the contestants, taking pleasure in the ways they are goaded with tempting snacks and punished with arduous exercise routines."[117]

These negative messages about those who are significantly overweight have taken hold among the public. One study suggests that just seeing an obese person triggers feelings of disgust, especially for individuals who have struggled with weight issues themselves.[118] About two-thirds of Americans who have been surveyed believe that individuals who are fat lack self-control.[119] Based on a number of studies, about 90 percent of the obese have been the subject of humiliating comments.[120] There is evidence that there is as much stigma associated with obesity as there is with AIDS, drug addiction, and criminal behavior.[121]

Such stigmatizing comments and action can lead to feelings of deep shame. More than a third of fat people would risk death to lose just 10 percent of their weight; three-quarters would take on such a risk if they could lose 20 percent.[122]

---

[113] SEEMAN & LUCIANI, *supra* note 14, at 73; (Editorial) *The Myth of the Shorter Lifespan*, GLOBE & MAIL, Jan. 4, 2013, at A10: "...[S]igns of a moral panic about obesity [are] all around."

[114] N. Onishi, *Japan, Seeking Trim Waists, Decides to Measure Millions*, N.Y. TIMES, June 13, 2008, at A1, A10.

[115] SEEMAN & LUCIANI, *supra* note 14, at 86–87.

[116] *Id.* at 87.

[117] FARRELL, *supra* note 63, at 119.

[118] SEEMAN & LUCIANI, *supra* note 14, at 88.

[119] RHODE, *supra* note 46, at 42.

[120] *Id.* at 29.

[121] *Id.* at 41.

[122] *Id.* at 6.

Ninety percent of formerly obese individuals would prefer to go blind than to be fat again.[123] What is more, such attitudes are not only emotionally stressful for the obese. They lead to concrete acts of discrimination against them. Even by an early age children have developed hostility to other kids who are obese. Fat kids are teased and ostracized.[124] In February 2012 a CNN commentator was suspended for homophobic comments. One columnist, discussing the slurs and the sanction, was shocked that a poll he displayed indicated that 33 percent of school children reported being bullied because they were or were thought to be gay, lesbian, or bisexual. What he did not note was that the highest figure—39 percent—was attributed to bullying because of body size.[125] Homophobia is to be everywhere condemned. Yet fat stigma may be an even more widespread problem.

There is evidence that fat people are discouraged from seeking medical attention and that they receive compromised services when they do.[126] A study of physicians' attitudes reported obese people as being viewed as: "awkward,... ugly, and unlikely to comply with treatment."[127] One study has indicated that just a 1 percent increase in a woman's BMI has measurable negative impacts on her family income and occupational prestige as assessed over time.[128] There is evidence that among white women in the United States an increase of two standard deviations in weight (about sixty-five pounds) is associated with a decrease of 9 percent of income.[129]

Such stigma is considered not only justified but a positive force spurring on the overweight to shed pounds. To those holding this view it is a "helpful and healthful prejudice to have."[130] They are bolstered in such views by statements such as the one by former U.S. Surgeon General Richard Carmona, who has exclaimed that weight levels would "dwarf" the attacks of 9/11 as the "terror within."[131] They are spurred on by Stanford Law Professor Richard Ford who asserts, without citing any source, that "Losing weight...for most [people is] only moderately challenging."[132] They felt permission to reject the possible

---

[123] *Id.* at 29.
[124] *Id.* at 41.
[125] C. Blow, *Real Men and Pink Suits*, N.Y. TIMES, Feb. 11, 2012, at A21.
[126] RHODE, *supra* note 46, at 42; T. Parker-Pope, *Overweight Patients Face Bias*, N.Y. TIMES, Apr. 30, 2013, at D5.
[127] SEEMAN & LUCIANI, *supra* note 14, at 75.
[128] *Id.*
[129] *Id.* at 76.
[130] M. Lasalandra, *Doctors Say Losing Weight Is Emphasized Too Heavily*, BOS. HERALD, June 1, 1998, at 20 (quoting Michael Fumento).
[131] KIRKLAND, *supra* note 63, at ix.
[132] R. FORD, THE RACE CARD: HOW BLUFFING ABOUT BIAS MAKES RACE RELATIONS WORSE 132 (2008).

candidacy of Governor Chris Christie in 2012 for president because: "He is just too fat."[133]

Let's go back to the start of the chapter and the picture of the young fat child with the caption "It's hard to be a little girl if you're not." The photo and slogan are part of a billboard campaign in Georgia, the state with the second-highest rate of obesity in the United States. Other billboards display a variety of fat children and similar messages warning of the dangers of and humiliation associated with obesity. The surgeon-in-chief of Children's Health care of Atlanta, the sponsoring institution, has insisted that "the most effective means are to use techniques that...are controversial."[134] The campaign brought loud protests, including from Alan Guttmacher, a child health expert at the National Institute of Health.[135] He warned that the campaign could backfire, reinforcing the very behaviors it was meant to change. Nevertheless, it was staunchly defended in some quarters: "[A]nti-stigmatizers are more worried about eroding kids' 'self-esteem' than combating an escalating health problem in a vulnerable population."[136]

This campaign returns us to a discussion of the centrality of norms. We do need to develop attitudes and behaviors that embrace healthy eating and exercise. Such norms are important for all ages but especially for children so that, right from the start, good practices are nurtured and become a habit. Moreover, as we have seen earlier in this chapter, stigma can have a role in changing behavior. Shifting norms have come to condemn smoking.[137] Such shunning of smokers has been an important part in suppressing the use of tobacco. The Atlanta campaign was modeled on an anti-methamphetamine one. That campaign may have been successful; we do use stigma to discourage drug consumption as well.

Stigma and shame can have a role in developing norms. But what that role is in any context can give rise to complex issues.[138] A current example, in another context, is the public rating of teachers in an effort to improve performance: a move strongly opposed by some educational leaders on the grounds that the shaming of teachers with low evaluations will do more harm than good.[139] But

---

[133] M. Kinsley, *Requiem for a Governor before He's in the Ring*, BLOOMBERG, Sept. 29, 2011, available at http://www.bloomberg.com/news/2011-09-30/requiem-for-a-governor-before-he-s-in-the-ring-michael-kinsley.html.

[134] B. Kay, *High Esteem Won't Cure Obesity's Ills*, NAT'L POST, Feb. 11, 2012, available at http://fullcomment.nationalpost.com/2012/02/11/barbara-kay-high-esteem-wont-cure-obesitys-ills/.

[135] K. Daley, *A Leading US Health Official Has Warned That a Campaign Started by a Children's Hospital to Fight Childhood Obesity Poses Health Risks*, BBC NEWS, Feb. 9, 2012, available at http://www.bbc.co.uk/news/world-us-canada-16958865; E. Renzetti, *It's Time to Shed the Tyranny of Dieting—Losing Weight Is a Losing Battle*, GLOBE & MAIL, Jan. 7, 2012, at A2.

[136] Kay, *supra* note 134.

[137] *Supra* Section IV(e)(1): Panics, Good Norms, and Consumption.

[138] BOGART, *supra* note 104, at 113 and 115–16; R. Reeves, *Shame Is Not a Four-Letter Word*, N.Y. TIMES, Mar. 16, 2013, at A19.

[139] B. Gates, *Shame Is Not the Solution*, N.Y. TIMES, Feb. 23, 2012, at A23.

norms and obesity are different than norms and smoking or the use of recreational drugs (drinking alcohol or gambling). Fat people have been subjected to censorious attitudes for a long time. During that period, the rates of obesity, however, measured, have not fallen and have, at times, increased. Such attitudes and behaviors have mostly added to, not lessened, the burden on fat individuals.

Obesity differs in several ways from smoking, imbibing of alcohol, taking drugs, or gambling. With these other forms of consumption the solution when problems arise is to stop or, better yet, especially in the case of drugs and smoking, to never start. The response may not be easy but it is straightforward: walk away. But we all have to eat and drink. Abstinence can never be a solution. There are a variety of issues for almost everyone about what to eat and drink, and in which combination and amounts.

Furthermore, there are financial incentives at play with other forms of consumption, such as smoking, that are not available in terms of addressing obesity. Abstaining from using cigarettes (or never starting) saves an individual a significant amount of money. No such monetary inducements are available in terms of weight; stopping eating/drinking is not an option. Indeed, there are often financial disincentives: consuming fresh fruits and vegetables can be more costly than many foods of dubious nutrition. Nutritious food and drink must also be available. Such is often not the case in the "food deserts" of inner cities where chips, soda, chocolate bars, and goodness knows what other dubious items are often at hand for the buying.[140]

What is more, weight can be not just about calories consumed but also can be about those expended. Here, too, there are a variety of issues about different exercises and sports, their duration, intensity, and so forth. Moreover, there are significant issues about the opportunities for physical activity, including time and physical spaces. In terms of the latter there are fundamental issues regarding how urban spaces have been configured and built in ways that may encourage physical activity, but that often actually discourage active lifestyles. Finally, the notion that weight, once gained, is shed with effort that is "only moderately challenging" is a pernicious myth.[141]

The point of all this is not to deflect concerns about obesity, especially in terms of children. Rather, it is to question whether yet more shame and embarrassment for fat people, as in the Children's Health care of Atlanta campaign, is a way to go. There are many questions about how to strengthen efforts to prevent obesity, in particular in terms of children. This is more so because of the complexities around eating and exercise, as just described. We'll pursue these questions in Part III. Most of those who have researched and thought about these issues consider positive support for parents, in terms of proper nutrition and active lifestyle, is the better way to proceed. Yes, parents must take

---

[140] WHITE HOUSE TASK FORCE, *supra* note 17, at ch. IV: "Access to Healthy, Affordable Food."
[141] FORD, *supra* note 132, at 132 and accompanying text.

responsibility. But they will be helped in doing so if given the tools. Meanwhile the Atlanta campaign has caused shame—but shame directed at those who would pillory children and their parents in this way?

3. Responses

The documentation of stigmatization, on the one hand, and the reactions to it, on the other, are gathering momentum. Stereotypes of fat people as lazy and out of control are being challenged on many fronts. This confronting of stigma has led to several different responses. They share common ground in protesting the harsh treatment of the obese. They then differ in their prescriptions for fighting that stigmatization. Let's look at three main ones.

i. Fight Stigma—Battle Weight

This response largely agrees with the allegations of stigma and prejudice against fat people. It allies itself with the overall conclusion about how such bias causes stress for the obese and makes responding to various issues affecting the overweight even more difficult. Consider this conclusion about the overall negative impact of such attitudes and actions: "Weight stigma is not a beneficial public health tool for reducing obesity...[It] generates health disparities, and interferes with effective obesity intervention efforts...[It is] both a social justice issue and a priority for public health."[142]

At the same time the emphasis of this response largely remains on weight loss as a primary solution for problems of the obese, anti-weight initiatives should be careful not to have stigmatizing effects and should, themselves, be part of the fight against prejudice toward fat people. That said, fat people should lose weight.

A novel contribution to this position is Seeman and Luciani, *XXL: Obesity and the Limits of Shame*.[143] They vociferously condemn the many ways fat people are stigmatized and subjected to discrimination. They provide a very long inventory, many items of which have already been referred to, of such attitudes and actions.[144] They are not shy about accusing those with power over the lives of fat people for promulgating such negative norms. Consider just their comments about doctors and the role they play in censuring large individuals:

> When obesity is framed as a lack of personal responsibility...this translates into stigma...Doctors internalize this shaming mentality...They see their obese patients as unmotivated or lazy. The heavier patients are, the less respectfully they're treated.[145]

---

[142] Puhl & Heuer, *supra* note 89, at 1019.
[143] SEEMAN & LUCIANI, *supra* note 14.
[144] *Id.* at 73–79.
[145] *Id.* at 75.

The point here is not to assess the accuracy of Seeman and Luciani's remarks about the medical profession, but, rather, to use them to demonstrate how condemnatory these authors are of anything that can be construed as stigmatization of fat people.

Yet that sympathy toward the obese does not alter their view of the central problem: too many people have way too much weight. They propose to tackle this core issue though a novel intervention: Healthy Living Vouchers (HLV). To what extent any kind of vouchers can and should be part of a response is a matter to which we will return in Part III. There we will discuss specifics of the Seeman and Luciani proposal. It raises many issues but by no means should it be dismissed out of hand.

Here we are citing these authors as an example of an approach that both condemns stigma toward the obese even as it insists that fat people must lose weight. By novel means, perhaps, but lose it they must: "The *participatory and accountable journey* to a weight loss option is what matters."[146]

ii. Weight Is Not the Problem—It's Society That Has Issues

This response insists that the primary focus should not be on weight, and certainly not its loss, but on the harm inflicted because of bias toward the obese. In its strongest form this reaction flatly rejects the contention that being obese is a problem for fat people; any issues arise from society's negative acts and attitudes toward large people.

The core of this response is that being fat is simply a physical characteristic. Some people are tall. Some have blue eyes. Some are fat. Or: "Most people naturally occupy a middle range of weights (and heights) whereas some people naturally weigh less and some people naturally weigh more (just as some people are naturally tall or short)."[147] A person's size is not and should not be taken to be a proxy for health. What is more, it should not be a basis for presumptions about who is worthy, attractive, or responsible, or who has any number of other positive or negative characteristics.

This response is a driving force behind the use of the word "fat" rather than "obese" as the description of large-size individuals. From this perspective calling someone "'obese' medicalizes human diversity [and]...inspires a misplaced search for a 'cure' for naturally occurring difference ... [It] fuels anti-fat prejudice...in all areas of society."[148] In contrast, "[T]here is the respect for the political project of reclaiming the word fat, both as the preferred neutral adjective (i.e., short/tall, young/old, fat/thin) and also as a preferred term of political identity."[149]

---

[146] *Id.* at 126 (emphasis in the original).
[147] M. Wann, *Foreword: Fat Studies: An Invitation to Revolution* to ROTHBLUM & SOLOVAY, *supra* note 49, at ix.
[148] *Id.* at xiii; A. Pollack, *A.M.A. Recognizes Obesity as a Disease*, N.Y. TIMES, June 19, 2013, B1, B5.
[149] *Id.* at xii.

This reaction challenges the linkage of weight to health. The 1993 study, discussed earlier, that substantially exaggerated the number of deaths associated with obesity is often cited as an example of the way that the medical profession and the wider society are prepared to all too easily conclude that fatness is equated with sickness.[150] Instead, the assertion is that, whatever ailments may be associated with weight in some fat people, these health difficulties, particularly psychological ones, can be attributed, at least in part, to the constant stress that fat people experience from the abuse that they suffer because of their large size.[151]

Such health complications may also be associated, in part, with the pressure to lose weight and the many failed attempts to do so. As we saw earlier in this chapter, some fat people can lose weight but very few people can maintain the loss. The claim is that not only does dieting not work over the long term, but that the yo-yoing of weight may, itself, contribute to any health problems large-size people may suffer.[152]

These issues for fat people are exacerbated by pressures from the weight loss and diet pill industries and from those involved with bariatric procedures. These forces have a strong economic interest in emphasizing the health risks of being obese and the need to lose weight at any cost and by any means. Over the last several decades they have been very successful: "Fear of fat is not new... What is new in the last fifty years...is the extent to which the diet and weight loss industry has moved from the sidelines to the center of American life, managing to dramatically increase its influence and profits without ever increasing product effectiveness."[153]

This perspective is skeptical of any interventions, including legal ones, designed to help individuals lose weight or not gain it in the first place. Such interventions are premised on a number of presumptions that should be questioned:

- Increased availability (and cheapness) of highly caloric food is a causal force in...increased consumption
- Food consumption and exercise are related to body size in a linear, regularized, and predictable way
- By obtaining new knowledge about food people will eat differently
- Humans are naturally or have been historically thin.[154]

---

[150] *Supra*, Section IV(c): The Physical Health Problems Related to Obesity Are Misrepresented
[151] RHODE, *supra* note 46, at 39–40.
[152] P. Lyons, *Prescription for Harm—Diet Industry Influence, Public Health Policy, and the "Obesity Epidemic,"* in ROTHBLUM & SOLOVAY, *supra* note 49, at 75, 81.
[153] *Id.* at 75.
[154] J. Guthman, *Neoliberalism and the Constitutionality of Contemporary Bodies*, in ROTHBLUM & SOLOVAY, *supra* note 49, at 189–90.

Some with this perspective do not oppose efforts to decry dense caloric food of questionable nutritional value and urban spaces that promote driving rather than walking. But these efforts and what they propose as explanations for obesity are "highly problematic."[155] Even efforts aimed at preventing people from becoming fat are questioned: "There is no nice, unstigmatizing way to wish that fat people did not eat or exist. Besides, 'obesity' prevention is a fallback position, a tacit admission that experts hope the same tips that have failed to produce weight loss will somehow prevent weight gain."[156]

There is one area where this view does approve of intervention. It invokes the law and would use it more robustly to protect large people from fat prejudice. If the problem, at least for the most part, is bias toward the obese then, in an age of rights, it is no surprise that there would be a claim for legal protections especially by those who have examined these issues and who are legally trained. Two important and recent attempts to address these issues are Kirkland's *Fat Rights* and Rhode's *The Beauty Bias*.[157] These issues and legal responses to them as part of "regulating obesity" are significant and central to an understanding of the potential and limits of law. As a result we devote the next chapter to these questions and to how they help us understand the complexities of engaging law as a response to obesity.

iii. Health at Every Size (HAES)

A third response to fat prejudice is to join in the fight against bias while, at the same time, establishing a perspective that is proactive in terms of achieving and maintaining health and fitness but which de-emphasizes weight and body size. This reaction underscores respect for all shapes and sizes of bodies while supporting efforts to have people eat and drink nutritiously and to be physically active. In other words: "A weight-neutral approach focuses on loving self-care and the decisions that people can make on a day-to-day basis that are sustainable for a lifetime. [This response] is not against weight loss; it is against the pursuit of weight loss."[158]

Health at Every Size (HAES) offers as an alternative public health model, one that offers a different view of weight and responses to it than the traditional conceptions of public health and obesity discussed earlier in this chapter.[159] HAES emphasizes self-acceptance and healthy daily living regardless of

---

[155] *Id.* at 189.

[156] Wann. *supra* note 147, at xvii.

[157] KIRKLAND. *supra* note 63; RHODE. *supra* note 46. Rhode is also supportive of legal interventions that would be guided by an approach like the one taken by the Health at Every Size Model (HAES) (*see* Section IV(e)(3)(iii) *infra*): RHODE at ch. 7: "Strategies for Change." However, her emphasis is on protection from appearance bias, including the victimization of fat people.

[158] Burgard. *supra* note 83, at 42, 44: the association for size diversity and health has registered "HEALTH AT EVERY SIZE" as a trademark. The references in this book are to the more general HAES movement.

[159] *Supra.* Section III: Obesity: A Public Health Issue?

whether an individual's weight changes.[160] HAES adherents claim that health risks can be reduced by social support, good nutrition, access to medical care, physical activity, and other factors regardless if the person loses weight. In contrast: "Policies which promote weight loss as feasible and beneficial not only perpetuate misinformation and damaging stereotypes, but also contribute to a healthist, moralizing discourse which mitigates against socially-integrated approaches to health."[161]

HAES advocates cite a two-year study in which a group of fat women were divided into two subgroups. Subgroup 1 was coached regarding dieting and exercise. Subgoup 2 was encouraged to eat a healthy diet, to listen to their body's clues, to exercise in fun ways, and to take part in fat acceptance discussions. Members in subgroup 1 initially lost weight, but by the end of the two-year period half had dropped out of the study and most had regained any weight that had been lost. Blood pressure, cholesterol, and other metabolic measures had not improved, and self-esteem had decreased. Those in subgroup 2 did not lose weight but most stayed in the study and exercised regularly. Blood pressure, cholesterol, and other metabolic measures had improved as had self-esteem.[162] Some medical researchers are also moving away from reliance on BMI as indicative of health status. Instead, they are working on devising systematic assessments of any risks associated with an individual's weight based on that person's physical state as determined by several indicators.[163]

HAES advocates assert that this model:

- De-emphasizes weight (while focusing on controllable choices) in health/medical communications, eliminating a source of stigma and anxiety for people of any weight.
- Does not ask people to control what may not be controllable. This prevents damaging cycles of body loathing, weight loss and regain, and feelings of ineffectiveness.
- Does not try to prevent "obesity" but rather bodily neglect and abuse.
- Offers a comprehensive approach to valuing and caring for bodies of every size.[164]

Much of what HAES advocates is attractive. Yet the goals of the HAES movement are, themselves, very difficult to achieve. What is more, the very things HAES advocates, such as good nutrition, exercise, good medical attention,

---

[160] FARRELL, *supra* note 63, at 11–13.

[161] Bacon & Aphramor, *supra* note 86, at 8.

[162] L. Bacon et al., *Size Acceptance and Intuitive Eating Improve Health for Obese, Female, Chronic Dieters*, 105(6) J. AM. DIETETIC ASS'N 929 (2005), *cited in* FARRELL, *supra* note 63, at 11–12.

[163] R. Padwal, *Using the Edmonton Obesity Staging System to Predict Mortality in a Population-Representative Cohort of People with Overweight and Obesity*, 183(14) CAN. MED. ASS'N J. E1059–66 (2011).

[164] Burgard, *supra* note 83, at 51.

fighting of fat prejudice, etc. are normally part of a weight-loss program, and HAES may be no more likely to succeed in getting people to implement them just because weight loss itself is not the goal. From whatever perspective it is viewed, the goal of enabling and motivating people to eat and drink well and to be physically active is a complex undertaking, not easily achieved.

Still the goals of HAES and related perspectives let us look at interventions in yet another way. We need to ask of any strategy or mix of strategies not only did individuals lose weight (and maintain that loss), but were there any positive effects in terms of health indicators broadly defined to include increased opportunities to eat nutritiously and to be more physically active? Many believe that affirmative answers to the second question, about health indicators, are at least as significant, if not more important, than weight reduction. We'll return to these questions and answers in great detail in Part III when we look at various interventions.

V. The Heavy Hand of The State?

Yet another reaction to obesity is to suggest that whatever responses may be appropriate, government regulation, at least of the traditional sort, is not acceptable. This reaction aligns itself with other forces that rail against the evils of big government generally.[165] It is no surprise that a main element of this reaction comes from the food industry. That opposition asserts such failings as infringement of free speech, mangling of consumer choice, and ineffectiveness of such interventions.

There are two other attacks on government interventions responding to obesity. The second reaction focuses on the health professions and others and their misdirected attempts to address medical and social ills by articulating and implementing a public health model, especially for obesity. The third reaction comes from those who, as described earlier, overwhelmingly view the problem as society's negative norms toward fat people. Even interventions directed at healthy eating and physical activity are suspect as just another way to control the lives of the obese.

These three reactions, taken together, pose significant challenges for the design and implementation of effective regulatory intervention. Those challenges persist whether the goal is decreasing rates of obesity or promoting the consumption of healthy food/drinks and active lifestyles regardless of weight loss. These reactions and their critiques underscore the need to pose and answer the question: what is the problem?

---

[165] J. Hacker & P. Peirson, Winner Take All Politics: How Washington Made the Rich Richer and Turned Its Back on the Middle Class (2010); J. Simpson, *Income Equality: Deep, Complex, and Growing*, Globe & Mail, Dec. 9, 2011, at A21; A. Hacker, *We're More Unequal than You Think*, N.Y. Rev. Books, Feb. 23, 2012, LIX:3, at 34.

In terms of the first reaction, the food-and-drink industry is very effective in using lobbying, lawsuits, financial contributions, public relations, and other strategies to shape issues to its liking. In particular that industry aims to persuade legislators and the public that the science relating diet to health is so uncertain that regulation promoting better eating and drinking and aimed, in any way, at its products is mostly unnecessary and would, in any event, be mostly ineffective. In any event, diet and weight are a matter of personal responsibility, accountability, and discipline. Generally, this industry aligns itself with a "political environment [that] emphasizes market forces, individual responsibility, and a perception of government intervention in health as paternalism."[166]

Marion Nestle is brilliant and relentless in documenting the questionable tactics of that industry.[167] In her estimation it makes many questionable claims, including the following:

- All foods can be part of healthful diets (especially theirs).
- Dietary advice changes so often that we do not need to follow it (unless it favors their products).
- Diets are a matter of personal responsibility and freedom of choice (especially freedom to choose their products).
- Advocacy for more healthful food choices is irrational (if it suggests eating less of their products).
- Government intervention is unnecessary, undesirable, and incompatible with democratic institutions (unless it protects and promotes their products).[168]

In addition, there is another tactic that the industry has employed. It suggests that any problems with obesity are caused, not by overeating, but by lack of physical activity.[169] The industry hauls out evidence of sedentary lifestyles and the harms to health to argue that it is inactivity, not consumption of its products, which is the main culprit. The industry also does such things as sponsor sports events and associations promoting exercise to demonstrate that it is interested in finding solutions.

Exercise is important, and there are many health benefits associated with it. The sedentary ways that have developed are a significant cause for concern. We'll return to these issues in Part III.[170] The point here is that the food-and-drink industry, in order to deflect attention away from criticisms aimed toward

---

[166] INSTITUTE OF MEDICINE, *supra* note 5, at 20 (describing that environment but not agreeing with that description).

[167] See earlier discussion of her work in this chapter: note 33 and accompanying text.

[168] NESTLE, *supra* note 33, at 358–59; see also, M. Mudd, *How to Force Ethics on the Food Industry*, N.Y. TIMES, Mar. 17, 2013, Sunday Review, at 4.

[169] OLIVER, *supra* note 35, at 144–45 and T. CAULFIELD, THE CURE FOR EVERYTHING!: UNTANGLING TWISTED MESSAGES ABOUT HEALTH, FITNESS, AND HAPPINESS 46 *et seq.* (2012).

[170] Chapter 7: Encouraging Physical Activity: Children at Play!.

it, directs attention to a related—but separate—set of issues, and ones for which it has little responsibility.

Apart from specifics, the industry has been adept at generally portraying regulatory initiatives as heavy-handed mangling of choice by meddlesome governments intent upon corralling consumer demands, and the food-and-drink industry's response to them in the name of unnecessary and unachievable interventionists' goals. Consider just one comment by one of its spokespersons:

> Controlling...of products deemed "unfit" does not work...Food consumption is not supply driven, it is demand driven, and consumers are in the driver's seat...you cannot force people to comply with the Dietary Guidelines and it is wrong to try. It is an unworkable, totalitarian approach.[171]

We will discuss a number of tactics to avoid or minimize regulation employed by the food-and-drink industry and others when we look at various issues in Part III, including taxes on junk food and beverages; subsidies of healthy foods/drinks; banning of promotional toys with meals, especially associated with kids; restrictions on advertising, particularly to children; and efforts to promote physical activity. As the IOM Report *For the Public's Health* observed: "[C]onsumer autonomy is based on an assumption that people are entirely free in the marketplace...[T]his overlooks what is known about human behaviour (such as underestimating risk, optimism bias)...[C]ompanies marketing products known to have deleterious health effects use highly sophisticated advertising and product labelling developed to exploit consumer vulnerabilities."[172]

But for the moment, in terms of the food-and-drink industry and its tactics, let's give the last word to Marion Nestle. In the face of all this pressure for regulation, the industry is trying to depict itself as a responsible market actor.[173] Prominent among such efforts is that of Pepsi, the largest food-and-beverage company in the United States, striving to be "the good company." It holds itself out as wanting to play a leading role in public health issues and, in particular, issues of excess weight.[174] Nestle has straightforward but drastic advice for that company. When asked about this positioning, she replied: "The best thing Pepsi could do for worldwide obesity would be to go out of business."[175]

---

[171] NESTLE, *supra* note 33, at 359 (quoting Dr. R. Applebaum of the National Food Processors Association).

[172] INSTITUTE OF MEDICINE, *supra* note 5, at 61.

[173] S. Strom, *McDonald's Menu to Post Calorie Data*, N.Y. TIMES, Sept. 13, 2012, at B1; S. Strom, *In Ads, Coke Confronts Soda's Link to Obesity* N.Y. TIMES, Jan. 15, 2013, at B7.

[174] J. Seabrook, *Snacks for a Fat Planet: PepsiCo Takes Stock of the Obesity Epidemic*, NEW YORKER, May 16, 2011, at 54.

[175] *Id.* at 65.

The second reaction, the misdirected efforts of a public health model, is well articulated by Seeman and Luciani.[176] We encountered their work earlier, in our discussion of the shaming of fat people.[177] Their focus is on Healthy Living Vouchers (HLVs); as we noted we'll come to a discussion of their prescriptions in Part III.[178] Of note here is that their espousal of HLVs are a reaction to what they see are the inadequacies of the public health approach to obesity.

As we have seen, Seeman and Luciani are unqualified in their denunciation of stigma directed at fat people. That said, in their estimation, obesity is the problem; weight loss is the solution. Thus, they have nothing to say about the HEAS model of public health. Their critique is reserved for the traditional public health model and how it wants to address obesity through weight loss and prevention of excess weight gain.

The basic error is how that public health model focuses on issues, generally, and obesity in particular: too little focus on individuals and individualized solutions. As they put it: "[T]oo much attention has been paid to sweeping social change, and too little attention to what individuals can do to address their own individual obesity challenges."[179] In their view adherents of the public health model are too much "system planners" who "are committed to shaping public attitudes; individuals are not their chief concern."[180] As a result this "lack of attention to individual differences to weight gain and prevention has led to a *maze of policy incoherence*."[181]

This overarching criticism then leads them to take issue with numerous government policies, actual and potential. Their goal is to demonstrate the futility of any number of interventions, including educational campaigns,[182] taxes on soda,[183] physical activity requirements in schools,[184] financial incentives,[185] and banning of junk food in some educational institutions.[186] In fairness they do indicate that they are not *against* some government programs (such as making fresh fruits available to schoolchildren).[187] But they insist regarding obesity that "No public policies so far seem to have made an appreciable dent."[188]

---

[176] SEEMAN & LUCIANI, *supra* note 14.
[177] *Supra* Section IV(e)(3)(i): Fight Stigma—Battle Weight.
[178] Chapter 7, Section V(b)(5): Vouchers to the Rescue?: The Canadian Children's Fitness Tax Credit.
[179] SEEMAN & LUCIANI, *supra* note 14, at 64.
[180] *Id.* at 62.
[181] *Id.* at 64 (emphasis added).
[182] *Id.* at 100–01.
[183] *Id.* at 99.
[184] *Id.* at 67.
[185] *Id.* at 84.
[186] *Id.* at 67.
[187] *Id.* at 105.
[188] *Id.*

In making a case for HLVs Seeman and Luciani are opponents, generally, of an approach (the public health model) that is the foundation for the case for government intervention in many areas and certainly obesity. Consider how at odds their prescriptions are with those who rail against "obesogenic environments" and who are certain that systemic responses are necessary: "[T]he obesity epidemic poses a significant public health challenge to local, national, and global organizations. Addressing the root causes...means...regulating a globalized economic system...including food...that profits from expanding markets and promoting energy-dense products."[189] At the same time, in taking their position against the public health model, Seeman and Luciani give broad support, intentionally or not, to industry arguments that government interventions aimed at "obsogenic environments" are ineffective, mangle individual choice, suppress self-control, and smother market initiatives.

The third reaction comes from those in the fat rights movement who believe that well-intentioned interventions will produce unintended negative consequences. They, too, have problems with the traditional public health/environmental account of obesity and the responses for which it advocates. At the same time their dissatisfaction is for very different reasons than those of Seeman and Luciani. Kirkland is a leading voice for such concerns, particularly in terms of effects on the poor and racial minorities.[190]

The environmental account means to shift responsibility away from individuals and to focus it on obesogenic conditions that lead to excess eating mixed with sedentary ways. Yet its emphasis on the ultimate goal of shedding pounds leads back to the individual. Kirkland in her groundbreaking work observes "[t]he environmental approach to fighting obesity is supposed to be collective...But because the animating problem is that poor people are fat, the focus on weight loss has become the metric of success. The aim then is to get the poor and the fat to make virtuous personal choices to combat a contaminated world."[191] The target of Kirkland's concerns are well-meaning elites, especially well-educated, white, and non-deviant body feminists.[192] She asks: "What if it is the case that many elites find the terms of the environmental account to be simply a more palatable way to express their disgust at fat people, the tacky, low-class foods they eat, and the indolent ways they spend their time?"[193]

There is a broad sweep to this criticism. Almost any suggestion that people should consider what they eat can be subject to censure. Consider the aforementioned Marion Nestle, a great foe of the merchandising antics of

---

[189] K. Raine, *Obesity Epidemics: Inevitable Outcome of Globalization or Preventable Public Health Challenge?*, 57(1) INT'L J. PUB. HEALTH 35–36 (2012).
[190] A. Kirkland, *The Environmental Account of Obesity: A Case for Feminist Skepticism*, 36(2) SIGNS 463–86 (2011).
[191] *Id.* at 467.
[192] *Id.* at 464.
[193] *Id.* at 474.

the food-and-drink industry with its relentless peddling of dense caloric substances of dubious nutritional value. It's true that one of her rallying cries is "eat less, move more." But her objective is not the condemnation of fat people but, rather, to expose an industry, driven by profit seeking, that shoves what seems is a limitless amount of junk food and drink at individuals, including impressionable children. Kirkland, in her *Fat Rights*, all but ignores the wealth of information and the vigor of argument in *Food Politics*. She dismisses the book and some others as "some widely publicized anti-fat books marketed to a mainstream audience."[194] Nestle gets similar treatment in other works that take a position similar to Kirkland's.[195]

Yet critics such as Kirkland and others are insightful, if provocative, as they oppose what they call "healthism" and the way it gives rise to such perspectives as the environmental account of obesity. "Healthism" is a "super value" that can trump other social concerns.[196] For Guthman it "conflates personal practices of self-care with empowerment and good citizenship."[197] In this depiction, a thin, fit body is an indicator of health regardless of what must be done by individuals to achieve that status.[198]

To be wary of "healthism" is not to be against health and collective efforts to improve well-being. Appropriate public health interventions to combat disease and alleviate suffering are to be applauded.[199] But "healthism" can distort our understanding of obesity and responses to it. Such warping occurs in several ways. One is the way our approach to fat establishes social privilege for an elite who are thin, nutritiously fed, and vocal about the state of their well-being: "[T]he implicit linking of good food, good bodies, and political activism allows those who are already privileged to achieve ever higher status by virtue of their bodies and food purchasing habits."[200]

Kirkland, at the conclusion of one of her works, does mention approvingly HAES, the alternative public health model we discussed earlier.[201] Given the core of that philosophy it may be that Kirkland would not oppose some interventions aimed at promoting nutritious eating/drinking and physical activity and not weight loss (or prevention). She ends with one last run at the environmental movement even as she recognizes its basis in admirable values: "Much of the environmental account is buoyed along by elite ethnocentrism about the superiority of our own habits, but the undercurrent is real concern for the suffering, deprivation, and dangers that bedevil poor people in our societies and

---

[194] KIRKLAND, *supra* note 63, at 30.
[195] Guthman, *supra* note 154, at 188–89.
[196] GUTHMAN, *supra* note 29, at 52.
[197] *Id.* at 191.
[198] *Id.* at 53.
[199] *Id.* at 64.
[200] *Id.* at 193.
[201] Kirkland, *supra* note 190, at 481.

around the world."[202] But how do we find ways to oppose "healthism" even as we recognize and support such "real concern"?

VI. Conclusion

Let's return, again, to the little fat girl in Atlanta. The size of children as they are developing is of concern—an issue that is well documented. The question is: what to do about it? A place to start would be to stop obsessing about weight and equating size with health. At the moment we have a set of norms buttressing stigma toward and discrimination against fat people. Somehow we need to shift to norms that encourage nutritious eating and drinking, active lifestyles, and a fundamental acceptance of bodies of many shapes and sizes.

For that transformation to occur, there will need to be great societal change. If we get things more or less right, law can have a role: a complicated and limited one. Perhaps law can even do something for that child in Atlanta. As we have seen, interventions are likely to be greeted with skepticism and opposition on a number of fronts. We'll examine particular possibilities and the controversies surrounding them in Part III. As a start, here, let's ask: which is the bigger problem—the little girl's chubbiness or the way society treats her? Such negative attitudes, the actions they breed, and the role of law in opposing them are the subject of the next chapter.

---

[202] *Id.* at 481.

{ 3 }

Appearance Bias–Fat Rights

I. Introduction

In April 2012 the media reported that a hospital in Texas was refusing to hire anyone with a BMI of 35 or over.[1] (Recall that, by conventional standards, anyone with a BMI of 30 or over is considered obese.)[2] The institution's policy indicated that an employee's appearance "should fit with a representational image or specific mental projection of the job of a health care professional ... free from distraction." [3] Proponents of the policy claimed that it was reasonable for the employees of a health care provider to project a healthy image. But critics were quick to underscore how this institution conflated health and weight, resulting in discrimination toward the obese. In rejecting the hospital's position Lyn Grefe, President and Chief Executive of the National Eating Disorders Association, put it bluntly: "You cannot tell by looking at someone whether or not they are healthy."[4]

Whatever the causes, whatever the responses, one fact seems clear: a significant number of people are fat. Many people who try to lose weight fail in their efforts. Many of those who do succeed will regain weight over several years. As we saw in Chapter 2, obese people are the targets of stigma in many forms in schools, at work, in social settings, in the media, etc. In this chapter we'll see how such negative norms can lead to acts of discrimination. We'll then pose and answer the question: should obese people be protected by human rights laws from such mistreatment?

---

[1] W. Leung, *Should Employers Discriminate Based on Workers' Waistlines?*, GLOBE & MAIL, Apr. 10, 2012, *available at* http://www.theglobeandmail.com/life/the-hot-button/should-employers-discriminate-based-on-workers-waistlines/article2396947/[hereinafter Leung].

[2] Chapter 2, Section: III: Obesity: A Public Health Issue?.

[3] Leung, *supra* note 1.

[4] *Id.*

The second part of the title of this chapter is the same as a book by Anna Kirkland.[5] Professor Kirkland explores many issues related to using human rights legislation to protect fat people from discrimination. We'll refer to many of her ideas in this chapter as we assess the extent to which the law does and should shield obese individuals from various acts of prejudice—acts that occur for the most part simply because of the way large people look.

Although discrimination against fat people is a main form of appearance bias, it is not the only one. People who are regarded as, for example, looking too old, too short, too homely, or, in the case of women, insufficiently sexualized, can also be the targets of such prejudice. We'll discuss issues involving the obese in this larger context of appearance bias to gain a fuller understanding of the several ways in which harmful norms privilege selected looks to the detriment of others. Issues involving fat people are set in that larger terrain of prejudice against many shapes, sizes, and looks that do not conform to misdirected standards. In the few jurisdictions that have responded directly in shielding fat people from discrimination, such legislation is often couched in terms of the more generally applicable prohibition against appearance bias. What are the justifications for such laws? Are there particular complexities involved in banning discrimination based on weight?

We conclude the chapter with a question related to ones asked throughout the book: what will be the effects of any laws designed to protect fat people from discrimination? We begin the chapter with a brief, general discussion of human rights laws and their efforts to protect individuals from unjustified discrimination.

II. Discrimination and Human Rights Laws

One of the defining characteristics of the last fifty years or so of postindustrial societies has been the ascendance of human rights. This rights consciousness has been accompanied by campaigns to have various claims protected by law. Historically disadvantaged groups and individuals, such as women, blacks and other visible minorities, and the people with disabilities have asserted their rights to be legally protected from discrimination.

How the "rights revolution" came to be is an interesting question. How, if at all, fat people can join this march toward equality also raises many issues that are the subject of this chapter. But first, a word about terminology. The claims that we are discussing we will refer to as "human rights." In the United States, in particular, these protections are often referred to as "civil rights." Some commentators view "human rights" as a more encompassing concept, including

---

[5] A. KIRKLAND, FAT RIGHTS: DILEMMAS OF DIFFERENCE AND PERSONHOOD (2008).

embracing claims on behalf of not just individuals, but also groups.[6] Others, generally sympathetic to such legal protections, dispute the individual/group distinction.[7] This is an important debate but one that largely does not concern us in respect of the discussion in this chapter. We use "human rights" because that is the more widely used term in various countries and in international documents concerned with issues of discrimination and protection of minorities.[8]

How did this "rights revolution" come to press its many claims?[9] There were a number of developments that, together, led to this transformation. We sketch them here. One was the reaction to the horror of World War II, especially the Holocaust. Such acts of inhumanity led many to believe that law must be invoked to protect, as best it could, religious and other minorities. Another was the turbulent struggle of Blacks in America to end the blight of segregation and other exclusions. Still another was the women's movement and its demands for equality between the sexes. During the 1970s, '80s, and '90s the LGBT (lesbian, gay, bisexual, and transgendered), people with disabilities, Aboriginals, and others joined the long struggle against discrimination.

In terms of the law there were three kinds of important developments. The first was the recognition of rights and protection from discrimination at the international level. The creation of various documents and institutions signaled that ending prejudice was a project of global concern and not simply of interest to particular societies embroiled in these issues.[10] The second were courts, in some countries, most especially the United States, who interpreted their bills of rights in ways that, often, advanced the claims of disadvantaged minorities against governments, such as opposing legislation that discriminated against them.[11] The third were legislatures that enacted human rights statutes that applied to both public and private actors and that prohibited discrimination based on sex, religion, disability, race, and so forth.[12] It is that development and its potential to protect fat people from acts of prejudice that most concerns us in this chapter.

---

[6] R. Abella, *International Law and Human Rights: The Power and the Pity*, 55 McGILL L.J. 871, 878–79 (2010).

[7] L. FRIEDMAN, THE HUMAN RIGHTS CULTURE: A STUDY IN HISTORY AND CONTEXT 15, 87 (2011).

[8] E.g., Ontario Human Rights Code, RSO 1990, ch. 19; Canadian Human Rights Code, RSC 1985, ch-6; Universal Declaration of Human Rights GA Res. 217 (III), UN GAOR, 3d Sess., Supp. No.13, UN Doc. A/810 (1948) 71; European Convention on Human Rights 4 November 1950, E.T.S. 5,13 U.N.T.S. 221 (entered into force September 3, 1953).

[9] C. EPP, THE RIGHTS REVOLUTION: LAWYERS, ACTIVISTS, AND SUPREME COURTS IN COMPARATIVE PERSPECTIVE (1998).

[10] Abella, *supra* note 6.

[11] EPP, *supra* note 9; W. A. BOGART, GOOD GOVERNMENT? GOOD CITIZENS?: COURTS, POLITICS, AND MARKETS IN A CHANGING CANADA (2005).

[12] *Supra*, note 8; Americans with Disabilities Act (1990), as amended, Title 42, ch. 126.

Do these struggles against discrimination have a common element? Lawrence Friedman thinks so. He suggests that they are all aspects of "plural equality." For Friedman that idea has steeped into the collective consciousness of many societies. Plural equality demands not only tolerance of everyone but also recognition of the worthiness of each of us. Friedman opines: "It is the translation into social terms, and into real life, of the ideals expressed in all the charters and manifestoes and declarations: that everybody is or should be equal in dignity and in rights to everybody else."[13]

Enter the claims of fat rights. Reactions by fat activists to the orthodoxies of the traditional public health model's response to obesity are comparatively recent. The fat rights claims are even newer, having gathered momentum only in the last decade.[14] Such claims do seem to fit well with Friedman's characterizations of plural equality. The case for legal protection of the obese from discrimination builds on arguments made by other rights' claimants. Those arguing for such protections assert that being fat, like, for example, sex, sexual orientation, or age, is an immutable characteristic and, therefore, should not be a barrier to equality of treatment, whether in terms of employment, education, access to health care, or the many other aspects of life.

But the case for fat rights is contentious. We'll explore the several dimensions of the controversy in the balance of the chapter. The claim is also being pressed after several decades of rights assertions.[15] Has fatigue set in? Justice Abella, of the Supreme Court of Canada, while protesting any such negative reactions, suggests that this possibility must be faced:

> Somehow we started to let those who had enough say "enough is enough," allowing them to set the agenda while they accused everyone else of having an "agenda," and leaving millions wondering where the human rights they were promised had gone, and why so many people who already had them thought the rest of the continent didn't need them.[16]

Just because a claim is being made after a long list of similar ones have pressed their case is not a basis for judging its merits. The balance of the chapter will have lots to say about the strength of arguments for protecting fat individuals from discrimination. Still the timing of such claims should not be ignored. Will society give these arguments a fair hearing? Or will fat rights, among other challenges, suffer from bad timing?

---

[13] FRIEDMAN, *supra* note 7, at 87.
[14] Chapter 2, Section IV(3)(ii): Responses: Weight Is Not the Problem—It's Society That Has Issues.
[15] W. OSIATYNSKI, HUMAN RIGHTS AND THEIR LIMITS (2009).
[16] Abella, *supra* note 6, at 880.

III. Appearance Bias: "What is Beautiful is Good"[17]

One night when Lynn McAfee was five years old, her psychologically troubled mother left her at the side of a road as punishment... [T]he terrified girl looked toward the nearby houses... and wondered if she should walk over and ask for help. "But I didn't," said Ms. McAfee, 62, who is now the director of medical advocacy for the Council on Size and Weight Discrimination. "I didn't think anyone would want a fat child."[18]

In her book, *The Beauty Bias*, Deborah Rhode explores the many dimensions of appearance bias, including but not limited to weight.[19] Looks matter right from the start. Infants stare longer at attractive faces. Parents and teachers believe children who are less attractive are not as good, smart, likeable, etc. as are kids who are better looking. Children, themselves, come to hold similar beliefs about their counterparts. By twelve many girls place more emphasis on being attractive than being competent. Dissatisfaction with looks may produce anxiety, eating disorders, and other dysfunctions. Generally, confusion over appearance can diminish self-confidence and social skills, which can negatively affect personal relationships and career opportunities as adults.

Attractiveness certainly does count for adults.[20] Less attractive adults are not as likely to be regarded as smart, happy, interesting, likeable, etc. For men, height is a proxy for many desirable characteristics: intelligence, competence, trustworthiness, and so forth. In contrast, unattractive men and women are treated less favorably in a variety of circumstances, including higher sentences and lower damage awards in simulated legal proceedings. Subjects in studies who are told to evaluate essays tend to give lower grades to those that are accompanied by a photograph of an unattractive author.

Candidates for political office with an inappropriate appearance tend to lose.[21] In the famous presidential debate between Kennedy and Nixon the former looked tanned and rested while the latter appeared tired and poorly shaven. Those who watched the exchange on television thought Kennedy had won; those who only listened to the candidates on radio concluded that Nixon was the victor. Given the subsequent history of Nixon, one is tempted to suggest that that there may be something to be said for appearance after all.

---

[17] D. Rhode, The Beauty Bias: The Injustice of Appearance in Life and Law 26 (2010).
[18] S. Begley, *Weight Stigma Hard to Overcome*, Globe & Mail, May 14, 2012, at L5.
[19] Rhode, *supra* note 17, at 26–27 and the sources cited.
[20] W. Immen, *The Skinny on Weight Discrimination*, Globe & Mail, Jan. 23, 2010, at B14.; L. Kwoh, *Want to be CEO? Being Fit Matters*, Globe & Mail, Jan. 23, 2013, at B17.
[21] L. Mlodinow, *Would You Vote for This Face?*, N.Y. Times, Apr. 22, 2012, at SR12.

Several studies have indicated that more "able looking" candidates, judged by a number of factors relating to appearance, are more likely to be supported independently of party or platform. The difference may be as high as twelve percentage points. As Mlodinow opines, "Few of us believe that appearance determines our vote, yet for a significant number of us, it may."[22]

Women are especially burdened. As Rhode puts it: "By virtually any measure, appearance is more important to women than to men."[23] Overweight females are subject to more severe judgments than males, they suffer greater income discounts, and obese women are twice as unlikely to marry as obese men. Male status is enhanced by dating an attractive woman; women with good-looking boyfriends are not so advantaged. One longitudinal study tracking ten thousand graduates of Wisconsin high schools found that overweight men experienced no barriers to getting hired and promoted. But fat women, for a variety of reasons related to reactions to being overweight, were less likely to earn college degrees. They also had jobs with lower earnings and social status than thinner female peers.[24]

In the employment setting, women can be subject to denigrating standards. In female-dominated jobs being unattractive is a disadvantage. Yet in upper-level positions, which have historically been male-dominated, beautiful women can be viewed as less competent and intelligent (though one expert in these issues, sympathetic to women, doubts that this "bimbo effect" is widespread).[25] There is some evidence that not only men but women who do recruiting also discriminate against attractive females.[26] Women employees can also suffer more from dress and grooming standards that sexualize them and expose them to humiliation, harassment, and even physical injury because of high heels, etc.[27]

Meanwhile the global grooming industry is huge, an estimated $15 billion just for perfume, with women spending disproportionate amounts for its products. Norms privileging a constrained sense of beauty urge the embrace of the famous dictate of Estee Lauder: "There are no homely women, only careless women. You have to want [beauty] very much and then help it along."[28] In 2007, Americans were injected with Botox 4.6 million times, had 285,000 operations to reshape their noses, and had 241,000 eyelid procedures.[29] Citizens of other countries are not so fascinated with such techniques. That said, in 2006 the English spent about $800 million on cosmetic interventions, leading the EU

---

[22] *Id.*
[23] RHODE, *supra* note 17, at 30.
[24] C. Glass et al., *Heavy in School, Burdened for Life*, N.Y. TIMES, June 3, 2011, at A19.
[25] D. HAMERMESH, BEAUTY PAYS: WHY ATTRACTIVE PEOPLE ARE MORE SUCCESSFUL 48 (2011).
[26] *Don't Hate Me Because I'm Beautiful*, ECONOMIST, Mar. 31, 2012, at 87; see also J. Hoffman, *'Fat Talk' Carries a Cost* N.Y. TIMES, May 28, 2013, D4.
[27] RHODE, *supra* note 17, at 97.
[28] *Id.* at 55.
[29] HAMERMESH, *supra* note 25, at 32.

on a per capita basis (and paying four times more for such procedures than they did in 2001).[30]

A great part of the appearance industry is, at the least, focused on fantasy. As Rhode opines: "[M]uch of the investment falls short of its intended effect or is induced by fraudulent or misleading claims."[31] Despite, or perhaps because of, such whackery, more money is spent in the United States on grooming than on materials to read.[32] Nine out of ten cosmetic surgery patients are women and, thus, they are exposed disproportionately to the health risks that may accompany these procedures.[33]

But not all commentators are upset by such a focus on appearance. Indeed, some want more attention paid to such matters not less. Catherine Hakim in *Honey Money* believes that it is time to recognize a fourth capital—erotic—to the three that have long been recognized: economic (what money one has), human (what one knows), and social (who one knows).[34] The traditional three capitals have long been viewed as significant determinants, taken together, of an individual's success. Hakim insists that we need to recognize and assess erotic capital, which, depending on the circumstance, can be as important as the other three.

She believes that it is especially significant for women and their personal and professional advancement. Women score higher on levels of physical and social attractiveness. Yet men are rewarded more for such attributes. Hakim means to alter this pattern. She asks: "Why does no one encourage women to exploit men whenever they can?"[35] Perhaps because most women believe that the proper response to human exploitation is to oppose it, not try to convert it to their own advantage.

Whatever the answer to the foregoing question, here's another query: if erotic capital is so critical, why has it taken so long to be recognized? The explanation, according to Hakim, is a strange alliance between patriarchy and radical feminism. The former has systematically trivialized women's erotic capital to discourage women from exploiting it. Women generally have more erotic capital so men have long denied its existence so as to contain women. In terms of the latter, radical feminists have more recently—and unwittingly—colluded with male chauvinist agendas by being contemptuous of anything that enhances beauty or lauds sex appeal.[36] And, just for good measure, Hakim has the following to say about issues that are the subject of this chapter: "'Lookism' ideology and the revolt of the 'fatties' are the latest expression of this denial of

---

[30] *Id.*
[31] RHODE, *supra* note 17, at 33.
[32] *Id.*
[33] *Id.* at 97.
[34] C. HAKIM, HONEY MONEY: THE POWER OF EROTIC CAPITAL (2011).
[35] *Id.* at 3.
[36] *Id.* at 7.

the social and economic value of erotic capital."[37] Other commentators are not as scathing. Nevertheless, they still believe that social pressure, or perhaps norms, can be brought to bear on people with obesity so that they will shed pounds: "stigmatization lite."[38]

We'll have more to say about Professor Hakim's ideas and her opinions on "lookism" and the "revolt of the 'fatties'" later on in the chapter.[39] For the moment her views make it clear that there is by no means universal agreement about whether appearance bias exists at all and, what if anything, should be done about how individuals are treated differently because of the way they look.

IV. "Good Clean Wholesome Female Sexuality" and other Examples of Appearance Bias

Appearance bias can take several forms, with different severity and consequences. We can think of it occurring along a continuum.[40] At one end are characteristics such as height and facial features that are unchangeable and are not otherwise protected grounds of discrimination in human rights law. At this end are also characteristics such as sex, race, and ethnicity that relate to appearance bias but that are separately protected grounds of discrimination.

At the other end are characteristics that usually are a matter of personal choice for which individuals need to take responsibility such as dress and grooming. However, these characteristics can be part of appearance bias if certain aspects are mandated under certain conditions—for example, dress and grooming codes in the workplace. This is especially the case if such codes disproportionately affect women, racial and religious minorities, etc. In between are characteristics such as weight that have both behavioral and genetic determinants and that are permanently changeable only with difficulty, if at all. Many such instances of appearance bias arise from situations involving fat people.

The quote in the subtitle, just above, comes from a Hooters Restaurant spokesperson who explained that that chain sells "all American sex appeal" as much as it sells burgers. But as Rhode observes, it is just that kind of appearance bias that forces on women grooming and dress standards that sexualize them in order to sell products, food, and services.[41] Any claims that such dress and grooming codes are simply responding to clients' preferences need to be rejected as either specious or, when they do in fact exist, not entitled to

---

[37] *Id.*
[38] D. Callahan, *Obesity: Chasing an Elusive Epidemic*, 43(1) HASTING CENTER REPORT 34–40 doi:10 1002/hast.114, 11 VARIETIES OF SOCIAL PRESSURE (2013).
[39] *Infra*, Section V: Resisting the Prejudice of Looks: Justifications for Invoking Law.
[40] RHODE, *supra* note 17, at 25–26.
[41] *Id.* at 13 and 107–09.

deference because they are part of the very bias that needs to be eradicated. Such instances may also be objected to on the basis of sex discrimination, but they also implicate appearance bias. We'll return below to justifications for using legal means to fight prejudice based on looks. Here let's examine just a few concrete instances of such behavior.

As the Hooters example illustrates many of these instances do not concern weight but they can involve dress and grooming codes that sexualize women. Some other examples are a television station that required female anchors to wear bows and ruffles; the Bikini Expresso, a drive-through coffee bar with waitresses wearing sheer baby doll negligees and matching panties; and the Heart Attack Grill with waitresses in "naughty nurses" costumes.[42]

Or, such codes may conflict with religious practices, such as the prohibiting of head coverings, which can cause issues for Muslim women and Jewish men. Or, they may fall disproportionately on racial minorities, such as prohibitions on braiding hair, which affects black women. Such requirements can also conflict with the expression of sexual orientation. A Florida high school required females to sit for graduation pictures in a scoop-neck dress. A lesbian student who had never worn skirts or dresses wanted to pose in a suit like the ones males graduates wore. As her lawyer explained, "She simply wanted to appear in her yearbook as herself not a fluffed up stereotype of what school administrators thought she should look like."[43]

At the same time many such instances do involve issues of weight.[44] We discussed some aspects of fat stigma in Chapter 2.[45] Such opprobrium appears to be spreading. Studies suggest that harmful perceptions of fat individuals may become the cultural norm even in societies where larger bodies have been viewed as attractive.[46] The following are some examples, in the United States, where those negative norms have led to acts of discrimination:

- The "Borgata Babes." An instance involving both sexualization and weight. An Atlantic City casino required cocktail waitresses to have an "hourglass figure." These women, once hired, could not have more than a seven percent weight gain and could not request a bigger costume size. Exceptions for the latter were made for women who had breast implants. They were reimbursed for the procedure and were given bigger bustiers.[47]

---

[42] Id. at 97–98.
[43] M. Brown, Gay Teen Sues School over Yearbook Photo, TAMPA TRIB., June 20, 2002, at M1 (quoting Karen Doering), in RHODE, supra note 17, at 98–99.
[44] H. Brown, For Obese People, Prejudice in Plain Sight, N.Y. TIMES, Mar. 16, 2010, at D6.
[45] Chapter 2, Section IV(e): Stigma, Shame, and Fat.
[46] T. Parker-Pope, Fat Stigma Is Fast Spreading around the Globe, N.Y. TIMES, Mar. 31, 2011, at A1, A3; A. Brewis et al., Body Norms and Fat Stigma in Global Perspective, 52 CURRENT ANTHROPOLOGY 269 (Apr. 2011).
[47] RHODE, supra note 17, at 98.

- During the confirmation process for her appointment to the Supreme Court a number of comments were made about Justice Sonia Sotomayer's size. She was characterized as "quite overweight" and it was said that she might not "last too long on the [C]ourt." No evidence was given to substantiate these concerns. Whatever the basis for linking weight and health, the Justice is nowhere near a level that might indicate increased risks of mortality.[48]
- A 240-pound aerobics instructor was denied a Jazzercise franchise. The company claimed that it only partnered with individuals with a "fit, toned body." The instructor was fit. She worked out six days a week and had no history of performance problems or lack of students. She was just large and wanted to be "judged on my merits, not my measurements."[49]
- An obese nursing student was expelled from her faculty. Her academic record was satisfactory. However, officials believed her weight prevented her from being a "role model [for] good health habits."[50]
- An obese woman was rejected for a job as an airport bus driver. The company doctor had concluded that her weight would prevent her from attending to the safety of passengers in the event of an accident or other emergency. The doctor acknowledged that the woman had no health problems and that he had not conducted any agility tests etc. His judgment was based solely on his seeing her "waddling down the hall."[51]

Hamermesh also introduces an important complication. His study focused on beauty, as judged by people's faces, the economic benefits bestowed by it, and the consequences for those judged to be below-average in terms of their facial characteristics. We'll return to his analysis of such financial impacts momentarily. The complication we want to focus on here is his finding that faces override bodies, so to speak.[52] If a person's face is judged beautiful that sense of attractiveness is not cancelled out if the individual is also overweight: "Beauty is, within bounds, more or less independent of physique."[53] If Hamermesh is right, fat people may be protected, somewhat, from discrimination if they

---

[48] *Id.* at 94.
[49] E. Fernandez, *Teacher Says Fat, Fitness Can Mix*, S.F. CHRON., Feb. 24, 2002 (quoting Portnick), *cited in* RHODE, *supra* note 17, at 18.
[50] J. Weinstien, *Nurse Ousted for Obesity Sues School*, ST. PETERSBURG Fla. TIMES, Apr. 8, 1989, at 3B (quoting Steven Snow), *cited in* RHODE, *supra* note 17 at 105.
[51] EEOC v Texas Bus Lines (1996), 923 F. Supp. 965, 967–68 (S.D. Tex. 1996), *cited in* RHODE, *supra* note 17, at 95.
[52] HAMERMESH, *supra* note 25, at 53–54.
[53] *Id.* at 54.

possess a beautiful face. His conclusion also suggests that those who are both fat and homely can face a lot of rejection.

Most human rights laws protect against prejudice based on characteristics over which individuals have no control, such as sex, race, disability, and age, or about which individuals should have a basic right to choose, such as religion. In some instances, claims against appearance bias can be joined with those based on these other characteristics to ground complaints. Thus, dress and grooming codes that sexualize women, the "Borgata Babes" and other examples described just above, can be objected to as appearance bias and as discrimination based on sex. In jurisdictions where sexual orientation is protected, the lesbian student who objected to the dress code for graduation pictures could claim to suffer from both appearance bias and discrimination based on sexual orientation.

In many of the instances described earlier, the situation was responded to either through a complaint process, because of media and public reaction, or through the victims' own persistence. Justice Sotomayer was confirmed despite much opposition. After a raft of media attention the casino with the "Borgata Babes" ultimately settled a lawsuit involving the negative impacts of its dress and grooming code (though the code remained otherwise in force).[54] The Florida school with the dress code for graduation pictures objected to by the lesbian student did alter its procedures to provide for students to show "good cause" why they should be exempted from the requirements (though these changes came too late for the student in question).[55] The obese nursing student was accepted at another nursing school, received supportive media coverage, graduated, and became a successful administrator in a children's hospital.[56]

Nevertheless, the number of situations in which there was no redress and the steep hurdles that were encountered in order to have a solution worked out suggest that much more could be done to resist appearance bias. As an instance of a claim that failed in the face of blatant discrimination, consider the case of the telemarketer who sought a direct "face to face" sales promotion in her company.[57] She had done very well, including being named "Telemarketer of the Year." But she weighed 270 pounds. The company promoted another woman with fewer credentials who was "thinner and cuter."[58]

The rejected applicant was told: "Lose the weight and you'll get promoted."[59] She sued charging sex discrimination. She lost because there were no fat men in the position she sought. Thus, it was concluded that the company did not engage in sex discrimination. They treated fat men and women alike: they

---

[54] RHODE, *supra* note 17, at 98.
[55] *Id.* at 116.
[56] *Id.* at 105.
[57] Marks v. Nat'l Commc's Ass. Inc. (1999), 72 F. Supp. 2d 322, 327 (S.D.N.Y. 1999), *cited in* KIRKLAND, *supra* note 5, at 9–10, 39–40, 163 n.15.
[58] *Marks*, 72 F. Supp. 2d at 327.
[59] *Id.* at 326.

promoted neither. As weight was not a protected ground, the court reasoned that there was no basis for a successful claim.[60] Or, as Kirkland puts it, as she underscores the unfairness of the telemarketer's treatment: "[F]atness is just like any other undesirable trait that employers are free to keep out of their workplaces, like...dirty uniforms or foul language."[61]

What are the financial costs of such discriminatory acts? That's a difficult question to answer, and will obviously vary depending on a variety of circumstances in different contexts such as employment, schooling, consumer transactions, and so forth. Hamermesh has examined such issues in terms of the workplace. He emphasizes the lack of current, reliable empirical information.[62] He also underscores that when it comes to earning power: "Looks do matter a lot, but other things matter much more."[63]

That said, how much more, overall, do good-looking people make than those who are below-average in appearance? For the United States, the answer is $230,000.[64] Taking 2010 figures and the average working rate of $20 per hour times 2,000 per year times 40 years he suggests the good-looking will earn about $1.69 million, whereas a below-average worker will earn just $1.46 million. Elsewhere he suggests an overall premium of about 5 percent for good-looking workers.[65] Given Hamermesh's own cautions, one should not rely on these figures for precise accuracy. They do suggest that, globally, the title of his book is appropriate: *Beauty Pays*.

That better-looking people earn more may cause some of us who don't look like Brad Pitt or Reese Witherspoon to grumble. At the same time, this premium enhances the case for legal protection from appearance bias. We will pursue this point below when we discuss the form such protections might take.[66] Harm comes from judging people on their looks rather than on their merits. Claims that looks are part of merits for any particular job have to be closely scrutinized. But how? Is there a role for law?

V. Resisting the Prejudice of Looks: Justifications for Invoking Law

Many of us might conclude that appearance bias is wrong. It is silly. It is cruel. It springs from fantasy fed by a warped and obsessed consumer culture. But at the same time we might hesitate about the law taking on this form of bias.

---

[60] KIRKLAND, *supra* note 5, 9, 39–40.
[61] *Id.* at 40.
[62] HAMERMESH, *supra* note 25, at 42–51.
[63] *Id.* at 47.
[64] *Id.*
[65] *Id.* at 64.
[66] *Infra*, Section VI: Banning Appearance Bias?.

Isn't beauty an asset that should be recognized? Why shouldn't people be well groomed? Shouldn't these issues be left to market forces to resolve one way or the other?[67] What would be the standard for holding that appearance bias should attract legal sanctions? How would such standards be enforced? Isn't appearance bias so often entangled with sexism, racism, religious prejudice, unequal treatment because of disability, or some other prohibited basis of discrimination that it can and should be addressed by founding objections on these other grounds?

The appearance of individuals has, in many periods, not been a law-free zone. For centuries there have been laws of the state, of business, and of religion that have regulated many dimensions of how persons are to dress and be groomed. In medieval Europe there were often sumptuary laws that limited certain clothes as the preserve of the aristocracy.[68] There are stipulated uniforms for the police, firefighters, and the armed services. Up to the recent past health care professionals, nurses and doctors, were to project that "all in white" look. Many employers have dress and grooming codes for wait, custodial, and other staff.

The extent to which the law should intervene to directly prohibit appearance bias discrimination may be debatable. But such a discussion should be aware of the extent to which state law and commercial power are already used to regulate appearance. The question may be not so much whether there should be laws to prohibit bias but, rather, laws to ensure lack of discrimination in the context of much regulation, public and private, that already exists.

Rhode believes that appearance bias should be directly prohibited. She suggests three goals that respond to discrimination because of looks.[69] First, the promotion of a more attainable, healthy, and inclusive sense of attractiveness. That sense should include greater variation in age, weight, race, ethnicity, etc. and workplace grooming requirements should tolerate that variety. Second, lessening discrimination based on appearance, including the sexualized double standards that especially burden women. Third, encouraging lifestyles that emphasize health, not just appearance.

In the larger context of these goals she cites three justifications for invoking the law to ban appearance discrimination.[70] First, this discrimination offends a right to equal opportunity: individuals should be assessed on their merits, not irrelevant physical characteristics. Second, such bias reinforces group subordination: it worsens disadvantages already present because of race, gender, ethnicity, and so forth. Third, constraints arising because of appearance can unduly restrict self-expression and cultural and other forms of identity.

---

[67] S. Clifford, *A Plus-Size Revelation: Bigger Women Have Cash, Too*, N.Y. TIMES, June 19, 2010, at A1, A3.
[68] A. HUNT, GOVERNANCE OF THE CONSUMING PASSIONS: A HISTORY OF SUMPTUARY LAW (1996).
[69] RHODE, *supra* note 17, at 147.
[70] *Id.* at 93.

Some resile from the idea of using law in this way. Hakim, in her analysis of erotic capital discussed earlier, is outraged by the suggestion.[71] "Fatties" and feminists have become entangled, as wrong-headed allies, in this misadventure.[72] There is no need for legal intervention. The obese, if they so choose, can simply decide to free themselves from their "unnecessary and indefensible" condition.[73] She declares: "The feminist espousal of such a dysfunctional campaign suggests that the movement has lost sight of its goals and has become a permanently negative ideology, irrespective of logic, the facts or reason...Talking about 'discrimination' seems odd for a condition that offers only disadvantages and can be changed at will."[74]

Aside from Hakim's broadside, a main objection focuses on burdens imposed on those subject to such prohibitions. Concerns range from constraints that will be imposed on employers, to the increased caseload imposed on agencies and courts because of the numbers and difficulties of the claims, to the blunting impact this questionable form of discrimination will have on more established grounds such as sex and race where much bias has still not yet been eradicated. One commentator states the objections in dramatic language: "[A] business community united in frustration at a bloated civil rights regime could become a powerful political force for reform or even repeal." [75]

Regarding constraints on employers, Rhode suggests this is exactly the point of the prohibition: to prevent those who hire from using appearance as a criterion for employment when there is no justifiable basis for doing so. Thus, dress and grooming standards meant to ensure cleanliness and neatness would be permissible, but banning ear rings for men and mandating stiletto heels for women would not be allowed.

What is more, those who hire usually would not be able to cite customer preference as the basis for justifying a certain kind of appearance. Consider the unsuccessful lawsuit of a news anchor who claimed that she was fired because she was "too old, too unattractive, and not deferential to men." The court took account of viewers' ratings. Rhode takes issue with this approach. She fears that the stereotype of female broadcasters as young and attractive will be perpetuated.

Instead, once audiences are exposed to older women not hired or promoted for their appearance, but on merit, they will accept them just as they have the Walter Cronkites and the Larry Kings.[76] There is some evidence of such acceptance. For example, in 2012 a Wisconsin news anchor responded publicly,

---

[71] HAKIM, *supra* note 34, and accompanying text.
[72] *Id.* at 130–32.
[73] *Id.* at 131.
[74] *Id.*
[75] R. FORD, THE RACE CARD: HOW BLUFFING ABOUT BIAS MAKES RACE RELATIONS WORSE 176 (2007).
[76] RHODE, *supra* note 17, at 107–08.

and with much support, to a viewer who made disparaging remarks about her weight.[77] Moreover, as Rhode emphasizes, employers would still have wide latitude to make hiring (and firing) decisions in the newscaster's and other jobs. But they would be steered away from doing so based on how someone looks when that appearance is irrelevant to the job.

In terms of the apprehension about increased workload for courts and agencies hearing such matters, Rhode cites the small number of complaints filed in the few jurisdictions that directly address appearance bias.[78] A 1992 ordinance in Santa Cruz bans discrimination based on a variety of factors, including height, weight, and other physical characteristics. For fifteen years after the ordinance was passed, there had been no complaints filed based on those factors. Thirty years after a similar ordinance was passed in Urbana, Illinois, there had also been no complaints filed. Michigan has a state-wide law banning weight and height discrimination. There are on average thirty complaints a year based on this provision, but many of these complaints are also based on other grounds of discrimination (sex, race, and so forth).[79]

Rhode suggests that if there is a problem, it may be with under- not over-enforcement. An optimistic explanation for the relatively few claims may be that the existence of the law itself prompts employers and others to discriminate less. Other possibilities may be the scope of the prohibitions, the difficulties regarding proving discriminatory behavior, the deference given to employers and others' decisions, and the lack of substantial damages awarded when claims are successful.[80] Still, Rhode insists these protections serve a purpose: "Even laws that are notoriously underenforced can serve a crucial role in designating public norms, deterring violations, and affirming social ideals."[81]

The charge that recognizing appearance bias will blunt efforts to fight established grounds of discrimination such as sex, race, and religion is made in a variety of ways. However, the essence of this allegation is captured in the following reaction: "The growing number of social groups making claims to civil rights protection threatens the political and practical viability of civil rights for those who need them most."[82]

We earlier discussed Hamermesh's economic analysis of the effects of the beauty advantage.[83] He is, generally, sympathetic to legal protection

---

[77] A. Stanley, *Female Stars Step Off the Scale*, N.Y. TIMES, ARTS & LEISURE, Oct. 11, 2012, at 1, 20.

[78] She also reviews efforts to address appearance bias in Europe and Australia: RHODE, *supra* note 17, ch. 6: "Legal Frameworks."

[79] *Id.* at 126–36.

[80] *Id.* at 139–40.

[81] *Id.* at 114.

[82] FORD, *supra* note 75, at 176; RHODE, *supra* note 17, at 110.

[83] HAMERMESH, *supra* note 25, and accompanying text.

against appearance bias and thinks that it will ultimately be realized.[84] He observes: "The causes of mistreatment of the bad-looking, and their results—inferior outcomes in a large variety of areas—seem little different either qualitatively or quantitatively from the mistreatment of other groups...be they racial, religious, or ethnic, and even a gender majority."[85] Yet, he too, worries about the impact on these other groups if legal protections are extended to combat bias based on looks. He cautions: "If we believe that there is either economic or political substitution of protection for one group against protection for another, concerns about these groups should make us think even harder about extending protection to the ugly."[86]

However, as Rhode points out, there is no evidence from the jurisdictions that have legal protections of appearance bias that efforts to combat other forms of discrimination had been compromised by the existence of these provisions. As she observes: "Jurisdictions with such ordinances...are not known for problems either of 'totalitarianism' or backlash against antidiscrimination policies."[87] As indicated earlier, to the extent to which there is a problem, it may be one of under-enforcement of appearance bias protections.

If legal protections against appearance bias were adopted in various jurisdictions, what might they look like? In particular, how could they protect fat people from discrimination? These questions are the focus of the next section.

VI. Banning Appearance Bias?

A) PROHIBITING PREJUDICE AGAINST LOOKS

Efforts, at least in the United States, to expand the present law to address appearance bias have largely proven unsuccessful.[88] Thus the best way to provide legal protection against appearance bias is to ban it directly. In the instances where discriminatory actions may also implicate other established grounds, such as gender or race, they can also be a foundation for a complaint. However, as we saw earlier, there can be instances of appearance bias that do not involve these other grounds and where a provision specifically banning such discrimination is necessary to address the objectionable actions.

Rhode proposes the following provisions in legislation to directly deal with appearance bias:

- Cover employment, housing, public accommodation, and related contexts.

---

[84] *Id.* at 169.
[85] *Id.* at 166.
[86] *Id.* at 167.
[87] RHODE, *supra* note 17, at 113.
[88] *Id.* at 118–25.

- "Appearance" should include
  - physical characteristics, and
  - grooming and dress that are not inconsistent with reasonable business needs.
- As with issues of disability, religion etc., there should be reasonable accommodation for appearance that does not cause undue hardship.
- A fair and inexpensive dispute resolution process should be available and there should be a right of appeal to the courts.
- Attorneys' fees and compensatory damages should be awarded to complainants who establish that appearance bias was the determining factor in the decision at issue.[89]

These proposals are meant to be of general application and are written in the American context. They would have to be adapted to the accepted practices of various jurisdictions. For example, if there are no overarching provisions for attorney's fees and costs for successful complainants in the applicable human rights statues, there would seem to be no compelling case to carve out an exception for appearance bias complaints.

As discussed earlier, it appears that good-looking people, as a group, are awarded something like a 5 percent premium on their lifetime earnings because of their looks.[90] That positive advantage becomes another reason to shield others from bias based on appearance. That significant advantage is not likely to be easily eroded by granting protections based on looks to individuals relating to specific instances of discrimination. Concerns that good-looking people would somehow be crowded out in the job market or insufficiently remunerated seem ill-founded. In any event they could be addressed.

For example, relevant Australian legislation, in the state of Victoria, contains protections from appearance bias. However, there are a number of exceptions, including discrimination that is necessary for dramatic, artistic, entertainment, photographic, or modeling work.[91] A further general exception could be created when appearance is demonstrated to be a legitimate requirement for the job. The point here is that those who want to take appearance into account would bear the onus of demonstrating that such considerations were legitimate in the particular circumstances.

The proposal by Rhode suggests a basis for explicitly protecting from appearance bias. Such a provision would address all the instances discussed earlier whether or not other grounds of discrimination were involved.[92]

---

[89] *Id.* at 154.
[90] HAMERMESH, *supra* note 25, and accompanying text.
[91] RHODE, *supra* note 17, at 135.
[92] *See* examples discussed above: Section IV: "Good Clean Wholesome Female Sexuality" and Other Examples of Appearance Bias.

Altering actions in respect of appearance will not be easy. Our attitudes toward looks may not be hardwired but they do run deep. Yet Rhode remains insistent: "[T]he costs of appearance discrimination are...considerable, and we have by no means reached the limit of what can be done to address them."[93] What impact law may have in this area is a matter we'll return to in the next section. First let's address in more detail the form of appearance bias that most concerns us: weight discrimination.

B) COMPLEXITIES OF BANNING WEIGHT DISCRIMINATION

As indicated earlier, efforts, at least in the United States, to address appearance bias using existing law have largely proven unsuccessful.[94] Such attempts have included trying to have obesity characterized as a disability under the federal *Americans with Disabilities Act* and related federal and state laws.[95] Except for a few instances involving the morbidly obese the cases have not been successful because the obese person has been found not to be impaired and, therefore, cannot invoke laws addressing disability.

At the same time many advocating for fat rights do not want to have to invoke such provisions. They object to the notion that fat people are disabled just because they are overweight. The equating of obesity with illness and impairment is something that they oppose in life and law. There was nothing wrong with the obese woman who applied to be an airport bus driver. What was wrong was the examining doctor's reactions toward her "waddling down the hall."[96]

The proposal of Rhode's in the last section to address appearance bias would include issues of weight. Thus, those complaining of prejudicial actions because of being fat could complain directly without getting involved in debates about whether, and under what circumstances, fatness is or should be considered a disability. Discrimination based solely on weight without further complications would be sufficient to trigger the protections of the relevant statute. Such a provision would appear to address the circumstances of the "waddling" bus driver applicant, as well as the large aerobics instructor, the "Borgata Babes," and the telemarketer discussed earlier.[97]

However, issues of weight discrimination would remain complicated. There is a general duty to accommodate in many human rights laws. If, for example,

---

[93] RHODE, *supra* note 17, at 146.
[94] *Supra* note 88 and accompanying text.
[95] *Americans with Disabilities Act* (1990), title 42, ch 126; *Americans with Disabilities Act Amendments Act* (1990), PL 110-325 (S 3406), § 37.2202(1)(a) of *Michigan's Elliott-Larsen Civil Rights Act* 453 (1976), s. 37.22202(1)(a); Mississippi House Bill (2009) 1530; New York (2009), NY AD 154; Virginia (2009), VA SB 1351 and HB 2557.
[96] *Supra* note 51 and accompanying text.
[97] *Supra* note 47 and accompanying text.

situations in the workplace make it difficult for a person to practice his religious beliefs or for a disabled person to do her job (for which she is otherwise qualified), there is a duty to accommodate. Such a duty is stringent and can only be relieved against when compliance would cause "undue hardship."

A duty to accommodate should also apply in situations involving the obese.[98] If a fat person is otherwise qualified and, in the case of a competition, is judged to be the best person for the job, then any necessary accommodations should have to be made because of the person's size to allow her or him to do that job. What might such accommodation entail?

Certain kinds of such accommodation, in and beyond the workplace, might be relatively straightforward. Or as Kirkland puts it: "Public accommodations may be as simple as creating a few larger-sized seats in airplanes, buses, and theaters, for instance. These accommodations are so obvious that they may not require much interaction and scrutiny."[99] The obese person requiring two plane seats and the media brouhaha that seems to invariably ensue could fade away, to be replaced with a few seats that could be opened up in some way when necessary to accommodate fatness.[100] Failure to make such accommodation may make air travel for fat people not only embarrassing and uncomfortable, but such trips may also be unsafe because of existing seating arrangements being inappropriate for the obese.[101] In the recommendation discussed in the earlier section, all appearance would be protected from discrimination.[102] That being the case, similar appropriate accommodations should be made for other "appearances" such as very short or very tall individuals.[103]

But situations can be more complex than the ones just referred to. Consider the fat woman in Michigan who applied to be a substitute school bus driver.[104] During the first day of the training program, it became clear that the only way she could position herself behind the wheel was to have it pressing into her abdomen. The next day she was dismissed from the program. The woman sued and lost despite the fact that Michigan legislation protects against discrimination based on weight (the only state, to date, to extend such protection).[105]

The court in that case found that the supervisor had no "discriminatory animus." Rather it "found [the woman's] weight to be a problem because it prevented [her] from driving the bus safely."[106] The employer refused to adjust the

---

[98] RHODE, *supra* note 17, at 154.
[99] KIRKLAND, *supra* note 5, at 145.
[100] McKay-Panos v Air Canada, [2006] 4 FCR 3, 2006 FCJ No 28 (F.C.A.)(QL).
[101] C. Negroni, *Americans' Growing Bulk Prompts Doubts about Safety of Airline Seats*, N.Y. TIMES, May 9, 2012, at 17.
[102] *Supra* Section VI(a): Prohibiting Prejudice against Looks.
[103] Of the jurisdictions in which there is legal protection from such discrimination, a few (such as Michigan) explicitly refer to height: *see* RHODE, *supra* note 17, at 132–34.
[104] Webb v. Bowman, 2001 Mich. App. LEXIS 742, Jan. 16, 2001 (unpublished opinion).
[105] *Supra* Section VI(a): Prohibiting Prejudice against Looks.
[106] *Webb*, 2001 Mich. App. LEXIS at 14.

bus seat or make other modifications, arguing that such changes could violate safety standards.

But should the applicant have been accommodated by making the modifications just described, or similar ones? As the employer is relieved from doing so only if it can establish undue hardship, a mere suggestion that alterations would violate safety standards does not seem sufficient.[107] The result, after all, is that an otherwise qualified person is not hired because of body size.

Kirkland explains why there might be such accommodations. In her view the perspective in such cases is: "conceding that fat people have bodies that depart from the norm, but insisting that the norm itself is unjust and serves to naturalize the privileges that thinner bodies in our culture enjoy."[108] In respect of the applicant bus driver, Kirkland asserts: "The idea that justice requires modifying the bus... would use a strategy capable of securing redistributions of resources backed by a political commitment to transform the lives and opportunities of fat people."[109]

Is society, in fact, ready to respond to the needs of the obese in such ways? Kirkland suggests that it should be. In asserting her position she leads us back to a central idea in this book: the role of norms.[110] In her view, to grapple with the lives of the obese and the injustices they suffer, we need to change norms. One that has to be altered is taking the constructed world as a given—something that fat people must navigate as best they can.[111] Another is accepting fat people in positions, in employment and otherwise, as representing part of diverse images of that job and not as obese people who somehow qualify for a thin person's position. As Kirkland asks of the Jazzercise instructor, discussed earlier, did "San Francisco succeed[..] in transforming social norms or just tweaking... to include a fatter instructor as long as she could do the job as well and in the same way as a thinner one[?]"[112]

Kirkland's comments regarding the centrality of shifting norms in respect of fat people and the complexities that she raises lead us back to a central question of the book regarding the effects of law: what will be the impact of efforts to legally protect fat people?

---

[107] The district had decided not to adjust the seat on the bus any further because it would require structural modification, possibly in violation of other safety standards (something the district had been unwilling to do for other applicants as well).

[108] KIRKLAND, *supra* note 5, at 45.

[109] *Id.*

[110] Chapter 1, Section V(b): Ideas for New Governance: Normativity and Its Offspring.

[111] KIRKLAND, *supra* note 5, at 45; *see also* at 40 and 43.

[112] *Id.* at 40.

VII. The Impact of Laws Banning Appearance Bias

A) LAWS AGAINST BIAS, LAWS PROMOTING HEALTHY EATING/DRINKING AND PHYSICAL ACTIVITY

For Kirkland thinking about obesity becomes an opportunity for reflecting on human rights: "Perhaps the unique status of fat as an identity—changeable but only with great difficulty, linked to behaviors sometimes but sometimes not, heritable in most cases but not all, the subject of moral panic as well as scientific study, sexualized and racialized in contingent ways—could help us to revisit other categories of antidiscrimination law that we presume we already understand."[113]

She eloquently maps out the issues that will need to be addressed to protect fat people from discrimination. As she herself acknowledges, how much protection there will be and its effectiveness remain to be determined.[114] She suggests that her "book is more like a field guide to the underlying presumptions of antidiscrimination laws than a plan for adding 'weight' to the list of protected traits."[115] A limit of her book, for our purposes, is that it is so focused on rights and their many complications.

Kirkland is right to insist that there is hyberbole, even "moral panic" around weight in many societies, particularly the United States.[116] What is more, she effectively condemns the censorious attitudes to those struggling with weight issues: "[M]ost people think that getting fat is primarily caused by bad behaviors like eating too much and failing to exercise. It is considered a garden-variety character flaw, like getting into too much credit card debt."[117]

However, it is no answer to these negative attitudes toward fat people to push aside calm efforts to help people eat better and be more physically active while, at the same time, confronting the excesses of corporate America. Interventions to promote healthy eating/drinking and to protect the rights of fat people should be complementary, not opposed, strategies. We can promote healthier ways and, at the same time, protect fat people from the sting of prejudice.

Kirkland says many insightful things in *Fat Rights*. At one point she observes: "The crux of the debate is whether fat per se deserves so much attention, or whether the real concern should be with the poor eating habits and sedentary lifestyles."[118] This is a wise observation, one that should inspire both fat rights and interventions that promote nutritious eating/drinking and regular physical exercise.

---

[113] *Id.* at 158.
[114] *Id.* at 147–59.
[115] *Id.* at x.
[116] Chapter 2, Section IV(e)(2): "The Greatest Threat": Stigma, Discrimination, and the Obese.
[117] KIRKLAND, *supra* note 5, at 110.
[118] *Id.* at 111.

Deborah Rhode sees these two strategies as capable of being pursued together. As we have seen she is adamant that appearance bias be prohibited. At the same time she is insistent that the banning of such discrimination must be accompanied by multiple initiatives to change norms that privilege a pinched sense of beauty, and to promote healthier lifestyles. She makes proposals regarding activism on the part of individuals and groups,[119] self-regulating behavior on the part of business and the media,[120] and law and policy, in addition to the banning of appearance bias.[121]

She understands that prohibiting discrimination on the basis of appearance, including weight, is critical, but it is only one of several measures that must be taken to address issues of appearance and health, including weight. The overarching goal is the one highlighted by Kirkland: altering norms toward appearance, including being fat. The following are some of Rhode's suggestions.

In terms of individuals and groups, she delivers a message central to this book. Individuals need to make healthy choices, be tolerant of many looks, and to demonstrate "their support for changes in social attitudes and policies towards appearance."[122] She points to citizen involvement in such things as the Body Project. This initiative supports females in designing their own plan of activism concerning issues of appearance. It has been suggested that participants can have a 60 percent lower incidence of eating disorders than others of the same age.[123]

In terms of business and the media, she urges the adoption of codes, similar to initiatives in parts of Europe, regulating the use of models so as to curb the promotion of unrealistically thin body images and harm to young women who engage in extravagant dieting in an effort to keep themselves dangerously thin.[124] She wants the media to take a more sophisticated and nuanced approach to reporting on weight issues. That perspective "would stress the complex causes of obesity and the rationale for focusing on health[ier] eating and fitness behaviors rather than simply weight reduction."[125] Regarding food conglomerates, Rhode believes that there is room for change based on the industry's own self-interest. Quite apart from any regulatory initiatives directed at that industry, she maintains it should exploit the potential of nutritious foods, which could be developed and marketed much more vigorously.[126]

---

[119] RHODE, *supra* note 17, at 146–50.
[120] *Id.* at 151–54.
[121] *Id.* at 154–61.
[122] *Id.* at 148.
[123] *Id.* at 150, citing S. Gupta, *Taking on the Thin Ideal*, TIME, June 5, 2008, at 50.
[124] *Id.* at 151.
[125] *Id.* at 152.
[126] *Id.* at 153.

Regarding law and policy, she makes recommendations in addition to her central one of passing laws to ban appearance bias.[127] One recommendation is to strengthen and enforce laws to target misleading advertising, particularly relating to weight-loss practices. Generally, such law enforcement activities need to be aimed at "the serious risks, low probabilities of success, and dubious health-related claims of many appearance related purchases."[128]

Another set of interventions would relate to the central issues raised in this book. They would focus on issues of weight and any associated costs. Prevention of children's excess weight gain, when that is possible, would be a particular objective. Rhode underscores the need to promote norms encouraging a healthy environment. Ratifying attitudes that punish fat people must be avoided. In sum: "A central challenge lies in crafting an environment that encourages sensible eating and fitness behaviors without demonizing those who fall short."[129]

B) ROUND UP THE FAT KIDS!

During the summer of 2011 and beyond there appeared several stories concerning obese children being removed from their homes.[130] Details differed, but one question ran throughout the reports and commentary: under what circumstances should fat kids be taken from their parents?

Particulars of these events are disturbing. One occurrence involved officials in Ohio physically removing an eight-year-old obese boy from his home. The young person was on the honor roll at school and at no risk for imminent danger. The child was placed in a foster home where his mother was permitted to see him only once a week for two hours.[131] Another involved state troopers in South Carolina removing an obese child from his home and his mother being charged with child neglect.[132] It has also been reported that placing "severely obese children into state care has been the norm for more than a decade in the United Kingdom."[133] That said, it was also claimed that in some such interventions children did receive good care outside the home even as parents were supported by social workers, dieticians, and other professionals so that the child could be returned to a positive home environment.[134]

---

[127] *Id.* at 154–61.

[128] *Id.* at 154.

[129] *Id.* at 155.

[130] B. Rochman, *Should Parents Lose Custody of Their Extremely Obese Kids?*, TIME, July 13, 2011, available at http://healthland.time.com/2011/07/13/should-parents-lose-custody-of-their-very-obese-kids/ [hereinafter Rochman].

[131] M. Sangiacomo, *Obese Boy to Return Home Saturday after Dropping 50 Pounds*, PLAIN DEALER, Feb. 28, 2012, *available at* http://blog.cleveland.com/metro/2012/02/obese_boy_returns_home_after_d.html.

[132] A. Picard, *Sometimes We Just Need to Step In*, GLOBE & MAIL, July 21, 2011, at L6.

[133] *Id.*

[134] *Id.*

A lightning rod regarding the controversial nature of such actions was an article appearing in the *Journal of the American Medical Association* that gave (guarded) support to them.[135] Any number of other experts responded expressing indignation for any support for such actions.[136] They pointed to such elements as obesogenic environments, on the one hand, and the need for special treatment programs for obese children, on the other, as key to understanding and addressing childhood obesity. One response opined: "It's inappropriate to suggest these agencies have a role to play in the treatment of severe obesity when we, as a health-care system, are failing. This very notion suggests such treatment is as simple as placing children in a substitute home environment and lays blame solely at the feet of the family."[137]

What's required in these situations is to separate out abuse from obesity. Most jurisdictions provide that children can be taken from their parents in situations of ill-treatment where there is clear danger to the child.[138] The standard for removal is exacting, but it can be met in dire situations. It's the equating of obesity with abuse that is wrong. If a child is being mistreated to an extent that meets the otherwise existing test, the fact that the child is obese is incidental to that determination. Obese children who are being severely abused should be removed. Obesity, itself, is not evidence of abuse.

Laws protecting against appearance bias would scarcely be a complete response to these situations. But such laws could be a clear reminder to officials that they can't draw conclusions about children and their home environments based on how a child looks. These laws could also promote other efforts that expend more resources on helping fat kids and their parents and fewer on attempts to police them. We'll look at some of these initiatives in the following chapters.

VIII. Conclusion

For decades a critical thrust of human rights laws in numerous societies has been to have people judged on their merits and not on irrelevant characteristics. People should be hired, admitted to programs, be subject to the criminal law, etc. based on their abilities, what they have actually done, etc. and not barred or, in the case of legal proceedings, more severely sanctioned because they are female, Black, Muslim, gay, and so forth. Such laws are meant to buttress

---

[135] D. Ludwig, *State Intervention in Life-Threatening Childhood Obesity*, 306(2) J. Am. Med. Ass'n 206-07 (2011).

[136] Rochman, *supra* note 130.

[137] S. Hadjiyannakis & A. Bucholz, *Is Obesity Cause for State Intervention?*, Globe & Mail, Aug. 15, 2011, *available at* http://www.theglobeandmail.com/news/opinions/opinion/is-obesity-cause-for-state-intervention/article2128249/.

[138] Child and Family Services Act, RSO 1990, c C11, ss 37(2), 40.

norms of tolerance that promote attitudes and actions that treat everyone as individuals to be judged based on their conduct and not on the color of their skin, or the religion they profess, etc.

Amendments to such laws to prohibit discrimination against the obese would confer these protections on fat people. With what impact? Uncertain—based on Rhode's analysis, though the situation could clarify as more jurisdictions adopted such laws. The main effect should be the same as other provisions protecting individuals from discrimination: buttress norms that promote tolerance and judgment of people based on their merits and their actions, not their sexual orientation or their country of origin, etc. Based on Rhode's findings there need be no fear of a flood of claims or protracted, frivolous litigation.[139]

Let's return to the Texas hospital story that opened this chapter. The hospital refused to hire anyone with a BMI over 35. Someone with that Body Mass Index would be a very large person. But what follows from this fact? Not a conclusion, as suggested by the hospital's policy, that a fat individual is not a well person who has no place working in a hospital. A law protecting against appearance bias would suggest that nothing inexorably follows from the fact that a person is obese, other than he or she is a large size. Difficult situations can arise, but health and weight are not to be confused.[140]

If fat people are otherwise qualified, they should be hired. It might be that some accommodations could be necessary for them to do their job because of their size. As discussed, accommodations are sometimes required for other workers such as those who have disabilities. Such flexibility is a complication that is more problematic, but such issues should be resolved in favor of fat people if reasonably possible. But in most instances no accommodation will be required: all that will be necessary is that employers take no notice of the size of the person and assess that person based on his or her ability to do the job.

Human rights laws are necessary to protect fat people from prejudice. Making the case for such provisions at a time of hostility to rights for the disadvantaged will be no easy task. But advocates such as Hamermesh, Kirkland, and Rhode point the way. At the same time such protections are just part of a legal role. The law can be used to stand up to aggressive marketing of the food-and-beverage industry, to promote nutritious eating/drinking, and to encourage physical activity. All the while, better health, not less weight, should be the central aim of any intervention. Concern for children should have priority in respect of this goal. These are ambitious objectives. To what extent can law be employed to achieve these ends, and with what success? These critical questions are the subject of Part III.

---

[139] *Supra*, Section V: Resisting the Prejudice of Looks: Justifications for Invoking Law.
[140] C. Abraham, *Fat and Fertility: Should Obese Women Have Access to Costly Reproductive Therapies?*, GLOBE & MAIL, Sept. 21, 2011, at A1, A10.

{ PART III }

Healthy Consumption, Active Living, and the Regulatory State

{ 4 }

Assessing Interventions

I. Introduction

Chapters 5 to 7 look at a number of legal interventions that respond to various issues discussed in the previous chapters. There are five overarching points that apply to all these interventions. They are useful to discuss here before we turn to an analysis of the specifics of these strategies in the chapters that follow.

The first concerns the goals of these interventions. In responding to this issue we revisit the fat/obesity debates, discussed in Chapter 2, and the discussion of the stigmatization of fat people and the need to protect them from prejudice, addressed in Chapter 3. These debates and discussions lead us to focus on children and how these interventions might address their particular needs. Kids are the future: supporting them should be the first priority.

The second point, related to the first, concerns gauging the effectiveness of the interventions that we will look at. The main criterion for assessment should be the extent to which these interventions, individually and taken together, promote healthy eating/drinking and physical activity. Encouraging weight loss and even the prevention of weight gain are secondary; moreover, such goals carry the danger of—unintentionally—contributing to the stigmatization of fat people. Can we shift norms away from prejudice toward fat people to an embrace of healthier eating/drinking and physical activity and acceptance of bodies of all shapes and sizes?

The third is the evidentiary basis for interventions. How do policy makers decide that they are justified in intervening? How do they know which strategies to employ? These questions lead us back to issues that we discussed in Chapter 1, regarding impact, and, again, to the fat/obesity debates in Chapter 2. We'll discuss the "precautionary principle" and its tilt toward intervention, especially applicable when children are concerned. Yet the reality is that trial and error looms large. A mix of interventions offers the best possibility even as educated guesswork plays a big part.

The fourth is the basis for selecting the interventions that are being evaluated. Numerous strategies are on the table; we can't cover them all. We've selected three general areas that illustrate the main issues that need to be tackled and that include a number of particular interventions within each. Interventions in these areas, together, may substantially respond to concerns relating to both healthier eating/drinking and exercise. The three are: marketing, fiscal policy, and promoting physical activity—especially for children.

The fifth is an explanation for not addressing four areas in the larger terrain of regulating obesity: prescription drugs for weight control, the weight loss/diet industry, bariatric surgery, and litigation aimed at the food industry. All these areas need scrutiny. Nevertheless, for reasons that will be given, they are put to the side in this book.

II. Goals of Interventions

A discussion of the goals of intervention takes us back to issues addressed in the three previous chapters. Are we trying to help individuals lose weight or, better still, not gain excessive weight in the first place? Are we trying to promote healthier eating/drinking and physical activity, with weight status deemphasized? Are we trying to protect fat people from stigmatization and acts of prejudice? To what extent are we willing to commit public resources to, and develop a sense of public responsibility for, achieving any of these objectives? Will interventions shift norms away from contempt for large individuals to embrace nutritious consumption and exercise by people of all sizes?

The traditional public health model has, for the last decades, been focused on weight as the problem and weight loss (or prevention of its gain) as the solution.[1] That approach has largely been a failure at least in terms of weight loss.[2] The statistics respecting fat people being able to lose weight and to keep it off are sobering. Something like 95 percent of those who can lose weight regain the pounds shed, if not more, within five years.[3]

Beyond this dramatic fact are ideas that challenge the simple contention that weight, up, down, or in a steady state, is a function of "calories in, calories out": if we take more calories in than we use, we gain; if we burn more calories than we consume, we lose. Explanations involving genes, metabolism,

---

[1] For example, F. SASSI, OBESITY AND THE ECONOMICS OF PREVENTION: FIT NOT FAT [in association with the OECD] ch.6: The Impact of Interventions (2010); J. Alston et al., *US Food Policy and Obesity, in* PUBLIC HEALTH—SOCIAL AND BEHAVIORAL HEALTH (J. Maddock ed., 2012), *available at* http://www.intechopen.com/books/public-health-social-and-behavioral-health/food-policy-and-obesity.

[2] Chapter 2, Section IV(d): Weight Loss? What Is Shed Is Almost Always Regained.

[3] L. Bacon & L. Aphramor, *Weight Science: Evaluating the Evidence for a Paradigm Shift*, 10 NUTRITION J. 69 (2011).

antibiotics, and obesogens suggest that some individuals are obese for reasons that go beyond "calories in/calories out." Among other complications such factors could be associated with fetal and infant development that may result in consequences that can last throughout a person's life.[4]

Yet healthier eating/drinking and physical activity can still be important in preventing excess weight gain in many individuals. Campaigns targeting prevention, bolstered by a mix of legal strategies focused on not gaining too many pounds, have, as yet, not been systematically attempted. Some informed opinion doubts that these campaigns can be effective.[5] Nevertheless, in terms of this objective, children become an important focus of attention: if weight can somehow be controlled from the first stages of life, issues of obesity will just never arise.[6] As a result, for this and other reasons explained in a moment, we will pay particularly close attention to the needs of the young when we examine various interventions in Chapters 5 to 7. In any event, good eating/drinking and an active lifestyle can bestow significant health benefits regardless of individuals' weight and for all ages.[7]

In Chapter 2 we discussed sharp reactions to any campaigns focused on weight loss and, for some, even prevention. However well-intended, such efforts are bound for failure and, as they stumble along, only add to the stigmatization of fat individuals. Some strands of this reaction question the idea of interventions at all, fearing they are bound to ostracize fat people no matter what the goals or intentions.[8]

Others, while opposing bias against fat people and the emphasis placed on weight loss, support efforts to help all people to be healthier regardless of their size. From this perspective interventions can be appropriate if their focus is the promotion of healthy eating/drinking and physical activity with issues of weight relegated to the sidelines.[9] Such interventions, to be effective, must also confront the need for public resources and public responsibility for the promotion of a healthier population.

A similar approach for children is appropriate. Interventions may assist in weight control, but that goal should be secondary. The primary focus should be on ensuring children eat and drink nutritiously and be physically active. If excessive weight gain is prevented, so much the better; a preoccupation with pounds is to be avoided. Again, a key point is the provision of adequate public resources when necessary to strengthen the effectiveness of such interventions.

---

[4] WHITE HOUSE TASK FORCE ON CHILDHOOD OBESITY REPORT TO THE PRESIDENT, SOLVING THE PROBLEM OF CHILDHOOD OBESITY WITHIN A GENERATION 17 (2010).
[5] *Dr. Sharma's Obesity Notes, Shifting to Second Gear in Obesity Prevention?* (Oct. 19, 2010), *available at* http://www.drsharma.ca/shifting-to-second-gear-in-obesity-prevention.html.
[6] R. Rabin, *Baby Fat May Not Be So Cute After All*, N.Y. TIMES, Mar. 23, 2010, at D5.
[7] *Canada's Alleged Obesity Epidemic*, GLOBE & MAIL, Jan. 15, 2010, at A16.
[8] Chapter 2, Section IV(e)(3)(ii): Weight Is Not the Problem—It's Society That Has Issues.
[9] Chapter 2, Section IV(e)(3)(iii): Health at Every Size (HAES).

There is another goal of regulation in this area: protection of fat people from prejudice, through human rights laws.[10] The case for such legal provisions in the present climate of skepticism for rights for the disadvantaged will be hard to make. At the same time these protections are only a part of a legal role in addressing issues affecting the obese.

The law can be used to stand up to aggressive marketing of the food and beverage industry, to promote nutritious eating/drinking, and to encourage physical activity. At the same time these other strategies need to be designed and implemented in ways that do not contribute to the further stigmatization of large individuals. We'll look at individual interventions where there is risk of contributing to such contempt: for example, a requirement to post caloric content of selections on menus and measuring and reporting on BMI of school children.[11]

Finally, we need to return to our discussion of "normativity" in Chapter 1. An important test for legal interventions is the extent to which individuals actually change behavior in ways consistent with the goals of the interventions. Regulation of smoking in Canada and the United States is seen to be (quite) successful because rates of smoking have been roughly halved, though about 20 percent of adults still light up.[12] But the real success of tobacco regulation is that it has been part of a shifting terrain of social control. Most people have changed their behavior and have done so willingly because of the drastic morphing of norms regarding smoking from a glamorous indulgence to a filthy, expensive, noxious habit.

An important test of regulation regarding obesity is the extent to which there are changes in behavior and shifts in norms. Will these shifts be away from obsession regarding weight and weight loss and contempt for large individuals—away from the acts of prejudice that accompany such attitudes? Will they be toward healthier eating/drinking, physical activity, and acceptance of individuals of all shapes and sizes? That shift in norms will strengthen regulatory efforts designed to regulate nutritious consumption and exercise; those interventions will buttress the changing norms. But the critical question remains: what are the chances of such changes occurring? Laudable goals—but ones that will be hard to achieve. To what extent can law be employed to attain these ends, and with what success? These critical questions are the subject of the next three chapters.

---

[10] Chapter 3: Appearance Bias–Fat Rights.
[11] Chapter 7, Section V(b)(4)(i)[three]: Measuring BMI.
[12] Chapter 1, Section IV. Consumption Encounters Law: *Permit but Discourage*.

III. Perspectives on Assessment

For most fat people losing weight is a losing battle for the long term. Prevention, especially for young people, is a possibility but one largely untested in a systematic and rigorous way. Thus, when we look at various interventions (described below), we will be skeptical that the goal can be weight loss (or even prevention of gain) brought about by some combination of reduced and expended calories (physical activity). The focus should be on the potential of these interventions to promote nutritious eating/drinking and exercise and the benefits they can bestow regardless of weight.

The goals of weight loss, on the one hand, and of healthy eating/drinking and physical activity, on the other, are distinct. True, most people have to eat/drink well and exercise to lose weight (or prevent its gain). So there is overlap between the two. But an essential difference is that the former fixes on loss of pounds as the end point. The latter sets it sights on nutritious eating/drinking and physical activity as goals, in themselves, with weight loss, should it occur, as an incidental outcome. What is more, this latter approach encourages acceptance of people in a variety of shapes and sizes. To repeat a remark from a spokeswoman for the HAES (Health at Every Size) movement discussed in Chapter 2: "[We are] not against weight loss; [we are] against the pursuit of weight loss."[13]

As we focus on these legal strategies and their potential for promoting healthier eating/drinking and exercise we will assess, to the extent possible, the financial costs of any of these interventions. The necessary expenditures for any intervention are a legitimate aspect of its evaluation. Costs also need to be assessed to make the critical point that improvement of individuals' health will necessitate the spending of public dollars.

Some of those studying these issues may be in denial on this point. The White House Task Force has many insightful things to say and is cited throughout this book.[14] Yet consider this vacillating statement regarding expenditures: "Reducing childhood obesity does not have to be a costly endeavour...While many of the recommendations in this report will require additional public resources, creative strategies can also be used to redirect resources or make more effective use of existing investments." What is meant by "redirect[ing] resources" and "more effective use of existing investments"? In terms of education? Health care? Wars? Enabling individuals, particularly those who are poor, to eat/drink better and to be more physically active requires public outlays. Not always—but often. Without such expenditures much of

---

[13] D. Burgard, *What Is "Health at Every Size"?*, in THE FAT STUDIES READER 42, 44 (E. Rothblum & S. Solovay eds., 2009).
[14] WHITE HOUSE TASK FORCE, *supra* note 4, at 8.

the discussion of such issues and responses to them will be only decorative assertions.

The increasing interest in prevention of obesity has focused on children: if weight is controlled in the earliest years it is likely not to be an issue for the rest of the individual's life. So we will pay particular attention to the impact on the young of the interventions we assess. Again, our benchmarks will not be just prevention but also the extent to which legal strategies promote healthier eating/drinking, physical activity regardless of weight, and acceptance of bodies of all shapes. We will also gauge the extent to which any of these interventions could have the unintended consequences of stigmatizing fat adults and children because of misplaced emphasis on weight and obsession with body size.

IV. Evidentiary Basis for Interventions

How do policy makers know when to invoke regulation to address a situation? Viewpoint is an important factor. Those who espouse the market triumphant are likely to be wary of interventions that are seen as interfering with its workings. We discussed this attitude in Chapter 2. In this depiction obesity is a matter of individual responsibility. Woe unto the government who would police the food/beverage, diet, and exercise industries in an attempt to better health, however that concept might be understood.[15]

Those open to regulation in any particular area are not deterred by claims for an unfettered market. Its own excesses, for example the 2008 meltdown and the havoc it wreaked, belie insistence that government should just stay clear. The general case for intervention is couched in various ways.[16] For example, some suggest that regulation is justified on the basis of certain economic arguments in respect of efficiencies, provision of information by the state, etc.[17] Others claim an overarching duty exists on the part of government to protect the health of its citizens, especially children.[18]

Still, for regulators, the question remains: when are particular circumstances appropriate for intervention? Ascertaining when particular regulation should be implemented in the midst of controversy regarding the nature of the problem and the efficacy of interventions raises critical issues—ones by no means unique to obesity.

---

[15] Chapter 2, Section V: The Heavy Hand of the State.
[16] C. Sunstein, *It's for Your Own Good*, N.Y. Rev. Books, Mar. 7, 2013, available at http://www.nybooks.com/articles/archives/2013/mar/07/its-your-own-good/?pagination=false.
[17] Alston et al., *supra* note 1, at 166–68.
[18] INSTITUTE OF MEDICINE, ACCELERATING PROGRESS IN OBESITY PREVENTION: SOLVING THE WEIGHT OF THE NATION 101–02 (2012).

To respond to such issues, in a number of areas, a central concept that has been advanced is the "precautionary principle."[19] The principle addresses two core ideas: first, the uncertainty of a cause-and-effect relationship between a product or activity and human health, and, second, the need for caution in the face of such uncertainty.[20] The principle has been recognized and applied in a number of areas, especially the environment.[21]

The precautionary principle has several formulations. Mild versions underscore the point that a lack of decisive evidence of harm should not be a reason for refusing to intervene to prevent such harm from occurring. Strong versions suggest that just a possibility of harm occurring is sufficient to justify regulation.[22] One version of the principle that has been incorporated in the literature on gambling is a milder version but one that shifts the onus to those who are raising doubts regarding negative consequences of gaming:

> When an activity causes threats of harm to human health...precautionary measures should be taken even if some cause and effect relationships are not fully established scientifically...[T]he proponent of an activity...bears the burden of proof.[23]

The principle has been criticized. A major critique is that any regulation that is prompted by the principle may impose negative effects of its own.[24] For example, there are good reasons to be cautious about new therapeutic drugs and to put them through stringent regulatory processes before they are approved so as to avoid negative effects. At the same time, such stringent processes impose costs and delays that prevent those drugs from assisting people who may urgently need them.

In Chapter 1 we talked about the IOM Report addressing the role of law in promoting health issues.[25] That Report embraces a version of the precautionary principle to bolster the case for legal interventions for a range of issues affecting health. After discussing the relevant issues at length, the Report asserts: "In the case of a policy targeting a major risk factor for poor health, the combination of a well-constructed hypothesis and high risk to the population may

---

[19] W. A. BOGART, PERMIT BUT DISCOURAGE: REGULATING EXCESSIVE CONSUMPTION 265–67 (2011).

[20] R. MacNeil, *Government as Gambling Regulator and Operator: The Case of Electronic Gaming Machines,* in CASINO STATE: LEGALIZED GAMBLING IN CANADA 144 (J. Cosgrove & T. Klassen eds., 2009).

[21] *See, e.g.,* THE PRECAUTIONARY PRINCIPLE IN THE 20TH CENTURY: LATE LESSONS FROM EARLY WARNINGS (P. Harremoës et al. eds., 2002).

[22] For various formulations, *see* C. Sunstein, *Precautions & Nature*, 137(2) Daedalus 49, 50–51 (2008).

[23] MacNeil, *supra* note 20, at 144, citing C. RAFFENSPERGER, FINAL WINGSPREAD PRECAUTIONARY PRINCIPLE STATEMENT (1998).

[24] Sunstein, *supra* note 22, at 53.

[25] INSTITUTE OF MEDICINE, FOR THE PUBLIC'S HEALTH: REVITALIZING LAW AND POLICY TO MEET NEW CHALLENGES(2011); Chapter 1, Section III(c): Legal Interventions to Promote Health.

call for applying the precautionary principle and for taking action even in the absence of definitive evidence."[26]

The need to protect children especially suggests erring on the side of intervention. Advocates of regulation argue that the consequences of failure to act can be particularly significant: the risk of damage done that will affect the young for the rest of their lives. The IOM Report, addressing well-being in general, agrees with such an assertion: "The evidence for various policy and other approaches is mixed and there are important remaining gaps in our knowledge, but the risk from not acting on what is known, or even partially supported by the evidence, can be great, as a generation of children grows up without some of the potentially essential ingredients for healthy development."[27]

Similar assertions have been made about children and the prevention of obesity. The IOM has also done a report on avoidance of excess weight in early childhood.[28] We'll discuss its findings and recommendations in some detail in Chapter 7.[29] For the moment what is of interest are its conclusions about the appropriate basis for intervention. It discusses the lack of research, until recently, into the issue of obesity and young children.[30] Despite this paucity it concludes that "the urgency of the issues of obesity in young children demands that action be taken."[31] The "best available evidence" is sufficient for action. ("The best available evidence—as opposed to waiting for the best possible evidence.")[32]

The point of this discussion is not to salute the precautionary principle, the IOM Report on law and health's version of it, or to endorse the IOM's Report on the young and obesity prevention's assertion about when intervention is justified. The goal here is to underscore the complexity surrounding many legal interventions, generally, and in terms of obesity, in particular. The costs of misdirected regulation are an ever-present hazard; they need to be minimized.[33] There is a large amount of guesswork and controversy both in terms of deciding when and how to intervene and in establishing the effects of various interventions, individually and taken together. There is a strong case for intervention to promote healthier eating/drinking and active lifestyles. But

---

[26] FOR THE PUBLIC'S HEALTH, *supra* note 25, at 101.

[27] *Id.* at 100.

[28] INSTITUTE OF MEDICINE, COMMITTEE ON OBESITY PREVENTION POLICIES FOR YOUNG CHILDREN, EARLY CHILDHOOD OBESITY PREVENTION POLICIES (2011).

[29] Chapter 7: Encouraging Physical Activity: Children at Play!.

[30] EARLY CHILDHOOD OBESITY PREVENTION, *supra* note 28, at 24–25.

[31] *Id.* at 25.

[32] *Id.* quoting INSTITUTE OF MEDICINE, PREVENTING CHILDHOOD OBESITY: HEALTH IN THE BALANCE 3 (2005).

[33] *Over-regulated America: The Home of Laissez-Faire Is Being Suffocated by Excessive and Badly Written Regulation,* ECONOMIST, Feb. 18, 2012, at 9; THE BEHAVIORAL FOUNDATIONS OF PUBLIC POLICY (E. Shafir ed., 2013).

be wary of those who claim that any such basis is straightforward and bound to produce just what is needed.

V. What's Being Assessed?

There are many legal strategies that have or could be invoked to promote nutritious eating/drinking and physical activity. We will not attempt to look at them all. We will examine several interventions in three areas: marketing; fiscal policy; and physical activity—in particular, strategies for children. These three areas allow us to look at laws to improve both healthy eating/drinking and active lifestyles. Each of them also cluster several kinds of interventions.

In terms of marketing, in Chapter 5 we will examine: educational campaigns to promote nutritious eating/drinking and physical exercise; mandated caloric labeling on menus and nutrition labeling on packaging for food and beverages; restrictions on marketing to children through self-regulation and legislative restrictions; and, the potential of merchandising in borderless cyperspace to undermine regulatory efforts of various jurisdictions in the real world.

Within fiscal policy, in Chapter 6 we will look at taxation of nonnutritious food and beverages (to discourage their consumption) and at subsidies (to promote healthy food and drinks). In terms of subsidies we will examine both generally applicable incentives to grow and market healthy foods, such as fruits and vegetables, and targeted assistance encouraging individuals with low incomes to consume healthier diets.

Concerning efforts to promote physical activity, Chapter 7 focuses on children and looks at strategies for: preschool, formal education, community efforts, the built environment, and use of the tax system to create incentives for participating in sports and other recreational activities.

We observed in Chapter 1 that it is the "mix" of the interventions that can be critical for the effectiveness of regulation. The classic example, in terms of consumption, is the many kinds of regulation invoked to discourage smoking. But a similar point can be made regarding efforts to curb excessive drinking or problem gambling.[34] The several strategies to promote good eating/drinking and physical activity are more likely to have a greater impact, taken together, than any one of them individually. Such interventions have not been invoked at all, or only partially, and for a limited time. So there needs to be a leap of faith here: whatever the outcomes produced by an individual intervention, healthy ways will increase because of the overall effects of several interventions over a period of time.

---

[34] Chapter 1, Section IV: Consumption Encounters Law: *Permit but Discourage*.

That said, when we examine regulation of marketing by the food-and-beverage industry we will look at an instance where one intervention, by itself, has had a marked impact. The province of Quebec in Canada forbids advertising to children in a variety of circumstances. Studies have demonstrated that the ban itself has led to significantly less consumption of unhealthy food by children affected by the prohibition. At the same time, it is unlikely that many other jurisdictions, especially in the United States, will engage in such drastic measures to curb marketing to young people. A "mix" of interventions—economically and politically acceptable—may have the greatest impact. Chapters 5 to 7 examine a combination of these legal strategies.

VI. Noted but not Examined

There are other areas, concerning weight issues, where law has a role. Four major ones are: prescription drugs, the weight loss–diet industry, bariatric surgery, and litigation against the food and beverage industry. Each of these raises important issues regarding obesity and the role of regulation. Whatever attention they have received, they should be more rigorously examined in terms of their impact and the effects that they are having on the lives of fat people.[35] They have contributed to the obsession with weight and weight loss in addressing issues of obesity. They have much less potential to promote healthier eating/drinking and active lifestyles, and for that reason they are put to the side in this book. However, let's take a brief look at them and some of the issues that they raise to provide important context for the interventions that we will be discussing in Chapters 5 to 7.

A) DRUGS

The significant benefits of drugs are part of the powers of modern medicine. From antibiotics to treat infections, to more sophisticated forms of anesthetics to address pain without substantial side effects, to various forms of chemotherapy that respond to the menace of cancer, pharmaceuticals have done much to alleviate human suffering. At the same time drugs are big business.[36] Motivations to use them to reap profits are an intricate part of development and marketing.[37]

---

[35] E. Mathieu, *Big Bucks, Few Controls in the Wild West of Weight Loss*, TORONTO STAR, June 19, 2011, *available at* http://www.thestar.com/life/health_wellness/nutrition/2011/06/19/big_bucks_few_controls_in_the_wild_west_of_weight_loss.html.

[36] T.CAULFIELD, THE CURE FOR EVERYTHING!: UNTANGLING TWISTED MESSAGES ABOUT HEALTH, FITNESS, AND HAPPINESS 194 *et seq.* (2012).

[37] C. Elliott, *Pharmaceutical Propaganda*, in AGAINST HEALTH: HOW HEALTH BECAME THE NEW MORALITY 93 (J. Metzl & A. Kirkland eds., 2010).

The financial potential of drugs to address obesity is evident. If excess weight, by itself, is the problem, and if a drug can be discovered that will suppress appetite so that pounds will be shed with no significant negative side effects, then there could be a vast market among the many who are obese or even just overweight. But the prospects for such sales have been, to date, fraught with perils.[38]

The pharmaceutical industry has a large financial incentive in bolstering the claim that weight is a proxy for health as a predicate for the need for a drug that will allow individuals to shed pounds. To that end the industry finances the research and other efforts of many experts on obesity.[39] Nevertheless, up to the present, efforts to discover a pill that will result in sustained weight loss and that has no substantial health consequences have been unavailing.[40]

The drugs that have been approved and marketed have not resulted in significant long-term weight loss or have been associated with important unwanted consequences, or both. An infamous example of such medication was "fen-phen." In the 1990s it was asserted that two drugs, Pondimin (fenflurimine) and Phentermine, when taken together were effective appetite suppressants. Some 6 million Americans were taking these drugs, or a variant (Redux), in order to lose weight. Then researchers established that these medications caused heart valve damage and other pulmonary issues. They were taken off the market, but not before many individuals had serious medical issues inflicted upon them.[41]

Other diet drugs have also caused substantial negative effects.[42] Critics have similar concerns about harmful consequences that could be caused by still other treatments such as Qsymia (formerly Qnexa). That drug was approved in 2012 by the Federal Drug Administration (FDA) despite widespread warnings, including by members of the agency's committees, of both its ineffectiveness and dangers.[43]

---

[38] L. Lucas & A. Rappeport, *Search for "Miracle Drug" in Fickle Diet Market Continues*, FIN. TIMES, May 8, 2012, at 19.

[39] E. OLIVER, FAT POLITICS: THE REAL STORY BEHIND AMERICA'S OBESITY EPIDEMIC 28 *et seq.* (2006).

[40] P. Lyons, *Prescription for Harm: Diet Industry Influence, Public Health Policy, and the "Obesity Epidemic,"* in THE FAT STUDIES READER, *supra* note 13, at 75.

[41] OLIVER, *supra* note 39, at 114. In addition, there was a flurry of litigation against the drug manufacturers, leading to multibillion dollar settlements; *see Fenphen Maker Agrees to 3.75 Billion Settlement*, CNN HEALTH, Oct. 8, 1999, *available at* http://articles.cnn.com/1999-10-08/health/9910_08_fen.phen_1_heart-valve-pondimin-diet-drug?_s=PM:HEALTH. The litigation continues some fifteen years after the drug was taken off the market; see Jef Feeley, *Pfizer Asks End to Fen-Phen Suits Linked to Lung Ailment*, BLOOMBERG BUSINESSWEEK, Aug. 23, 2012, available at http://www.businessweek.com/news/2012-08-23/pfizer-asks-end-to-fen-phen-suits-linked-to-lung-ailment.

[42] C. Weeks, *Why Did It Take So Long to Get This Diet Pill off the Market?*, Globe & Mail, Oct. 25, 2010, at L1, L4.

[43] A. Pollack, *U.S. to Review Diet Treatment Once Rejected*, N.Y. TIMES, Feb. 16, 2012, at B1, B6; A. Pollack, *Side Effects of Diet Pill Still Concern Regulators*, N.Y. TIMES, Feb. 18, 2012, at B1, B2; A. Pollack, *In Reversal, F.D.A. Panel Endorses a Diet Pill*, N.Y. TIMES, Feb. 23, 2012, at

The FDA has been vigilant in terms of diet pills. Up until the approval of Qsymia and one other drug, the FDA had not approved any other such medication for years.[44] But there was great pressure to do so. Pharmaceutical companies can look to huge potential profits if a treatment can be found that effectively suppresses appetite over the long term. The public sees a straightforward solution to a straightforward problem: fat, regardless of the underlying state of health.

A legal and administrative framework exists for approval of drugs. But many issues arise around a critical question: are all costs being weighed appropriately against claimed benefits in the case of diet pills?

B) WEIGHT LOSS–DIET INDUSTRY

"Why not eat pistachios at midnight when the moon is full?"[45]

Such is the tongue-in-cheek comment of obesity expert Dr. Jules Hirsch on the many fad diets over the years that have led to long-term failure for most people who have tried them. The weight loss–diet industry has long played upon the desperate longing of fat people to shed pounds and to keep them off.[46]

There has been a large amount of quackery over the years directed at having the consuming public believe that there is a tried-and-true path to slimness. The reality is much different. Yet the weight loss–diet industry continues to prey upon the hopes of those struggling to shed pounds. Rhode, whose book *The Beauty Bias* we discussed at length in Chapter 3, documents much of this chicanery.[47] Here are just a few of the schemes that she tells us about that have been recently investigated by the Federal Trade Commission (FTC):

- Siluette Patch—made from seaweed, eliminates fat deposits on contact;
- Fat Seltzer Reduce—dietary supplement eliminates fat without diet or exercise;
- Himalayan Diet Breakthrough—contains Nepalese Mineral Patch; causes as much as thirty-seven pounds of weight loss in eight weeks without diet or exercise.[48]

B1, B5; A. Pollack, *Medicine for Obesity Needs Study, Panel Says*, N.Y. TIMES, Mar. 30, 2012, at B1, B2.

[44] A. Pollack, *FDA Approves Qsymia, A Weight Loss Drug*, N.Y. TIMES, July 17, 2012, at B3; see also A. Pollack, *Prescription Drug to Aid Weight Loss Wins F.D.A. Backing*, N.Y. TIMES, June 27, 2012, at B1.

[45] G. Kolata, *In Dieting, Magic Isn't a Substitute for Science*, N.Y. TIMES, July 10, 2012, at D5, D6.

[46] A. Newman, *Poignant Endorsements in Weight-Loss Campaign*, N.Y. TIMES, Dec. 19, 2012, at B3.

[47] D.RHODE, THE BEAUTY BIAS: THE INJUSTICE OF APPEARANCE IN LIFE AND LAW 32–35 (2010).

[48] *Id.* at 33–34.

More-established weight loss programs, such as Jenny Craig and Weight Watchers, do not make such outlandish claims. Moreover, they, and some new schemes, are making some attempts to shift the emphasis away from a preoccupation with calories toward more nutritiously sound eating generally.[49] Yet, the fact remains that their success is in large part predicated on their customers' failure. They rarely report overall long-term success rates, which are mostly dismal.[50] These companies do well when hapless consumers' weights yo-yo from repeated efforts to lose pounds. Or, as has been observed: "profitability depends on failure...and failure [is what] happens."[51]

There are laws in place to protect consumers from fraudulent practices and misleading advertising. Yet in this area and others these laws are often under-enforced. Rhode documents some imaginative efforts by public authorities to warn of scams regarding weight loss and fitness products.[52] Nevertheless, much more could be done. A place to start would be to provide adequate resources to enforce existing provisions. Another strategy might be to strengthen laws to require disclosure, and publicizing of success rates of diet programs.

Meanwhile preoccupation with weight compels individuals to give themselves over to any number of schemes that insist that pounds can be shed and kept off, whatever the reality. One of the saddest aspects of these delusions is the children being swept into various regimens.[53] A book published in 2011 about a child losing weight, *Maggie Goes on a Diet*, generated much controversy.[54] America's obsession with pounds and appearance extends even to the very young.[55]

C) BARIATRIC SURGERY

Bariatric surgery is dramatically on the rise. Such procedures were once reserved for the extremely obese. Those turning to these procedures now include teenagers, especially young women. The threshold at which these surgeries are performed suggests that there is increasing pressure to lower the level of obesity. Yet they are expensive, invasive procedures that can be associated with a variety of negative outcomes, the long-term effects of which are unclear. Whatever the

---

[49] E. Gootman, *Weight Watchers Upends Its Points System*, N.Y. TIMES, Dec. 3, 2010, available at http://www.nytimes.com/2010/12/04/nyregion/04watchers.html?_r=1; N. Laporte, *A Weight-Loss Strategy from an Unlikely Pair*, N.Y. TIMES, BUSINESS WEEK, Sept. 2, 2012, at 3.
[50] Lyons, *supra* 40, at 78 79.
[51] RHODE, *supra* note 47, at 50 quoting Susie Orbach.
[52] *Id.* at 141.
[53] K. Dell'Antonia, *Putting a 7-Year-Old on a Diet*, N.Y. TIMES, Mar. 27, 2012, available at http://parenting.blogs.nytimes.com/2012/03/27/how-to-or-how-not-to-put-your-child-on-a-diet/.
[54] P. KRAMER, MAGGIE GOES ON A DIET (2011); J. Fain, *Children's Book Author and Filmmaker Weigh In on Kids' Dieting Controversy*, HUFFINGTON POST, Oct. 14, 2011, available at http://www.huffingtonpost.com/jean-fain-licsw-msw/paul-kramer-maggie-goes-on-a-diet_b_1003714.html.
[55] *See* DARA-LYNN WEISS, THE HEAVY: A MOTHER, A DAUGHTER, A DIET (2013).

merits of these surgeries, they have little to do, for most people, with nutritious eating/drinking and physical activity, including the prevention of excess weight gain. These techniques, used too freely, could be a dangerous substitute for the long and hard path to healthier eating/drinking and more active lifestyles.

There are a number of such procedures. The two main ones are gastric bypass and gastric banding.[56] The former restricts the stomach and bypasses part of the small intestine. The latter places an inflatable ring around the stomach so as to restrict intake of food. Other techniques are developing. One is sleeve gastrectomy: the stomach is stapled into a narrow tube and the rest is removed. Another is gastric imbrications (placation): the stomach is constricted by folding and sewing; as a result no part of it is actually removed.

From 1984 to 2004 the numbers of such surgeries that were performed, in the United States increased by 804 percent: 13,386 to 121, 055. By 2011 those greatly increased 2004 figures had doubled to between 200,000 and 250,000 operations a year.[57] Bariatric procedures have been estimated to now be a $6-billion-a-year enterprise in the United States.[58]

In 2011 the FDA expanded the criteria for performing some of these operations. Previously banding procedures were available for individuals with a BMI of at least 40 (35 with an existing severe condition associated with their obesity), or those who were overweight by at least 45 kg. Allergan, a maker of a band, applied for extension of the techniques to those with a BMI of at least 30 with a preexisting condition related to obesity. Despite protests the application was successful.[59] With that ruling some 27 million more Americans were eligible for this operation.[60]

Until recently these techniques were rarely employed on young people, but such statistics are rapidly changing. A survey of New York City and surrounding area hospitals, published in 2012, revealed that the percentage of patients under twenty-five who are operated on in this way varies. Nevertheless, the low was still as high as 4 percent of all such individuals undergoing the procedure, and in one hospital it reached as much as 19 percent.[61] In 2012 studies were

---

[56] A. Pollack, *Hoping to Avoid the Knife: Surgery-Free Devices Scarce for Weight Loss*, N.Y. TIMES, Mar. 17, 2011, at B1, B6.

[57] L. Alderman, *After Surgery to Slim Down, the Bills Can Pile Up*, N.Y. TIMES, Jan. 1, 2010, at B5.

[58] A. Hartocollis, *Young, Obese and Drawn to Surgery: Weight Procedures on Teenagers Rising, Despite Doubts*, N.Y. TIMES, January 8, 2012, at A1, A20.

[59] American Society of Bariatric Physicians, *Bariatric Physicians Question FDA Recommendations to Lower BMI Requirements for Lap-Band Surgery* (2011), *available at* http://www.prnewswire.com/news-releases/bariatric-physicians-question-fda-recommendations-to-lower-bmi-requirements-for-lap-band-surgery-112960679.html.

[60] M. Mitka, *FDA Action Allows More Obese Patients to Qualify for a Bariatric Procedure*, 305(13) J. AM. MED. ASS'N 1287 (Apr. 6, 2011); A. Pollack, *Panel Votes to Expand Surgery for Less Obese*, N.Y. TIMES, Dec. 4, 2010, at B1, B2.

[61] Hartocollis, *supra* note 58, at A20.

being conducted to gauge the effectiveness of such interventions on children as young as twelve.[62] Also, in that year Allergan (the same company, just discussed, that successfully applied to the FDA to loosen criteria for surgery) was seeking permission from the FDA to market its band to patients as young as fourteen; the existing limit is eighteen.[63] After much protest from a variety of groups the company withdrew its application.[64] Further manoeuvers on its part and others wishing to expand such surgery remain to be seen.

Bariatric surgery was, initially, quite dangerous, with a substantial risk of mortality compared with many other operations. In addition there were frequent and serious complications and often failure to permanently lose substantial amounts of weight.[65] However, more recently, with the advent of banding techniques, the surgery may now be less risky. Moreover, there appear to be positive outcomes, other than weight loss, in many cases depending on the procedure employed. Some who have this surgery experience significant reduction in metabolic syndrome and insulin resistance.[66] Women who have had bypass surgery may give birth to children who have lower blood pressure and higher insulin resistance than children of these same mothers born before the surgery.[67] Generally, babies born to mothers who have had bariatric procedures are less likely to grow up obese than if these women had not lost significant weight.[68]

That said, bariatric surgery remains expensive and can give rise to many untoward outcomes. In the United States it costs $15,000 to $30,000 depending on the procedure that is used and where in the country it is done.[69] Necessary expenditures that can accrue in the wake of the surgery can also be daunting.[70] Whatever the financial outlays, these techniques too often fail: 25 percent of gastric banding patients have not lost weight two years after surgery.[71]

Those who are successful frequently experience side effects. One study has suggested that as many as 90 percent of patients have effects such as pain or vomiting. Patients who have undergone these operations must engage in long-term lifestyle changes and have constant nutritional monitoring if they are to

---

[62] *Id.* at A1.

[63] *Id.* at A20.

[64] S. Amour, *Allergan Pulled Teen Lap-Band Plan as Criticism Mounted*, BLOOMBERG NEWS, Oct. 3, 2012, *available at* http://www.bloomberg.com/news/2012-10-03/allergan-pulls-teen-lap-b and-plans-as-criticism-mounts.html.

[65] OLIVER, *supra* note 39, at 54–56.

[66] C. Weeks, *Surgery More Effective for Treating Obese Teens*, GLOBE & MAIL, Feb. 10, 2010, *available at* http://www.theglobeandmail.com/life/parenting/surgery-more-effective-for-treating-obese-teens/article571664/.

[67] A. Picard, *Why Mom's Weight-Loss Surgery is Good for Baby*, GLOBE & MAIL, Oct. 29, 2012, *available at* http://www.theglobeandmail.com/life/health-and-fitness/health/why-moms-weight-loss-surgery-is-good-for-baby/article4699181/.

[68] *Id.*

[69] Alderman, *supra* note 57.

[70] *Id.*

[71] *Id.*

have safe and long-lasting weight loss. Nonetheless, almost 30 percent regain the weight they initially lost or have the procedure reversed. One study has indicated that there is a fivefold increase in suicides among these patients, most within five years of the operation. These techniques cause nutritional deficiencies requiring lifelong supplements of calcium, vitamin B12, foliate, and so forth.[72] There appear to be even more such complications when lap-band surgery is performed on young people.[73]

D) LITIGATION

"Litigation and the threat of [it] can be powerful forces in changing policies and practices that affect obesity."[74]

There is a widespread view that litigation is a forceful tool in altering the behavior of individuals, corporations, and governments.[75] Moreover, unlike most other aspects of regulation, it is not controlled by public actors; individual citizens and interest groups of varying political beliefs can invoke it to further wide-ranging agendas.[76] This account of lawsuits as a powerful, freewheeling presence (not dependent on government intransigence) for reconfiguring actions has been embraced by a good many addressing obesity. They often find inspiration in what is said to be litigation's critical role in taming the cigarette industry. A front page story in 2012 in *The New York* Times proclaimed "Lawyers ... against Big Tobacco Target Food Makers."[77]

The food and beverage industry and their political allies share some of these views about the force of lawsuits. The proposed *Personal Responsibility in Food Consumption Act*, in the House of Representatives, and the *Commonsense Consumption Act*, in the Senate, would have banned lawsuits for claims against that industry based on weight gain and related issues.[78] However, these bills met with fierce resistance from plaintiffs' lawyers and various advocacy groups and ultimately were not enacted. But their very existence demonstrated the widespread belief in the power of lawsuits to threaten the food-and-beverage industry.

---

[72] American Society of Bariatric Physicians, *supra* note 59, and the studies cited therein.
[73] Hartocollis, *supra* 58, at A20.
[74] INSTITUTE OF MEDICINE, LEGAL STRATEGIES IN CHILDHOOD OBESITY PREVENTION 51 (2011).
[75] S.FARHANG, THE LITIGATION STATE: PUBLIC REGULATION AND PRIVATE LAWSUITS IN THE US (2010).
[76] BOGART, *supra* note 19, at 56–58.
[77] S. Strom, *Lawyers from Suits against Big Tobacco Target Food Makers*, N.Y. TIMES, Aug. 18, 2012, at A1, A4.
[78] W.MCINTOSH & C.CATES, MULTI-PARTY LITIGATION: THE STRATEGIC CONTEXT 137 (2009); *Personal Responsibility in Food Consumption Act* of 2005, H.R. 554, and *Commonsense Consumption Act* of 2005, H.R. 2183.

Yet there are sound reasons to question the effectiveness of lawsuits, generally, and their role in respect of obesity, specifically. Many of the claims with regard to the power of litigation focus on tort actions. At base, a tort is a wrong, other than breach of contract, which the law will redress by an award of damages or some other remedy. Tort litigation is to contour all sorts of economic and social behavior reflecting an abundance of confidence in its ability to shape human conduct. A prominent commentator some time ago contended that: "It is...no exaggeration to see American tort law as the major means for setting norms and standards for social and economic behaviour."[79]

Despite such flourishes the empirical evidence concerning actual impact, in several contexts, suggests that the effects of tort lawsuits are often at odds with almost any goal assigned to them.[80] A major study assessed the effects of tort litigation in America in a number of areas, including medical malpractice, automobile accidents, and environmental injuries. That study confirmed the disparity between the actual impact of tort litigation and various claims about its effects, including when such assertions are measured against comparable regulatory or compensatory schemes and the outcomes they produce. The study concluded: "[t]he...system performs unevenly in deterring the causes of personal injuries, so its scope should be restricted to situations where its effect seems likely to justify its high cost."[81] What is more: there is a significant body of evidence that finds that the effects of litigation in still other contexts, such as attempts to promote various progressive causes, have, generally, not produced the hoped-for changes.[82]

There is some evidence that the threat of tort liability can be effective in deterring commercial establishments from serving alcohol to impaired customers.[83] In contrast, litigation against tobacco companies has not substantially altered the industry.[84] Smoking in Canada and the United States has significantly declined over the last several decades because of shifting norms and various regulatory efforts. But the cigarette companies remain largely unbowed as they continue to peddle their poisons globally. McIntosh and Cates surveyed the effects of litigation against these corporations as a means of regulation up to 2009. They concluded, "[T]he industry would appear to have changed very

---

[79] P. S. Atiyah, *Tort Law and the Alternatives: Some Anglo-American Comparisons*, 1987 DUKE L.J. 1002, 1018 (1987); BOGART, *supra* note 19, at 320–22.

[80] D. Dewees & M. Trebilcock, *The Efficacy of the Tort System and Its Alternatives: A Review of Empirical Evidence*, 30 OSGOODE HALL L.J. 57 (1992); R. Epstein, *The Social Consequences of Common Law Rules*, 95 HARV. L. REV. 1717 (1982).

[81] D.DEWEES, D.DUFF & M.TREBILCOCK, EXPLORING THE DOMAIN OF ACCIDENT LAW: TAKING THE FACTS SERIOUSLY 413 (1996).

[82] G.ROSENBERG, THE HOLLOW HOPE: CAN COURTS BRING ABOUT SOCIAL CHANGE? (2d ed. 2008). W. A. BOGART, GOOD GOVERNMENT? GOOD CITIZENS?: COURTS, POLITICS, AND MARKETS IN A CHANGING CANADA (2005), Ch. 2 The Ascendance of Courts.

[83] BOGART, *supra* note 19, at 35–38.

[84] *Id.* at 58–61.

little."[85] Litigation against gambling establishments on behalf of those who wager excessively is just starting, but is already encountering all manner of opposition. Its impact on the gaming industry is hard to predict.[86]

Litigation's effect on obesity could also be complicated and unpredictable. The Report, quoted at the beginning of this subsection, about lawsuits and the threat of them as "powerful forces" also acknowledged that resort to the courts can be "narrow and idiosyncratic."[87] In contrast, it suggested that "legislation and regulation are much more flexible ways of changing policies and practices."[88] At the same time the prospect of litigation as a response to a wide variety of issues tends to dazzle all interests caught up in such debates. Intense dustups over lawsuits, pending and potential, and their intended and actual effects can deflect attention away from other strategies that may be more effective and that can be implemented through legislative, administrative, and self-regulatory initiatives.

There is a clear role for government and private parties in turning to the courts, or just the possibility of doing so, to respond to misleading practices on the part of the food-and-beverage, exercise, and weight-loss industries. One example was the reaction of public officials to alleged misleading practices in the "Smart Choices" food program, which permitted cereals such as Fruit Loops to be so designated. Such scrutiny, with the possibility of legal action, led to the initiative being shut down. Another instance involved Rice Krispies suggesting that it "now helps support your child's immunity" during an influenza outbreak. Again, investigation by public officials, with the possibility of legal action, led to the claim being removed from the labeling.[89] Even more recent examples involve scrutiny of "energy drinks" and their claims regarding improvement of physical and mental health and related issues.[90]

Actual litigation against the industry has proceeded on other fronts. Much of it has resulted in victories for plaintiffs.[91] These cases include efforts to remove transfats from foods and soft drink vending machines from schools. Yet there is little evidence that such lawsuits have resulted in people either losing weight or eating and drinking more nutritiously and being more physically active. Reviewing such cases in 2009, McIntosh and Cates concluded "[T]he

---

[85] MCINTOSH & CATES, *supra* note 78, at 94.
[86] BOGART, *supra* note 19, at 314–22.
[87] INSTITUTE OF MEDICINE, *supra* note 74, at 51.
[88] *Id.*
[89] *Id.* at 4 for both examples.
[90] B. Meier, *Energy Drinks Promise Edge, But Experts Say Proof Is Scant*, N.Y. TIMES, Jan. 2, 2013, at A1; B. Meier, *Energy Shot's "No Crash" Claim Is Disputed by Watchdog*, N.Y. TIMES, Jan. 3, 2013, at B1; B. Meier, *More Emergency Visits Linked to Energy Drinks*, N.Y. TIMES, Jan. 12, 2013, at B3.
[91] MCINTOSH & CATES, *supra* note 78, at ch.5: "The Politics of Food Litigation."

modifications requested of big food have either cost little and/or redounded to the goodwill of the industry."[92]

Causation can be a significant issue in litigation involving the food-and-beverage industry. As we have seen in Chapter 2, obesity is attributable to many factors. Because that is the case, it is frequently difficult to show that any particular nonnutritious food or beverage has resulted in individuals being very overweight or has resulted in them, generally, eating and drinking food and beverages of dubious nutritional value and being sedentary. Haltom and McCann, in comparing litigation against the tobacco industry and purveyors of fat food/beverages, comment on the complexities of causation regarding the latter lawsuits: "the dangers of fast food are inseparable from the effects of other life choices about exercise, overall diet, and the like as well as genetic predispositions. Demonstrating how fast food contributes to heart attacks thus is more difficult than making the causal linkage between a lifetime of smoking and lung cancer."[93]

These difficulties with causation and related issues may blunt the effect of such lawsuits. They may even set back efforts to promote healthy eating/ drinking and active lifestyles. Haltom and McCann systematically studied the newspaper coverage of litigation against the fast-food and related industries. On the whole such coverage did not bolster the charge that the food-and-beverage industry is the cause of health problems. Rather, such stories tended to underscore the idea that fat people should accept individual responsibility for their weight, health, and so on. The authors concluded that such lawsuits were unlikely to contribute to battles against the food-and-beverage and related industries, and could even have a negative effect: "[L]itigators who seek to reassign responsibility for widespread harms may impede and divert the very agendas that they would set...[We] doubt that tort litigation to increase consumer health against corporate profit...will be able to surmount obstacles from mass communication."[94]

The point here is not to suggest that lawsuits against the food-and-beverage and related industries have no effect in changing behavior. Rather, it is to emphasize that outcomes produced by such litigation will be complicated and may even produce consequences that are at odds with activists' agendas. Moreover, prospects of litigation as a response to a wide variety of issues can preoccupy all interests caught up in these debates. Intense confrontations over lawsuits, pending and potential, and their intended and actual effects can deflect attention away from other regulatory strategies that may be more effective and

---

[92] *Id.* at 145.
[93] W. Haltom & M. McCann, *Framing Fast Food Litigation: Tort Claims, Mass Media, and the Politics of Responsibility in the United States*, in FAULT LINES: TORT LAW AS CULTURAL PRACTICE 97, 103 (D. Engel & M. McCann eds., 2009).
[94] *Id.* at 114.

that can be implemented through legislative, administrative, and self-regulatory initiatives.

These limits of litigation suggest that it should be viewed, at most, as only one element of several that constitute the regulatory "mix." Lawsuits can be "powerful." They can also distract attention from more effective and long-lasting initiatives while adding to the obsession with fat as the problem and weight loss as the solution.

VII. Conclusion

If we can put our obsession with weight to the side we may see the role of law in this area in a different light for the achieving of other goals: the promotion of healthier eating/drinking and of exercise and the protection of fat people from discrimination. At the same time law's effects may be more limited and unpredictable than many of its champions would have us believe, even as it still may play a part in achieving these other goals.

With these basics in mind, let's turn to examining three areas of intervention: marketing, fiscal policy, and promoting physical activity. The health of kids will be a priority as we look at each.

{ 5 }

Just the Facts?: Educating, Mandating Information, Controlling Advertising, Restricting Marketing to Children

I. Introduction

The power of advertising to influence our lives has long been a matter of debate. So, too, has been the role of government in policing the boundaries of various promotional techniques. Those who market tend to shield themselves by invoking the right to free speech at least so long as the message is not deceptive. Such freedom allows consumers to make informed choices regarding the vast array of goods and services on offer. And "choice" is a great rallying cry in market-driven economies. Any controls, if at all, should come about by advertisers and their associations engaging in self-regulation.

In contrast, many who warn against the dangers of advertising in steering consumers and inducing them to buy unnecessary or even harmful products and services are much more open to regulation. Such policing would include suppressing deceptive practices, but would also extend to marketing that promotes goods and services that can be harmful either because they are bad, in and of themselves, or damaging when consumed in excessive amounts. Concerns about free speech, to the extent that they are acknowledged to be applicable, are offset by the harm that such products can do. An additional attraction is that these interventions, mostly, require small government expenditures, especially as compared to some of the other strategies that we will discuss in Chapters 6 and 7.

Tobacco and alcohol are two areas, in terms of consumption, where arguments on behalf of stringent regulation of advertising have largely prevailed. Tobacco's toxic and addictive properties have made it a comparatively easy target of such activity. Among other restrictions, television and radio advertisements have been banned for some time, and mandatory warnings on packaging are becoming ever more graphic and gruesome.[1] Alcohol is a more difficult instance because it is probably not harmful, and may even have health-giving properties, when consumed in moderate amounts. Nevertheless, the scourge of alcoholism, the prohibition of underage drinking, and the carnage caused by drinking and driving have led to strong restrictions and mandatory labeling (warning of dangers to pregnant women, etc.) in many jurisdictions.[2]

Restrictions on advertising of nonnutritious foods is yet another matter. Junk foods have a parallel with alcohol: not harmful in moderate amounts; potentially habit forming but by no means for everyone. But the parallel is not complete: consuming excessive amounts of nonnutritious food is not a major cause of mayhem on the roads, there are no age restrictions on eating and drinking (nonalcoholic beverages), and physical activity (or lack thereof) may be a separate determinant of an individual's weight. Fatness does not approach the status of illness the way alcoholism does. Indeed, as we saw in Chapter 3, many fat people abhor the notion that there is something pathological about them just because they are big.

Thus far, the food and beverage industry has been comparatively successful in asserting that there is a large realm of individual responsibility in terms of what is consumed on a day-to-day basis. Nevertheless, many of those interested in promoting nutritious eating and drinking point to the food and beverage industry and its relentless peddling of substances of dubious value. Such advocates question whether there should be limits placed on that industry's capacity to invest millions in unrestricted promotional activities.

One way of responding to such industry tactics would be to require mandatory warnings about the hazards of nonnutritious eating and drinking and sedentary ways. This is a legal tactic that has been employed most prominently with cigarettes and also with alcohol. It is not one that has been widely employed against the food-and-beverage industry. France has tried a variant of this technique. Advertisements on television and radio are to be accompanied by brief messages such as "For your health, eat at least five fruits and vegetables a day" and "For your health, exercise regularly." Companies whose advertisements do not carry such warnings are required to pay a levy of 1.5 percent of their advertising budget to a governmental body that promotes healthy living. An interesting idea. However, there appear to be no rigorous assessments of the impact of this intervention nor has there been widespread interest in its adoption.[3]

In terms of interventions we begin with a discussion of educational campaigns to promote nutritious eating/drinking (and physical exercise). Such promotions spring off a basic idea: give people knowledge—"just the facts"—and they will modify their behavior in response to such information. Whether from

---

[1] W. A. BOGART, PERMIT BUT DISCOURAGE: REGULATING EXCESSIVE CONSUMPTION 58–61 (2011).
[2] Id. at 26–31.
[3] R. JOLLY, MARKETING OBESITY? JUNK FOOD, ADVERTISING AND KIDS, Research Paper No. 9 39 (Australia: Parliamentary Library 2011).

the perspective of the rates of obesity or what we know about the unhealthy eating/drinking habits and sedentary lifestyles of far too many, such efforts, to date, have not had much success. Advocates would argue that that is because we have not tried hard enough, including in terms of dedicating adequate resources to these programs.

There have been some legislated requirements to provide information that have been adopted in some jurisdictions. We will discuss two of these: caloric labeling in menus and nutrition labeling on packaging for food and beverages. Both are born of the idea that knowledge is power: if you give consumers information—"just the facts"—they will act on it. A noble concept. One that, too often, does not mirror reality. Such is the case, mostly, with these two interventions. But we will also discuss some recent recommendations for front of package labeling (FOP) that, if implemented, have potential to promote healthier eating/drinking.

Anyone being lured into consuming junk food is of concern. However, children have special needs and vulnerabilities. Moreover, to the extent that obesity can be prevented, the best hope would appear to be in equipping the very young with healthy eating and drinking habits and with a zest for regular physical activity. As a result, kids have been the focus of the greatest amount of debate and of some legislative activity in some jurisdictions. We will discuss various efforts to restrict advertising targeting children, especially for food and drink. Here the emphasis is on preventing young people from being manipulated by an absence of facts about food and drink of dubious nutritional value and by games, characters, and other forms of entertainment that build loyalty to unhealthy products. In particular, we will look at a long-standing ban on such advertising in the province of Quebec and various studies assessing its effects on the eating habits of children in that society.

Finally, we look at the Internet and the ploys food companies are using to merchandise unhealthy products, especially to children. The freewheeling ways of cyberspace create their own problems. At the same time, regulatory efforts in the real world, in whatever jurisdictions they are taking place, can be undermined by the virtual one and its borderless expanse.

II. The Power of Advertising

Ideas about the centrality of consumption to capitalist economies and the effects of it on social ordering have been around for some time; nowhere more so than in America.[4] Veblen coined the phrase "conspicuous consumption"

---

[4] This paragraph and the next one depend heavily on L. COHEN, A CONSUMERS' REPUBLIC: THE POLITICS OF MASS CONSUMPTION IN POSTWAR AMERICA Prologue, 9–11 (2004). This section, *generally*, is based on BOGART, *supra* note 1, at 143–58.

as he asserted that personal display of wealth was engaged in by all classes, to the extent of their ability to do so, as pale mimicking of the luxury attained by the elite.[5] In the 1950s Potter asserted that advertising was about far more than the promotion of various goods and services: it was among the forces that "fix the values and standards of society."[6]

In 2004 Cohen titled her analysis of the roles of citizens and consumers colliding and blending in the United States *A Consumers' Republic*: "[A]n economy, culture, and politics built around the promise of mass consumption, both in terms of material life and the more idealistic goals of greater freedom, democracy, and equality"[7] Other American commentators speak of the "progress paradox."[8] Despite the fact that wealth in developed countries has grown over the last several decades such affluence has not led to greater levels of happiness for most people. Instead, individuals are trapped by a relentless need to consume, by a distorted sense of choice: "[T]he American beacon of freedom shines in the allure of fast-food, large cars, and grand homes."[9] Bruni, writing of the many extremes in the day-to-day life of the Republic, has called America the "Land of the Binge."[10]

If many societies and their economies are premised on consumption (some would say excessively so), it is little wonder that many individuals become enmeshed in some form of dependence whether in terms of alcohol, gambling, drugs, and so forth, as yet other aspects of intemperate demands. But it is also true that the majority do not. However strong the messages are regarding ever-more consumption, many individuals manage to stick to the path of moderation. So a central question is: how does excessive consumption develop? Why is it that some individuals can easily eat, drink, gamble, and so forth in moderation while others have such a difficult time doing so and are drawn into harmful patterns of use?

Orford's model of "excessive appetites" emphasizes the multiple determinants of excessive appetites, including underscoring the significance of social context. The individual makes choices with regard to consumption but those choices are made amidst a larger terrain where numerous messages about eating, drinking and so forth are delivered by family, peers, religions, and associations. Industries involved in various consumptive activities also have a huge

---

[5] T. VEBLEN, THE THEORY OF THE LEISURE CLASS: AN ECONOMIC STUDY OF INSTITUTIONS (1899).
[6] D.POTTER, PEOPLE OF PLENTY: ECONOMIC ABUNDANCE AND THE AMERICAN CHARACTER 177 (1954).
[7] COHEN, *supra* note 4, at 7.
[8] G. EASTERBROOK, THE PROGRESS PARADOX: HOW LIFE GETS BETTERWHILE PEOPLE FEEL WORSE (2003); E. OLIVER, FAT POLITICS: THE REAL STORY BEHIND AMERICA'S OBESITY EPIDEMIC (2006).
[9] OLIVER, *supra* note 8, at 184.
[10] F. Bruni, *The Land of the Binge*, N.Y. TIMES, SUNDAY REV., Feb. 10, 2013, at 3.

role in such messages. Heyman, in a controversial book regarding choice and addiction, makes similar points.[11]

These industries use myriad advertisements that promote a range of food, drink, and products and that urge ever more consumption. For these companies there is a simple bottom line: more consumption of what they offer means increased profits and higher share prices. In market economies it is to be expected that corporations should seek ever better financial results. But crucial questions also arise about limits that should be put on the promotion of food, drink, and products that, at a certain point, are deleterious to individuals' health.

Producers start from a basic position: they respond to demand; they do not create it. Consumptive habits have their source in consumers' desires. Millions of individuals, making myriad choices every day, send innumerable signals regarding the food, drink, and products that they prefer. Industries react to such signals sent by consumers' preferences by endeavoring to make and market those items for which there will be a successful market. Promotion is about responding to demand and persuading people that a particular product or service should be purchased among a competitive array. Such a posture is aided and abetted by the notion of "consumer sovereignty": rational, informed persons who weigh the costs and the benefits of their actions should be free to eat, drink, gamble, smoke, and to do goodness knows what else as they so choose, bearing the various costs that may ensue.[12]

These claims asserting a simple relationship between consumers and industries have drawn fire. Critics insist that these industries not only react to demand but also create it. Through a variety of techniques, those peddling consumables persuade individuals that they have needs that a particular product can satisfy. Cohen documents the development of mass and segmented marketing during the 1950s and beyond. A major element of which was "planned obsolescence": concerted efforts to develop products and services that were accepted as continually needing replacement with some "improved model."[13]

Those concerned with overconsumption are especially worried about how various foods, drinks, and products that can be consumed to excess are marketed in ways that are designed to promote the development of appetites that are bound to lead to dependence among a significant percentage of individuals.[14] Whether regarding fast food, candy, soft drinks, or other "junk" foods, the industry's answer is almost always the same: we give them what they want.

---

[11] G. HEYMAN, ADDICTION–A DISORDER OF CHOICE (2009).
[12] S. Cnossen, *Economics and Politics of Excise Taxation*, in THEORY AND PRACTICE OF EXCISE TAXATION: SMOKING, DRINKING, GAMBLING, POLLUTING, AND DRIVING 1, 3–4 (S. Cnossen ed., 2005).
[13] COHEN, *supra* note 4, at 293–94.
[14] D. KESSLER, THE END OF OVEREATING: TAKING CONTROL OF THE INSATIABLE AMERICAN APPETITE (2009).

Advocates of good nutrition disagree. Nestle's *Food Politics* recounts how the industry manipulates consumers and governments so as to merchandise ever more food, especially of the junk variety.[15] She analyzes the various strategies that the industry uses to sell foods and drinks. A prominent one is to keep the "public puzzled." The basics for nutritious eating are simple and have been largely unchanged over the last several decades in terms of health: eat more or less the same amount of calories that the individual will burn on a daily basis; consume a diet rich in fruits, vegetables, and multigrains and low in fats and sugars; and be physically active. But such basics are not glamorous and require people to exercise and to steer clear of soft drinks, chips, salted nuts, chocolate bars, French fries, and all the other food and drink of dubious nutritional value that is constantly being offered by an industry that is far more interested in profits than it is in health.

To compound the problem the industry is all too willing to aid and abet confusion over what constitutes healthy foods.[16] Such tactics include funding research on the effects of single nutrients. The research, itself, may be valid, but any results may only confuse people about essentials. Reports regarding the effects of calcium on bone loss may be more newsworthy than tried-and-true messages regarding how, overall, such things as nutrients, food, drink, and exercise influence the amount of calcium in the body.[17]

In addition, the industry argues that nearly all its products have some nutritional value so there should not be a threshold established by regulation regarding what constitutes good food.[18] In the end, most food companies would have people believe that "there is no such thing as a 'good' food (except when it is theirs); ... there is no such thing as a 'bad' food (especially not theirs); ... all foods (especially theirs) can be incorporated into healthful diets; and that balance, variety and moderation are the keys to healthful diets—which means that no advice to restrict intake of their particular product is appropriate."[19]

Another tactic is to spend gargantuan amounts on advertising and promotion. By the turn of this century food companies were laying out some $33 billion annually on such activities. Most of these dollars are used to advertise and promote highly processed, elaborately packaged, and fast foods; in contrast only 2.2 percent is spent by those distributing fruits, vegetables, grains, or beans.[20] Children are a main target of such advertising and promotion. There are many forms of such marketing; over the last decades television ads have

---

[15] M. NESTLE, FOOD POLITICS: HOW THE FOOD INDUSTRY INFLUENCES NUTRITION AND HEALTH 4 (2007) ; M. MOSS, SALT SUGAR FAT: HOW THE FOOD GIANTS HOOKED US (2013).

[16] L. Beck, *The Results Are In: We're a Nation of Mindless Eaters*, GLOBE & MAIL, Oct. 15, 2008, at L4.

[17] NESTLE, *supra* note 15, at 20.

[18] OLIVER, *supra* note 8, at 169.

[19] NESTLE, *supra* note 15, at 21.

[20] *Id.* at 22–23.

been prominent.[21] Foods have been engineered to be high in fat, salt, and sugar so as to promote cravings for them. Consumption, for many, has become a pastime: "eatertainment."[22]

Yet another tactic of the food industry has been to promote larger portions. Increased sizes make marketing sense because food is inexpensive compared to other factors such as labor costs. Larger sizes are often less expensive for consumers on a per unit basis: the large size of McDonald's French fries is 40 percent cheaper by ounce than the smaller one. Nestle summarizes the "consume plus" strategy: "Taken together, advertising, convenience, larger portions, and...the added nutrients in foods otherwise high in fat, sugar, and salt all contribute to an environment that promotes 'eat more.'"[23]

All that said, there are contrary forces in play. Government, public health officials, and activists are putting pressure on the industry to change its ways. Big Food, itself, is taking some steps to alter what it promotes and how it merchandises, especially to children. Let's look at these efforts. What, if any, differences are such modifications bringing about?

III. Truth in Calories: Mandatory Menu and Package Labeling

A) EDUCATING ABOUT NUTRITIOUS EATING AND DRINKING

The claims of education can sometimes be as grand as those of law. Give individuals knowledge and they'll see the light: from buying securities to positive attitudes to human rights. It's easy to see why so many want education to have such benevolent force. It's much less intrusive than many forms of law (perhaps even if provision of the information is mandated), it can be comparatively inexpensive, and, the hope is that it springs off the power of individuals to chart their own course wisely based on good civic values. Such efforts also seem to reflect much of the "new governance," discussed in Chapter 1, with its emphasis on a less intrusive and controlling government.[24]

These campaigns are also beloved by many normativists. These are the folks we also talked about in Chapter 1 who believe that the effectiveness (or lack thereof) of law is largely explained by understanding its relationship with norms. It is the altering of norms that is critical in changing behavior. Law is simply one—though important—way of accomplishing that transformation.

---

[21] *Id.* at 176–78.
[22] E. Kolbert, *XXXL—Why Are We So Fat?*, NEW YORKER, July, 20, 2009, at 73, 75; E. ABBOTT, SUGAR: A BITTERSWEET HISTORY (2008).
[23] NESTLE, *supra* note 15, at 26. For some recent, contrary developments see: S. Strom, *Farewell to the Big Feast*, N.Y. TIMES, Feb. 7, 2013, at B1, B2.
[24] Chapter 1, Section V(a): *Looking at the State in a Different Way: New Governance.*

Education is, of course, another means of shaping behavior, of "cultivating conscience."[25]

Educational campaigns certainly can have force. Think of consumption and, in particular, smoking. The relentless public health campaigns combined with the mandatory warnings on packaging (in conjunction with other regulatory efforts) have had a significant effect in alerting consumers to the dangers of tobacco. Anyone in the 2010s who claimed not to know that smoking was addictive and toxic would be reacted to with dismay. But, generally, about 20 percent of adults in Canada and the United States still smoke. Eighty percent have gotten the message and complied with it. But what to do about that other 20 percent?[26]

There are three issues with educational efforts. One is providing information that is accessible and understandable. A second focuses on the role of government and of purveyors of the product: regarding the latter, to what extent should they be required to place messages on their products warning of health implications, etc.? There are some such limited requirements regarding food and beverages. We will discuss two of them: caloric labeling on menus and nutrition labeling on food/drink packaging.

A third issue is the extent to which people actually change their behavior based on relevant information. It's behavioral change that can be the critical test for these educational interventions. It's one thing for public health types to devise clear and snappy ditties to educate people about this or that issue ("don't drink and drive"; "buckle up"; "just say no"; "butt out"; "know your limit—play within it"). It's another for people to be ditty conformists.

Social norms marketing campaigns seeking to discourage college students from excessive use of alcohol, including binge drinking, have had very mixed results. In some instances there is evidence of an increase in drinking, possibly because of an overreliance on such efforts and too little use of traditional policies restricting alcohol on campuses.[27] Three decades ago a review of several government educational campaigns in a variety of areas questioned not only their effectiveness but also the way they deflected attention away from other interventions.[28] The authors suggested that, often, the popularity of such campaigns "rests more on...ideological grounds than on solid empirical evidence supporting their ability to alter consumer behavior."[29]

---

[25] L. STOUT, CULTIVATING CONSCIENCE: HOW GOOD LAWS MAKE GOOD PEOPLE (2011); see discussion of this work in Chapter 1, Section V(b): *Ideas for New Governance: Normativity and Its Offspring.*

[26] BOGART, *supra* note 1, at 127–38.

[27] *Id.* at 40–44.

[28] R. Adler & R. Pittle, *Cajolery or Command: Are Education Campaigns an Adequate Substitute for Regulation?*, 1 Yale . J. of Reg. 159 (1984).

[29] *Id.* at 161.

Proponents of social marketing campaigns suggest a more complex assessment is in order.[30] They begin by underscoring how inadequately funded many of such campaigns are, especially when compared with industry efforts to promote consumption, whether of cigarettes or soda or playing of electronic gaming machines. That said, they claim that educational campaigns can have positive effects when "they are carefully crafted, well-tested, fully funded, highly targeted (in terms of audience and behavior), and sustained over a long period of time."[31]

The public health community has been trying to educate individuals about food—its nutritional value, its calories, etc.—for a very long time. There have been official efforts at nutrition labeling in the United States since 1941.[32] The food pyramid, instructing about food groups and the proportions in which they should be consumed, has also been around for decades. Its updates have sometimes generated controversy even as it has been continuously put before the public as an exhortation to eat well.[33]

But what of the results? Given the clamor about obesity over the last decades, educational campaigns about eating have not had adequate impacts. As we saw in Chapter 2 there have been many factors at play regarding the "obesity epidemic" and the waging of "war" upon it. But, the public health community believes that more can be done. Wansink believes educational efforts focused on specific individuals and their eating habits can lead to changes in consumption.[34] The Institute of Medicine's *Weight of the Nation* report recommends a general campaign to promote good nutrition and physical activity. It suggests the following elements:

- Narrowly targeted audiences
- Narrowly defined goals for behavior change
- Tailored messages
- Several years duration
- Use of multiple media platforms—television, Internet, mobile, etc.
- Support from communities, nongovernmental organizations, and companies

---

[30] INSTITUTE OF MEDICINE, MEASURING PROGRESS IN OBESITY PREVENTION: WORKSHOP REPORT 67–71 (2012).
[31] INSTITUTE OF MEDICINE, ACCELERATING PROGRESS IN OBESITY PREVENTION: SOLVING THE WEIGHT OF THE NATION 181 (2012).
[32] INSTITUTE OF MEDICINE, FRONT-OF-PACKAGE NUTRITION RATING SYSTEMS AND SYMBOLS: PROMOTING HEALTHIER CHOICES Annex "Milestones of Nutrition Labeling" 129 (2012).
[33] NESTLE, *supra* note 15, at 5–9 and 380–81.
[34] B. Wansink, *Turning Mindless Eating into Healthy Eating*, in THE BEHAVIORAL FOUNDATIONS OF PUBLIC POLICY 310 (E. Shafir ed., 2013).

- Sufficient funding to conduct extensive message-testing, secure experts, and purchase advertising in media that are highly rated among target audiences[35]

Such a campaign would be a costly and lengthy experiment. But it should be tried: a big challenge to Big Food.

Now let's look at two initiatives where information to promote healthy eating and drinking is, or could be, specifically mandated by law: menus that post caloric content of selections and nutrition labeling of various food products purchased at retail outlets, particularly front of packaging (FOP) labeling. Again, we'll ask: how effective are they at altering behaviors? And what are the goals sought to be achieved?

B) CALORIC DISCLOSURE ON MENUS

The premise behind requiring disclosure of calories of items on menus is simple: when people are alerted to how many each selection contains they, in the interest of their health, will select the ones with lower amounts. Official reports seem optimistic about such efforts.[36] Does such disclosure work? To a limited extent.

New York City was one of the first to experiment. Since 2008 restaurants and coffee shop chains with over fifteen outlets have had to post the caloric content of various items next to the item's price on menus. The nationwide health care reform legislation the *Patient Protection and Affordable Care Act* requires that by 2013 caloric content be posted for vending machines and for restaurants with twenty or more locations nationwide.[37] There are other efforts underway. For example, in 2011 a voluntary program for caloric labeling was begun in Britain.[38]

A number of studies have examined New York's initiative. The first study came to the conclusion that such requirements had no impact on consumer behavior. The survey compared customers' behavior in low income communities in New York to a sample of consumers in Newark, New Jersey, a city that does not have such labeling. Only about one in seven indicated that they made use of the information. Overall, there was not a significant change in calories bought per customer.[39]

---

[35] INSTITUTE OF MEDICINE, *supra* note 31, at 246. *See also* WHITE HOUSE TASK FORCE ON CHILDHOOD OBESITY REPORT TO THE PRESIDENT, SOLVING THE PROBLEM OF CHILDHOOD OBESITY WITHIN A GENERATION 26–28 (2010). Regarding the sixth bullet, in the text, and community activity, see: INSTITUTE OF MEDICINE, CHALLENGES AND OPPORTUNITIES FOR CHANGE IN FOOD MARKETING TO CHILDREN AND YOUTH: WORKSHOP SUMMARY (2013) at 33-49.

[36] INSTITUTE OF MEDICINE, *supra* note 31, at 259; WHITE HOUSE TASK FORCE, *supra* note 35, at 26.

[37] *Patient Protection and Affordable Care Act* (2010), H.R. 3590, at para. 4205(b)(H).

[38] Babbage, *New York's Calorie Counting*, ECONOMIST, July 28, 2011, at 12.

[39] B. Elbel et al., *Caloric Labeling and Food Choices: A First Look at the Effects on Low-Income People in New York City*, 28 HEALTH AFFAIRS w1110 (2009). A study done in the state

A second study ("the second New York study"), published in 2011, was larger in scope and compared customers' behavior before and after the requirements came into effect.[40] Again, overall, there was no difference in the average of calories purchased. However, there were effects for those who did use the information. Only about one in six said they did so. But those who did purchased 11 percent (or ninety-six) fewer calories; other studies have also found similar reduction in calories purchased.[41]

Of particular interest, in this second study, was that chains that introduced lower calorie menu items tended to have customers who reduced calories purchased. For example, those eating at "Au Bon Pain" with its "Portions" menu reduced calories by 14 percent. Another study, involving a field experiment (the "field experiment") where more healthful options were made easier to order, produced similar results. Of note here, though, is that information about caloric content made little difference to choice; convenience in choosing the low calorie option appeared to be the determining factor.[42]

What do we make of these studies and their results? Caloric labeling seems to have limited influence on what people choose to purchase. Moreover, even for those individuals who did choose items with fewer calories, questions remain. Was the item chosen healthier? A diet soda will have fewer calories than apple juice, but it will not be the healthier option. When items with fewer calories were selected, was there compensation elsewhere? (I had a Diet Coke at the food outlet so I can have a chocolate bar later in the afternoon).

Given the results of the second New York study and the field experiment studies, it may be that making a low calorie selection easy may be at least as important a factor as calorie information. There is some indication in the media that restaurants also believe that low calorie selections have increased their market visibility.[43] The authors of the field experiment underscore this possibility, and in doing so return us to "the nudge" discussed in Chapter 1.[44] A "nudge"

---

of Washington regarding similar legislation yielded similar results: E. Finkelstein, *Mandatory Menu Labeling in One Fast-Food chain in King-County Washington*, 40 Am. J. Prev. Med. 122 (2011). Both studies are cited in T. Dumanovsky et al., *Changes in Energy Content of Lunchtime Purchases from Fast Food Restaurants after Introduction of Calorie Labelling: Cross Sectional Customer Surveys*, 343 Brit. Med. J. d4464 (July 2011) [hereinafter Dumanovsky].

[40] Dumanovsky et al., *supra* note 39.

[41] E. Pulos & K. Leng, *Evaluation of a Voluntary Menu-Labeling Program in Full-Service Restaurants*, 100 Am. J. Pub. Health 1035–39 (2010); B. Bollinger et al., *Calorie Posting in Chain Restaurants*, National Bureau of Economic Research: Working Paper No. 15648 (2010), *available at* www.nber.org/papers/w15648 Both studies cited in Dumanovsky et al., *supra* note 39.

[42] J. Downs et al., *The Psychology of Food Consumption: Strategies for Promoting Healthier Food Choices*, 99(2) Am. Econ. Review Papers and Proceedings 1 (2009); G. Loewenstein, *Confronting Reality: Pitfalls of Calorie Posting*, 93 Am. J. Clinical Nutrition 679 (2011); K. Blumenthal & K.G. Volpp, *Enhancing the Effectiveness of Food Labeling in Restaurants*, 303(6) J Am Med Ass'n 553 (2010).

[43] S. Strom, *supra* note 23.

[44] Chapter 1, Section V(a): *Ideas for New Governance: Normativity and Its Offspring*.

promotes changes in behavior sought to be achieved by "choice architects" without foreclosing options for individuals being "nudged." Promoting such changes in this area may have particular complications.[45] The field experiment suggests that one factor that may be important in these initiatives is to provide easy access to low calorie selection at the same time that caloric information is provided.

But there is a further question that springs off our discussion in Chapter 2.[46] If the purpose of caloric information is just to have people select lower calorie items, this initiative may go nowhere. Those who object to the obsession with weight loss/gain prevention will likely rail at intervention as just another piece of evidence of our collective fixation with weight. How is it ever going to be established that individuals lost weight because of information provided to them? Even if it can be shown that (at most) a minority pay attention to such information and act upon it at the time, can it be demonstrated that they don't compensate and have higher calorie foods/drinks later on? Even if they don't, how can it be shown that reduction of calories at a restaurant leads to weight loss and reduction that is maintained over time?

The results of the studies to date seem to indicate that ease of selection may be more influential to customers' choices. If that is the case, why not spend more time and effort promoting *healthier* selections (many of which may be less caloric). Instead of obsessing about calories, why not devise a labeling system that alerts clients to these choices (featured prominently), in the hope that they will focus on nutrition and not be fixated on calories? Let's turn to such an effort in terms of the labeling on the front of packaging.

C) FRONT OF PACKAGE LABELING

The idea behind front of packaging (FOP) labeling is also simple: give consumers clear, uniform information about nutrients and they will purchase healthier food products. Moreover, as the emphasis on FOP initiatives is on overall nutrition, this form of labeling is not fixated on calories and can place more emphasis on overall healthy food/drink choices. Again, though, there are those two issues that we've raised: providing consumers with information and, then, having them act on it. Although a very good idea, FOP and related labeling has, at best, produced very mixed results. The Institute of Medicine of the National Academies has made recommendations to make FOPs more effective.[47] Time will tell if these recommendations will be implemented and, if so, whether they will have greater impact.

---

[45] T. Marteau et al., CHANGING BEHAVIOR THROUGH STATE INTERVENTION, 337 BRIT. MED. J. a2543 (2008); T. Marteau et al., Judging Nudging: Can Nudging Improve Population Health?, 342 BRIT. MED. J. d228 (2011).
[46] Chapter 2, Section II: What's the Problem?
[47] INSTITUTE OF MEDICINE, *supra* note 32.

Nutrition labeling of food has had a long history and has witnessed many efforts to provide simple, clear, and accurate information to consumers to guide their food/drink purchases.[48] Nutrition facts panels (NFPs) appearing on the side or back of packages were heralded in their time as a breakthrough that would give purchasers nutrient and caloric information in some detail, yet in a fashion that was accessible and straightforward. However, studies have demonstrated that NFPs have had limited effects. Consumers have a difficult time processing the information contained in NFPs, particularly in the midst of busy, large food stores.[49]

In addition, there have been inadequate educational campaigns, mostly due to lack of funding, to promote NFPs and to instruct the public in their use. Of special concern are those with low literacy and numeracy skills, who comprise some 90 million adults in the United States: "Adults with low health literacy skills are less inclined to use nutrition labels and are at greater risk for diet-related health outcomes...[T]he nutrition label is not serving the needs of those who would benefit most from it."[50]

Because of these findings and other factors there have been several experiments in a number of countries with FOPs. The hope is that FOPs, appearing on the front of packages and containing simple symbols indicating nutritional quality, would be more helpful to consumers, who would then respond to their guidance.[51] Moreover, there is support among consumers for such a system.[52] The IOM reviewed a number of studies, field and non-field, examining FOPs' effectiveness in various societies. It concluded that the FOPs, to date, have had only limited impact, especially in actual shopping (field) environments (as opposed to controlled [non-field] settings).[53] One of the most prominent, the traffic light system used in Great Britain (green/yellow/red, with green for foods of highest nutritional content), was found to be among the least effective.[54]

Despite all this, the IOM concluded that a further refined FOP rating system could be effective if labels can "stand out and capture attention in...[a] busy and competitive food package environment."[55] As a result, it recommended a system with the following characteristics:

1. A simple symbol, signal, or one that instantly conveys meaning without written information, percentages, or other nutrition data or statistics;
2. Placement of the symbol in the same location on all food packages;

---

[48] *Id.* at ch.4: "Consumers' Use of Nutrition Information and Product Choices."
[49] *Id.* at 34–35.
[50] *Id.* at 35.
[51] M. Bittman, *My Dream Food Label*, N.Y. TIMES, SUNDAY REVIEW, Oct. 14, 2012, at SR6–7.
[52] INSTITUTE OF MEDICINE, *supra* note 32, at 35.
[53] *Id.* at 44–56 and 59–68.
[54] *Id.* at 45.
[55] *Id.* at 67.

3. A design that maximizes the symbol's visual contrast with existing elements of packaging;
4. Assurance that the symbol is sufficiently prominent in size to compete effectively with other package elements and attract consumer attention; and
5. A complementary campaign that guides consumers to look in a specific location for the specific symbol.[56]

To enhance the effectiveness of this FOP regime the IOM also recommends that promotion, evaluation, and monitoring accompany the implementation. Such efforts should include the techniques of social marketing so that consumers are more aware of these innovations and act upon them.[57]

Whether this system will be implemented and if implemented, whether it will be successful, remains to be seen. The goals are attractive—more so than caloric labeling. FOPs, done right, place the emphasis on nutrition; not exclusively on calories. If effective, FOP could be one element of the regulatory mix moving us away from obsession with weight and toward healthy eating/drinking.

But will this new incarnation of FOPs—should it be implemented—be effective? The IOM's own assessment suggests that nutrition labeling, no matter how it is done, has up to this point had little effect on consumer choice. So history is not on the side of these interventions. The IOM rightly urges a significant and well-funded educational campaign to accompany implementation, something often lacking regarding previous efforts.[58] But its optimistic pointing to social marketing gives pause when it does not mention the instances where this technique has had little positive or even negative impacts.[59] Beyond any of their own frailties FOPs run up against the harsh realities brought about by the limited economic resources of far too many consumers. To its credit the IOM acknowledges such difficult circumstances: "[W]hen food choice is constrained by economic considerations, healthier food choices will likely not receive attention if they are not affordable."[60]

D) CONCLUSIONS

Efforts to educate consumers about calories and nutrition have spanned decades and have involved a variety of innovations. On the whole, the results in terms of shifting food and drink selection have been disappointing. One of

---

[56] *Id.* at 68.
[57] *Id.* at ch. 8: "Promotion, Evaluation, and Monitoring for Front-of-Package Symbol Systems."
[58] *Id.* at 34–35.
[59] *See* notes 27–30 and accompanying text.
[60] INSTITUTE OF MEDICINE, *supra* note 32, at 56.

the latest innovations, posting calories on menus, appears not all that effective. What is more, it may just be adding to the obsession individuals can have with calories as the standard for determining what is to be eaten/drunk rather than an item's nutritional value.

Nutritional labeling efforts start from the right premise: alert the consumer to healthy choices in eating/drinking with calories being but one consideration. Yet, these efforts also have not had nearly the desired impact on consumers and their purchasing habits. The IOM's recommendations for FOPs, including educational campaigns and evaluations for effectiveness, hold promise as part of the regulatory mix promoting healthy eating and active lifestyles. Will they be implemented?

IV. Marketing: The Special Case of Children

A) EFFECTS OF ADVERTISING

The law has long taken the view that children, because they are not fully capable of moral and other judgments, may need special safeguards and even restrictions whether in terms of voting, driving a car, or smoking cigarettes. This concern for the welfare of young people extends to the influence of marketing by the food-and-beverage industry. Children can be a target for such promotional activities for three reasons: they are a "primary market" as they can spend money themselves, they are an "influence market" because they can shape parental purchases, and they are a "future market" because they will become adult consumers.[61]

There are many issues of concern regarding TV advertising targeting kids. Three main ones are: the number of hours of TV watched by many children, the endless repetition of commercials, and the lack of ability of young people to distinguish marketing from program content.[62] Bombardment of children by advertising has generally risen over the years. Food commercials are overwhelming for those of dubious nutritional value. A mid-1990s' study did not find any commercials for fruits, vegetables, bread, or fish.[63] Nestle reviewed many studies of how TV advertising affects children and other factors, concluding: "Marketers will do whatever they can to encourage even the youngest children to ask for advertised products in the hope of enticing young people to become lifetime consumers."[64]

---

[61] INSTITUTE OF MEDICINE, FOOD MARKETING TO CHILDREN AND YOUTH: THREAT OR OPPORTUNITY? 153–54 (2006); M. Mello, *Federal Trade Commission Regulation of Food Advertising to Children: Possibilities for a Reinvigorated Role*, 35(2) J. HEALTH POL. POL'Y. & LAW 227, 232 (2010).

[62] NESTLE, *supra* note 15, at 180.

[63] *Id.* at 181–82.

[64] *Id.* at 195.

Children are inundated with promotion of foods and drinks of dubious nutritional value as the industry insinuates itself into their lives. Television commercials and programs blend together so that their messages seem to be one. A senior marketing executive has astutely (and ominously) observed: "It isn't enough to just advertise...You've got to become part of...[children's] lives."[65]

In the United States food-and-beverage companies spend millions each year to promote their products. Whatever other restrictions there should be on such marketing, a fundamental requirement is surely that claims made in promotions be accurate. Public officials try to hold the food-and-beverage industry to that basic standard. For example, a company's claim that its sugary cereal improved child attentiveness was successfully challenged by the U.S. Federal Trade Commission on the grounds of false advertising.[66] There needs to be even more such scrutiny supported by necessary resources and political and civic backing.

Companies use a wide range of marketing tools, including broadcast, print, and Internet advertisements; product packaging and labeling; point of purchase displays; transmissions to personal digital devices; giveaway items; sponsorship of entertainment events, sports teams, and athletes; product placement; character licensing; etc. Nearly 60 percent of total expenditures on youth marketing is spent on products that are high in calories and saturated fat such as carbonated beverages, fast food, candy, and baked goods. Much of youth advertising is still spent on television, print, and radio advertising.[67] At the same time the power of the Internet and digital media is looming. We'll discuss the influence of cyberspace momentarily.[68]

Those advocating regulation of advertising to children make three main assertions. First, there is strong evidence of the association between marketing of food and drinks and the consumption pattern of children. Such association can be a significant contributing factor to obesity. Second, restricting such advertising is justified because it exploits the development of children's cognitive abilities and capacity for judgment. Third, parents have only limited power to counteract the substantial influences of such marketing upon their kids.[69]

The food-and-beverage industry contests any close connection between advertising and children's consumption. Many of those concerned with the welfare of kids say otherwise: "There is broad consensus among child health

---

[65] OLIVER, *supra* note 8, at 167, citing K. BROWNELL & K.HORGEN, FOOD FIGHT: THE INSIDE STORY OF THE FOOD INDUSTRY, AMERICA'S OBESITY CRISIS, AND WHAT WE CAN DO ABOUT IT 102 (2003).

[66] INSTITUTE OF MEDICINE, FOR THE PUBLIC'S HEALTH: REVITALIZING LAW AND POLICY TO MEET NEW CHALLENGES 61–64 (2011); *See* also Chapter 4, Section VI: Noted but Not Examined.

[67] Mello, *supra* note 61, at 228 and the sources cited.

[68] *See* Section IV(b)(3): The Challenges of the Internet and Digital Media.

[69] Mello, *supra* note 61, at 232.

experts that the food environment generally and food marketing in particular are major contributors to childhood obesity."[70]

In 2006 the Institute of Medicine in the United States released a report on food marketing.[71] The relevant committee reviewed 123 studies done over three decades on the relationship between exposure to food advertising and children's diet and related issues. The Report concluded:

- There is strong evidence that television advertising influences the food preference and purchase requests of children aged two to eleven.
- Children's purchasing requests are often successful, creating a causal link from food advertising to food intake.
- There is moderate evidence that television advertising affects the beliefs of children aged two to eleven about the healthfulness of particular foods.
- There is strong evidence that television viewing is associated with adiposity in children and adolescents.
- Generally, children aged eight and younger do not effectively understand the persuasive intent of advertising, and children aged four and younger cannot consistently discriminate television programming from advertisements.[72]

B) ATTEMPTS TO REGULATE MARKETING TO CHILDREN

1. Self-Regulation

Self-regulation can embody the "new governance" we discussed in Chapter 1.[73] Direct "command and control" by the heavy hand of the state recedes. Those most directly affected by policy goals can determine how they, themselves, will meet those objectives. The costs of such efforts are borne by those involved with such self-regulation; the state is freed of such expenses. Let's look at the food-and-beverage industry and its promotions as a case study regarding these lofty claims with regard to marketing directed at young people.

The industry has long taken the position that any controls on children's advertising are best left to it. In recent years the industry, in several countries, has taken

---

[70] Mello, *supra* note 61, at 230.
[71] INSTITUTE OF MEDICINE, *supra* note 61.
[72] *Id.* at 257–98 as summarized in Mello, *supra* note 61, at 231–32. *See also* R. Watts, *Protecting Children from Unhealthy Food Marketing*, British Heart Foundation and Children's Food Campaign (2007), available at http://www.childrensfoodcampaign.net/BHFnonbroadcastreport.pdf; and JOLLY, *supra* note 3, at 8–12.
[73] Chapter 1: Section V(a): Looking at the State in a Different Way: New Governance; *see also* Section V(b) Ideas for New Governance: Normativity and Its Offspring.

such measures.[74] There have been a number of such developments in the United States.[75] Let's look at those initiatives and the results they have produced.

In America a number of major media companies, such as Disney, have limited their licensing, including characters, to curtail the promotion of unhealthy foods. In 2006, the Children's Food and Beverage Advertising Initiative (CFBAI) was launched by the Council of Better Business Bureaus and the National Advertising Council. As of 2010, major companies pledged not to advertise to children under twelve at all, and another eleven had adopted minimum nutritional standards for the types of foods that they will advertise to such children.[76] The initiative also addresses licensed characters, movie tie-ins, use of celebrities to promote products, and so forth. These companies have also agreed to other restrictions such as limiting products depicted in interactive games.

There has also been activity by the Children's Advertising Review Unit (CARU), another industry organization. CARU's guidelines do not restrict advertising but are directed at unfair and deceptive practices. In 2006 and 2009 its guidelines were revised to further respond to unfair marketing; for example, mealtime depictions of food should be nutritionally balanced. There have also been other initiatives such as one involving large food manufacturers and distributors in respect of the nutrition formulation of various products.[77]

Such efforts are significant. Nonetheless, they are limited and subject to a number of criticisms.[78] For example, CARU's guidelines do not address the impact of the volume of advertising and, in any event, its efforts have not been subject to external review. CFBAI efforts do involve significant restraints on the types of products that can be advertised to children, and to that extent are an improvement on CARU's efforts. However, many companies have not agreed to adhere to CFBAI's standards. Moreover, the constraints themselves contain important limitations. For instance, pledging companies are still free to determine what constitutes advertising directed to kids under twelve and what are "healthier dietary choice" products. Mello reviewed such initiatives in 2010, and summarized the shortcomings: "the focus on advertising practices for the kinds of products that may be advertised, the inconsistent adherence of different companies to the articulated advertising standards, and the paucity of strong enforcement mechanisms."[79]

---

[74] Regarding Australia: see JOLLY, supra note 3, at 26–28 and Canada: see id., at 38; B. Jeffery, *The Supreme Court of Canada's Appraisal of the 1980 Ban on Advertising to Children in Quebec: Implications for Misleading Advertising Elsewhere*, 39 LOYOLA L.A. LAW REV. 237, 245–53 (2006); and M. Potvin Kent et al., *Self-Regulation by Industry of Food Marketing Is Having Little Impact during Children's Preferred Television*, 6 INT'L J. PEDIATRIC OBESITY 401–08 (2011).

[75] Mello, supra note 61, at 233–36.

[76] WHITE HOUSE TASK FORCE, supra note 35, at 29.

[77] INSTITUTE OF MEDICINE, supra note 31, at 254. For efforts by the Walt Disney Company and others, see INSTITUTE OF MEDICINE, CHANGE IN FOOD MARKETING, supra note 35, at 23-33. But see also: B. Barnes and B. Stelter, *Nickelodeon Resists Critics of Food Ads* N.Y. TIMES, June 19, 2013, B1, B5.

[78] Mello, supra note 61, at 235–36; S. Clifford, *A Fine Line When Ads and Children Mix*, N.Y. TIMES, Feb. 15, 2010, at B4.

[79] Mello, supra note 61, at 236.

In 2011 the Federal Trade Commission released the voluntary nutrition principles of the federal Interagency Working Group on Food Marketed to Children.[80] These efforts were rejected by the food-and-beverage industry and the U.S. Chamber of Commerce. The efforts were opposed because of the alleged negative impacts on jobs, interference with First Amendment rights, and limits they would impose on marketing of healthy foods (a claim specifically refuted by others' analysis).

Self-regulation of promotion: an embodiment of the "new governance" or decorative statements while the industry basically continues its tried-and-true ways of peddling its wares? We'll return to that question at the end of this chapter.

2. Legislative Initiatives

i. No Tax Deductions and No Toys

One way to discourage behavior is through the tax system. We'll come to a thorough exploration of that strategy when we discuss taxes on junk food.[81] Thus far there has been little interest in using the tax system to police advertising to children. A proposal was made in the United States in 2009 that would prohibit a tax deduction for advertising and marketing directed at children.[82] However, it has not been enacted, and does not appear to be being pursued.

Another way to discourage efforts directed at children is to target particular marketing techniques of the food-and-beverage industry. Around 2010, some municipalities in the United States began focusing on McDonald's, especially on one of its promotional techniques: including toys with "Happy Meals." To some child advocates Happy Meals typify the luring of kids into a life of junk food. McDonald's has long been the purveyor of fast food that some love to hate. From lawsuits over being scalded by excessively hot coffee to the documentary *Super Size Me*, McDonald's has been depicted as representing so much of what is wrong with the fast food industry.[83] Its targeting of children may cause the most ire. As many as 37 percent of children in the United States put McDonald's at the top of fast food chains (nearly four times as many as those

---

[80] Interagency Working Group on Food Marketed to Children, *Interagency Working Group on Food Marketed to Children*, preliminary proposed nutrition principles to guide industry self-regulatory efforts: Request for comments 2011, *available at* http://www.ftc.gov/os/2011/04/110428foodmarketproposedguide.pdf.

[81] Chapter 6, Section III: Junk Food and Beverage Taxes.

[82] Representative Dennis Kucinich, HR 4310—To amend the Internal Revenue Code of 1985 to protect children's health by denying any deduction for advertising and marketing directed at children to promote the consumption of food at fast food restaurants or of food of poor nutritional quality: referred to U.S. House of Representatives Committee in December 2009. *See also* JOLLY, *supra* note 3, 40.

[83] D. McGinn, *San Francisco Toy Ban Takes the "Happy" out of Happy Meals*, GLOBE & MAIL, Nov. 3, 2010, *available at* http://www.theglobeandmail.com/life/health-and-fitness/san-francisco-toy-ban-takes-the-happy-out-of-happy-meals/article1216457/.

favoring the second-place Subway). As Roy Bergold, a former McDonald's head of advertising, put it: "Go after kids."[84]

Enter the Happy Meal. A cheeseburger with fries and soda, and the ever-present toy, contains 640 calories, more than half the U.S. Department of Agriculture daily allowance for a sedentary child of four to eight years. True, McDonald's has added healthier choices. But a study by the Center for Science in the Public Interest of forty-four outlets found that French fries were served with 93 percent of the orders.[85]

Incensed by this manipulation of children, a few cities have taken action. Litigation was also filed by the Centre for Science in the Public Interest over the use of toys as bait for children's appetites. In November 2010, the San Francisco Board of Supervisors passed a measure requiring that meals sold with toys meet a minimum standard of nutrition; Santa Clara had passed a similar measure in May of that year.

Advocates of these measures praised them in ringing tones. A sponsor of the San Francisco initiative declared: "This is a tremendous victory for our children's health." Opponents were just as dramatic in their denunciation. A McDonald's spokeswomen said: "We are extremely disappointed with this decision. It's not what our customers want, nor is it something they asked for."[86] Beyond denunciation, the fast food industry was the beneficiary of legal activism of another sort. Some lawmakers in the more junk-friendly Florida and Arizona were promoting, as of March 2011, a ban on such bans. One lawmaker typified the reaction: "Government needs to stay out of the way of free enterprise."[87]

It is far from clear where such bans are headed. Nor, is it apparent what, if any, effects they will have. They could discourage at least some children and their parents from ordering (not so) Happy Meals. Or, they might represent another occasion for extreme sets of opinions while the larger issues raised by advertising to children are mostly ignored. Let's turn to some experiments that have attempted to address those central questions and to tackle advertising directed at children on a more comprehensive basis.

---

[84] Editorial, *Not So Happy Meals*, N.Y. TIMES, Dec. 20, 2010, at A28.
[85] *Id.*, citing Center for Science in the Public Interest, Kids' Meals: Obesity on the Menu, Aug. 2008, *available at* http://cspinet.org/new/pdf/kidsmeals-report.pdf.
[86] McGinn, *supra* note 83 (both quotes).
[87] W. Leung, *Ban Backlash: US Politicians to Prohibit Bans on Happy Meal Toys*, GLOBE & MAIL, Mar. 21, 2011, *available at* http://www.theglobeandmail.com/life/the-hot-button/ban-backlash-us-politicians-to-prohibit-bans-on-happy-meal-toys/article612710/.

ii. Restricting Advertising

[one] Generally

The United States, since 1990, has limited commercial time during any hour of children's programming to twelve minutes on weekdays and ten minutes and thirty seconds on weekends.[88] Regulations also require a buffer between ads and programs.[89] A number of other countries, including the United Kingdom, Sweden, Finland, and Norway have prohibited or significantly restricted advertising to children. The available evidence suggests mixed results. It also indicates the difficulty of assessing the effectiveness of any one intervention when there are so many factors at play.

Sweden banned television and radio advertising to children in 1991. However, because of a series of developments, such advertisements on satellite channels from other countries are not banned. Yet obesity rates have also risen since the introduction of the ban. Those supporting the restrictions fault the presence of television advertising from other countries. Those opposing such constraints point to the increased levels of fatness to argue that they are ineffective.[90]

Norway banned television advertisements to children twelve and younger in 1992. Between 1975 and 1995, it also reversed a general trend to high-fat diets. However, this shift was accompanied by a number of interventions, including food subsidies, price manipulation, retail regulation, and clear nutrition labeling. Thus, it is difficult to say what the impact of the ban on advertising actually was.[91]

Quebec, the predominantly French-speaking province in Canada, has had a ban on advertising to children in specified circumstances for over three decades—long enough to develop a substantial track record. What's more, the effects of the ban have been rigorously evaluated. Let's look at the Quebec experience in some detail.

[two] Quebec

A. The Experiment and Its Constitutional Validity

A ban on advertising to children thirteen and under has been in effect in Quebec since 1980.[92] To determine whether an advertisement is directed at such children, the context of any promotion is assessed. Relevant factors in such evaluations

---

[88] Children's Television Act (1990), Pub. L. 101-437, HR 1677, s 303.

[89] M. Richtel, *In Online Games, a Path to Young Consumers*, N.Y. TIMES, Apr. 21, 2011, at A1, A15.

[90] JOLLY, *supra* note 3, at 36–37.

[91] *Id.* at 37. *See also* C Hawkes, *Marketing Food to Children: The Global Regulatory Environment*, WHO, 2004, *available at* http://whqlibdoc.who.int/publications/2004/9241591579.pdf (last viewed Oct. 12, 2010).

[92] Office de la protection du consummateur, Loi sur la protection du consommatuer, Quebec, Gouvernement du Quebec, 1978; Consumer Protection Act, RSQ. 2012, ch. P.40.1, ss 248-249 but also ss 87-91. For other developments *see*: INSTITUTE OF MEDICINE, CHANGE IN FOOD MARKETING, supra note 35, at 45-47.

include: the nature and intended purpose of the goods advertised, the manner of presenting such advertisement, and the time and place it is shown.[93]

During television programs where children comprise more than 15 percent of the audience, targeting children is not permitted. That said, the law does not ban all advertisements to children. Noncommercial messages are permitted even when children are more than 15 percent of the audience. So too are commercial ones where children are not targeted, such as commercials for cars. Similarly, advertising focused on children can be broadcast but only during programs primarily viewed by adults.

The legislation was attacked as an infringement on free speech. That assault was unsuccessful. The validity of the act was upheld by the Supreme Court of Canada in 1989.[94] Concerns about free speech are often a brake on interventions to regulate advertising, particularly regarding consumption, and especially in the United States.[95] Thus, the Supreme Court of Canada's rebuffing of such attacks and its reasoning in doing so are significant. The importance of the decision is underscored because of its reliance on findings by agencies in the United States regarding the impact of advertising and marketing to children. Such conclusions might not be sufficient to be a basis for constitutional validity, should similar legislation be enacted in the United States, in the view of American courts.

Based on other relevant decisions the Court had to decide whether the legislation in question was responding to pressing and substantial issues and whether: (1) the act was rationally connected with those objectives; (2) it only minimally impaired the right to freedom of expression; and if so (3) the impairment was in proportion to the objectives of the legislation.[96] In deciding that all tests of constitutional validity regarding free speech were met, the Court relied on the findings of a 1981 Federal Trade Commission report on advertising to children.[97]

After reviewing this report that Court observed that it "provides a sound basis on which to conclude that television advertising directed at young children is *per se* manipulative. Such advertising aims to promote products by convincing those who will always believe."[98] In terms of minimal impairment the Court also relied on the report to justify the legislation's prohibition: "Because the Report found that children are not equipped to identify the persuasive intent of advertising, content regulation could not address the problem."[99]

---

[93] *Id.*, s 249.
[94] Attorney General of Quebec v. Irwin Toy Ltd. [1989] 1 SCR 927, 988-992, paras. 71–76 (QL).
[95] Mello, *supra* note 61, at 257–59.
[96] *Irwin Toy*, *supra* note 94, at 992–97; R v. Oakes [1986] 1 SCR 103.
[97] FEDERAL TRADE COMMISSION, FINAL STAFF REPORT AND RECOMMENDATION IN THE MATTER OF CHILDREN'S ADVERTISING, Fed. Reg 48, 710, 48, 712 (Oct. 2, 1981).
[98] *Irwin Toy*, *supra* note 94, at 989.
[99] *Id.* at 995–96.

B. The Impact of the Ban

There have been three studies of the effectiveness of the prohibition on advertising to children in Quebec. The findings vary but that is, in part, because they are measuring different effects. Overall they do indicate that the legislation has been effective in reducing the consumption of calorically dense foods by Francophone children in Quebec. The last study we will discuss used a methodology that led the authors to conclude that the restrictions on advertising were directly associated with Francophone children in that province eating significantly less junk food.

Two preliminary points should be noted. First, because of constitutional and other constraints the ban primarily applies to French-language television originating in Quebec. Second, Quebec is predominately French speaking but does have both a Francophone (FP) and Anglophone (AP) population. French programming originating in Quebec would be mostly watched by FPs. At the same time the AP segment has access to English-language television from the United States, other provinces in Canada, etc.

A 1990 study measured brand recognition among FPs and APs to assess the effectiveness of the ban.[100] AP children did have a stronger toy and cereal brand recognition. However, the study made no attempts to assess effects on consumption or to compare Quebec children with children in other provinces (where there are no such comparable bans).

A 2010 study did content analysis of television viewing by AP and FP children in Quebec and English children in Ontario.[101] The effects of such viewing on the various groups will be discussed momentarily. One finding of the study suggests that there may be significant violations of the ban. As much as 30 percent of French language programming may contain advertising that targets children. The authors suggest this level of noncompliance may be because of weakness in enforcement, especially because the system depends on the filing of complaints instead of systematic monitoring by responsible officials.[102]

In any event, the study found that overall the content of advertising watched by FP children was significantly different than both AP groups. Fun and the appearance of media characters were used significantly less frequently, and there were fewer beverage/food contests, and less sponsorship announcements.[103]

However, as the authors of this study point out, the differences just described do not tell us what, if any, are the effects on consumption by these three groups

---

[100] M. Goldberg, *A Quasi-Experiment Assessing the Effectiveness of TV Advertising Directed to Children*, 27(4) J. MKTG. RESEARCH 445–54 (1990).

[101] M. Potvin Kent et al., *Food Marketing on Children's Television in Two Different Policy Environments*, 6(2-2) INT'L J. PEDIATRIC OBESITY e433-e441 (2011).

[102] *Id.* at 437, *but compare* T. Dhar & K. Baylis, Fast-Food Consumption and the Ban on Advertising Targeting Children: The Quebec Experience, 48(5) J. MKTG. RESEARCH 799, 801 (2011).

[103] Potvin Kent, *supra* note 101, at 437 and 439.

of children. The final study sheds light on differences in consumption patterns.[104] This study was even more sophisticated as it added both French- and English-speaking groups in Ontario and also households without children in both provinces as control groups for FP and AP children in Quebec. The study examined expenditure on fast food for the various groups.

It found that the ban reduced fast food expenditures by something like 17 million fewer such meals eaten per year.[105] Francophone households were significantly less likely to purchase fast food if they lived in Quebec rather than Ontario and, on average, they spent substantially less.[106] (For AP households with children there were no significant differences between Ontario and Quebec. For AP and FP households without children there was an insignificant difference both in terms of purchase occurrence and the amount spent.[107]) The study acknowledges that these findings do not shed light on health outcomes for the various groups because of these differences in consumption patterns of fast food meals—issues they intend to pursue.[108] The study also questions the continuing effectiveness of the ban directed at television as children, including Francophone youth, as they spend more time using video games, computers and the Internet.[109]

That said, these findings are significant regarding the capacity of a single legal intervention to push toward healthier eating and drinking. But what other jurisdictions will be willing to take such measures? How effective can such measures be as various information technologies become more accessible and cyberspace proliferates?

3. The Challenges of the Internet and Digital Media

i. Untameable Cyberspace?

The Internet is not governed by a central authority at least in conventional ways.[110] The Net grew out of public funding and academic research. No central gatekeeper guards access to it. Anyone can use its protocols; there is no membership requirement. No one owns it: "[n]ot a single line of computer code which underpins the [N]et is proprietary; and nobody who contributed to its development has ever made a cent from intellectual property rights in it."[111]

---

[104] Dhar & Baylis, *supra* note 102.
[105] *Id.* at 810.
[106] *Id.*
[107] *Id.*
[108] *Id.* at 811.
[109] *Id.*
[110] This section is based on BOGART, *supra* note 1, at 273–76.
[111] J. NAUGHTON, A BRIEF HISTORY OF THE FUTURE: THE ORIGINS OF THE INTERNET xii (1999).

Still the World Wide Web is not a lawless land.[112] True the law may have effects that differ to an important extent.[113] Nonetheless, in the first instance, "real" law extends to activities online. Trafficking in child prostitutes is not immunized because it is done on the Web. A sales transaction on the Net attracts applicable taxes. There may be complications caused by the virtual world such as determining jurisdiction of courts and problems with giving effect to judgments.[114] These complexities may require special responses, such as particular legislative provisions and international action.[115] That said, similar issues can arise in the real world as well.

Yet characteristics of the Internet give rise to questions about enforceability of any regulation. First, intrinsic to the Internet is its ability to transcend borders: thus Finland can scarcely dictate what is available in Australia. Some suggest that individual nations should not attempt to police this unbordered space: "[Governments cannot] credibly claim a right to regulate the Net based on supposed local harms caused by activities that originate outside their borders and that travel electronically to many different nations."[116] Second, regulation has traditionally differentiated between public and private communications. Yet the Internet is both a private conduit, for messages between individuals, and a public one.[117]

Individual governments may still be critical in terms of the control of the Net.[118] There is an "arms race between geography-specifying and geography-defeating technologies."[119] Cyberspace may seem to be a borderless world. But there are also counter indications. A major study concluded that there is a global trend of increasing government filtering of the Net: the number of countries engaging in such activity, the variety of sites limited by governments, and the sophisticated methods employed to make such blocks effective.[120]

---

[112] *Developments in the Law: The Law of Cyberspace*, 112 Harv. L. Rev. 1574 (1999); J. Boyle, *Foucault in Cyberspace: Surveillance, Sovereignty, and Hard-Wired Censors* (1997), *available at* http://law.duke.edu/boylesite/foucault.htm.

[113] L. Lessig, *The Law of the Horse: What Cyberlaw Might Teach*, 113(2) Harv. L. Rev. 501 (1999), challenging the assertion that analyzing the "law of cyberspace" as something separate from other law causes confusion regarding activities involving the Net: *see* F. Easterbrook, *Cyberspace and the Law of the Horse*, 1996 U. Chi. Legal Forum 207 (1996).

[114] M. Geist, *Internet Jurisdiction: The Shifting Adjudicatory Approach*, 3 Isuma 1, 87 (Spring 2002); M. Richtel, *Courts Are Split on Internet Bans—Some Judges Say Cybercrime Justifies Limits on Convicts*, N.Y Times, Jan. 21, 2003, at A1, C2.

[115] Government of Canada, *Illegal and Offensive Content on the Internet* (Feb. 2001), *available at* http://publications.gc.ca/collections/Collection/C2-532-2000E.pdf.

[116] D. Johnson & D. Post, *Law and Borders—The Rise of Law in Cyberspace, Symposium: Surveying Law and Borders*, 48 Stan. L. Rev. 1367, 1390 (1996).

[117] Bogart, *supra* note 1, at 275.

[118] J. Goldsmith & T.Wu, Who Controls the Internet?: Illusions of a Borderless World (2006, 2008).

[119] *Id.* at x.

[120] *Id.* at viii, citing R. Deibert et al., Access Denied: The Practice and Policy of Global Internet Filtering (2008).

Issues regarding the regulation of the Internet and the effectiveness of such laws loom large in several areas regarding consumption. Gambling, and most especially problem gambling, gives rise to many such issues. The laws of the real world reach the virtual one in limited ways. Meanwhile the very activity that is regulated in the former—wagering—proceeds apace in the latter with few safeguards.[121] Cyberspace is also increasingly being used to market food and drink. Again, promotions directed at children are of particular concern.

ii. Children and Advergames

The food-and-beverage industry has taken advantage of the Internet and forms of digital media and their freewheeling ways to aggressively promote its products. Kids are often targeted.[122] Many of the restrictions that apply to television, the traditional medium of choice for that industry, are not applicable to cyberspace. In addition, jurisdictions, such as Quebec, which have imposed stringent restrictions may see their efforts undermined by the borderless Internet: a webpage from a U.S. food company is as accessible in Montreal as it is in Boston.

The food-and-beverage industry has been quick to exploit young people's increasing use of the Internet and other digital media to peddle its products.[123] Such child-focused promotions appear on commercial websites, in terms of third-party Internet advertising (banner advertising on other companies' websites), online videos, and social media. By 2006 U.S. food-and-beverage companies spent $76.6 million annually on Internet advertising that targeted kids and adolescents.[124]

A favorite ploy of the industry is advergames: online activities using fun to promote a brand, increasing its exposure and positive associations with it.[125] According to one study, in 2009 companies spent about $676 million producing these enticements.[126] The majority of food and beverages promoted in the advergames studied contained high levels of sugar, sodium, and/or fat; almost three quarters involved candy, soft drinks, etc. Only 3 percent had information about nutrition or health.[127]

---

[121] BOGART, supra note 1, at 273–86.

[122] J. Chester & K. Montgomery, *Interactive Food & Beverage Marketing: Targeting Adolescents in the Digital Age*, 45 J. ADOLESCENT HEALTH S18 (2009), available at http://digitalads.org/documents/PIIS1054139X09001499.pdf.

[123] P. Klass, *Endless Barrage of Hard Sell*, N.Y. TIMES, Feb. 12, 2013, at D4.

[124] Federal Trade Commission, *Marketing Food to Children and Adolescents: A Review of Industry Expenditures, Activities, and Self-Regulation* (2008), available at http://www.ftc.gov/os/2008/07/P064504foodmktingreport.pdf.

[125] Richtel, supra note 89.

[126] M. Lee et al., *Playing with Food: Content Analysis of Food Advergames*, 43(1) J CONSUMER AFFAIRS 129–54, 130 (2009).

[127] Id. at 129.

Adults who play advergames demonstrated increased positive brand attitudes and recall for the featured product.[128] The effects on children appear to be even greater. Studies suggest that up to 1.2 million children visit such sites every month and spend up to an hour on each site. Such sites mostly promote candy, high-sugar cereals, and fast food. After playing advergames children tended to consume nutritionally poor foods and fewer fruits and vegetables. Children who repeatedly play advergames appear to be most influenced by them.[129]

iii. Conclusions

The virtual world raises even more challenges than does the real one in terms of marketing to children. Based on the studies just described, the CFBAI pledges (discussed above) do not appear to be a restraint on such marketing techniques.[130] First, those conditions apply to "advertising primarily directed to children under 12"; promotions to audiences composed of 35 percent or higher of such children. That definition is often meaningless in terms of the Internet; the percentage of children in the studies was never greater than 34.5 percent. Second, though the product examined in the studies' experiment promoted a "better for you" alternative, that activity actually increased unhealthy snacking by the children who participated. That finding buttresses concerns that promoting somewhat less unhealthy food in advertising targeting children will not lessen the negative impact of such marketing techniques. As a result, one set of authors argues that advergames should be considered, by definition, as advertising directed to children. Thus, they would be subject to similar restraints as licensed characters.[131]

In the United States, self-regulation and agencies such as the Federal Communications Commission and the Federal Trade Commission, especially if its jurisdiction is extended to cover a range of issues affecting children, have much to do to restrain promotions to kids.[132] Whether there is the civic and political will to draw such boundaries is very much a question. Meanwhile the freewheeling ways of cyberspace and ready access to it by children everywhere pose a further threat to efforts in other jurisdictions, such as Quebec, to blunt the effects of such promotions. For children whose native tongue is not English, the widespread use of that language in the virtual world may be something of a brake. But for how long, as English becomes the common day-to-day language

---

[128] J. Harris et al., *US Food Company Branded Advergames on the Internet: Children's Exposure and Effects on Snack Consumption*, 6(1) J. CHILDREN & MEDIA 51, 52 (2012).
[129] *Id.* at 55, 63–64.
[130] *Infra* Section VI(b)(i) Self-Regulation; the studies are found in Harris, *supra* note 128, at 64 for points discussed in text.
[131] Harris, *supra* note 128, at 64.
[132] WHITE HOUSE TASK FORCE, *supra* note 35, at 31–33.

in so many spheres? The unbounded Internet may pay only little heed to various societies' efforts to safeguard children.

V. Conclusion

Educational campaigns, calories on menus, front of package labeling, forbidding toy giveaways with children's meals, restricting of advertising, especially to young people, either through self-regulation or legislation: all these have been tried. With what impact? Except for the instance of Quebec it's difficult to say.

General educational campaigns promoting healthy eating and drinking (and physical exercise) have, to date, been largely ineffective. The IOM proposes an ambitious campaign and suggests essential elements, including a significant period of time and substantial funding: a worthy experiment that should be tried.[133] Caloric labeling appears to have limited impact on what people choose. It may also be objectionable in the way it emphasizes weight rather than health.[134] Nutritional labeling efforts are preferable because they underscore healthy eating/drinking rather than calorie counting. Yet they, too, have not had anywhere near the desired effect. The IOM recommendations have potential, and they should be tried.[135] But will they be implemented?

Restriction of advertising is riven with controversy, particular in the United States. In the last decade there have been interesting initiatives regarding self-regulation. However, they have done little to curb promotion of unhealthy food and beverages, on the one hand, and to promote nutritious foods and drinks, on the other.[136] Meanwhile the Internet and other digital media threaten to undermine regulatory efforts even further.[137] Quebec and its banning of advertising to children appears to have had tangible success in curbing the consumption of junk food among children affected by the ban.[138] But how many jurisdictions are willing to take this drastic measure? For how long would any such measures be effective as unbounded cyperspace gives access to children of all jurisdictions to the aggressive promotions campaigns peddling all manner of unhealthy products?

The IOM's *Weight of the Nation* contains an excellent discussion of the negative impacts of advertising to children. Yet it concludes with a lackluster prescription, claiming effects scarcely supported by evidence it cites: "Implementing

---

[133] *Supra* Section III(a): Educating About Nutritious Eating and Drinking?
[134] *Supra*, Section III(b): Caloric Disclosure on Menus.
[135] *Supra*, Section III(c): Front of Package Labeling.
[136] *Supra*, Section IV(b)(1) Self-Regulation
[137] *Supra*, Section IV(b)(3): The Challenges of the Internet and Digital Media.
[138] *Supra*, Section IV(b)(2)(ii)[two] Quebec.

a common set of guidelines that includes all forms of marketing and extending [those] guidelines to the age of 17 will accelerate reductions in the consumption of nutrients that are currently overconsumed relative to the 2010 Dietary Guidelines for Americans and may increase the consumption of nutrients that support a healthy diet and are currently underconsumed."[139] Is this the best the Republic can do?

---

[139] INSTITUTE OF MEDICINE, *supra* note 31, at 255.

{6}

Fiscal Interventions: Fat Taxes and Subsidies

I. Introduction

Government can have an enormous influence on society through fiscal policy. Levying taxes and spending money can shape issues from child care to pensions, from social assistance to research and development. But these powers can be controversial from a number of perspectives, the more so in this age of cash-starved governments and disgruntled citizens who pay the levies.

Fiscal policy has been a focus for health advocates for some time. As the battle against obesity has intensified, so too has interest in ways that taxes and the spending power (most notably as subsidies) might be used to promote healthier eating/drinking and active lifestyles. The latter could include tax deductions for athletic club memberships, provision of exercise facilities for employees, government grants to build community recreational facilities, underwriting the cost of amateur sports, etc. The potential to promote physical activity has not been as developed as it could be. That said, in the next chapter we will examine a Canadian experiment using tax credits to promote children's physical activity.[1]

In contrast, ideas for using the taxing and spending power to promote healthy eating/drinking are revving up. Several innovative suggestions are being discussed. Two stand out: the first focuses on taxing nonnutritious foods in order to suppress consumption, a classic example of *permit but discourage*.[2] A particular target for these levies are sugar-sweetened beverages (SSBs), basically soda. There are significant issues regarding the effectiveness of such taxes and, in any event, their acceptability with consumers.

The second focuses on subsidies: incentives to shape behavior. At the forefront are two very different kinds. One involves a reordering of farm policy

---

[1] Chapter 7, Section V(b)(5)[iii]: CFTC.
[2] Chapter 1, Section IV: Consumption Encounters Law: *Permit but Discourage*.

so that agricultural producers are encouraged to produce more nutritious foods such as fruits and vegetables. Another focuses on poor individuals and families to provide incentives to purchase healthy foods and beverages. A pilot program in America run through SNAP (Supplementary Nutrition Assistance Program) holds much promise. Yet, for reasons we'll discuss, the more effective these kinds of subsidies are, the more costly they are. Such additional demands on SNAP resources are being made alongside threats to cut its overall budget.

As with other interventions, claims are asserted about the power of taxes and subsidies to bring about weight loss. There is scant evidence that they can do so in terms of permanent and significant shedding of pounds. Properly designed and implemented, they may help individuals to be healthier. This more realistic goal should be kept at the forefront of efforts to utilize fiscal policies.

II. Taxes and Consumption

A) POLICY ARGUMENTS

"For generations, when we believe something is bad for the population but not so bad that it should be outlawed, we tax it."

– Danish official commenting on that country's 2011 fat tax[3]

Taxation has many uses as a tool of policy making. Taxes can be employed to provide incentives for and to impose disincentives upon a myriad of activities: investing in certain equities, saving for retirement, supporting the rearing of children, and so forth. The progressive system of taxation itself reflects notions of equity as appropriate in achieving societal goals: those who earn more pay proportionately more tax.

Excise taxes are especially relevant in regulating consumption. Generally speaking these taxes are imposed upon specific goods and services (as opposed to, say, retail sales taxes that apply generally to all goods and services sold). Excise taxes can have several objectives: one is to discourage consumption.[4] Because of their targeted nature, these taxes can be levied on almost anything

---

[3] M. Bittman, *How about a Little Danish?*, N.Y. TIMES. Oct. 4, 2011, available at http://opinionator.blogs.nytimes.com/2011/10/04/how-about-a-little-danish/; T. Pearce, *Eat It Butter: Denmark Rolls Out Fat Tax. But Will It Work?*, GLOBE & MAIL, Oct. 2, 2011, *available at* http://www.theglobeandmail.com/life/the-hot-button/eat-it-butter-denmark-rolls-out-fat-tax-but-will-it-work/article617903/.

[4] S. Cnossen, *Economics and Politics of Excise Taxation, in* THEORY AND PRACTICE OF EXCISE TAXATION: SMOKING, DRINKING, GAMBLING, POLLUTING, AND DRIVING 1, 5 (S. Cnossen ed., 2005).

where policy makers have determined that, for a variety of reasons, there should be less use of the goods or services.

Excise taxes have been imposed on a variety of forms of consumption to discourage excess (and to raise revenues). Properly designed ones should be considered as part of the regulatory mix. However, there are issues regarding effectiveness, equity, and "a license to do."[5] There appears to be a range of effectiveness regarding the capacity of taxes to discourage consumption from significant (in the case of smoking) to questionable (in the case of nonnutritious food and drink)—issues that we discuss in detail in this chapter. There can be substantial impacts in terms of evasion: the tax on junk food in Denmark, referred to at the beginning of this subsection, has since been repealed. A major reason was the amount of evasion by Danes shopping in neighboring countries that do not have the tax.[6] Finally, excise taxes that would otherwise be effective can be negated if they are kept too low, something that has occurred for years in the United States in terms of alcohol. We'll discuss experiences with tobacco and spirits and the lessons to be learned before turning to the mixed results, so far, in terms of nonnutritious food and drinks.

In terms of equity excise taxes have a disproportionate impact on those with lower incomes. This greater effect on purchasing power may have the intended result, including curbing consumption by those who are poorer. However, for those in this group who continue to consume, there will be less money for the essentials of day-to-day existence.[7]

Concerns regarding "a license to do" focus on how excise taxes may be viewed as official tolerance of the targeted activity: the consumer pays the tax and, in exchange, can legally use, eat, smoke and, so forth, doing as much as the individual chooses. We discussed the importance of "normativity"—the relationship between law and norms—in Chapter 1. The fear, here, is that, to the extent that excise taxes are viewed as a "licence to do," norms sanctioning excessive consumption can be undermined.[8] This is a valid concern but may focus on the role played by excise taxes by themselves. However, that tool is used in combination with other strategies such as public health campaigns warning of the dangers of undue use and prohibition of the activity in situations where it can harm others (smoking in enclosed spaces, drinking and driving). Used in the right combination, the fiscal punch of such taxes can buttress norms and other forms of regulation that are clear in their message regarding

---

[5] W. A. BOGART, PERMIT BUT DISCOURAGE: REGULATING EXCESSIVE CONSUMPTION 54–56 (2011).

[6] T. Thanh Ha, *Denmark Scraps Contentious "Fat Tax,"* GLOBE & MAIL, Nov. 13, 2012, at L6; *Denmark to Abolish Tax on High-Fat Foods*, Nov. 10, 2012, *available at* http://www.bbc.co.uk/news/world-europe-20280863.

[7] B. Frey, *Excise Taxes: Economics, Politics, and Psychology, in* THEORY AND PRACTICE OF EXCISE TAXATION, *supra* note 4, at 232.

[8] *Id.* at 238.

curbing excess. Whether such levies play that role is a question that we will return to in our discussion of SSBs (sugar-sweetened beverages).[9]

B) LESSONS FROM TOBACCO AND ALCOHOL

The lessons from excise taxes on tobacco and alcohol are instructive in discussions of taxing junk food and drink. Advocates of fat taxes point to the success of levies on tobacco as proof that these interventions can work to suppress consumption. However, the experience with taxes on tobacco also sheds light on two more specific issues: the potential for evasion and the importance of the regulatory mix. Taxes on alcohol, at least in the United States, are an object lesson in a simple reality: it is not enough to impose such taxes; they must be levied at a sufficient level in order for them to be effective.

Laws aimed at lowering the rate of smoking are a tale of regulation interacting with shifting public attitudes and social norms in terms of tobacco. Smoking has gone from a glamorous, sophisticated pastime to a filthy, dangerous addiction. Changing public attitudes have been both cause and effect of legal intervention: as more people came to view smoking as unhealthy, expensive, and disgusting, support grew for regulatory intervention aimed at further curtailment; as regulation intensified, more people accepted, in terms of their own views and behavior, the obnoxiousness of cigarettes.

Legal intervention to suppress smoking is also an excellent illustration of the regulatory "mix" as governments resorted to a range of tools in order to achieve the policy goal of curtailing the use of tobacco. The full spectrum of tools was employed: from educating the public regarding the dangers of smoking to prohibitions of the sale of cigarettes to children and of smoking in public places. In addition there were legislative restrictions placed upon the advertising of cigarettes, requirements mandating ever more graphic and explicit warnings regarding the dangers of smoking on packaging, increased taxation of cigarettes, and various attempts to use litigation to compensate for the harm done by tobacco and to deter cigarette companies from peddling their poisons.

However, some strategies aimed at curbing tobacco consumption did not produce the effects hoped for. Taxes had substantial effects in suppressing consumption.[10] But there were also unintended consequences.[11] A case in point was Canada's experiment with big tax hikes on cigarettes in the late 1980s and early 1990s. Those hikes essentially backfired because of evasion. These increases resulted in the unintended consequence of promoting smuggling of cigarettes

---

[9] *Infra*, Section III(c): Experiments with SSBs (Sugar-Sweetened Beverages).
[10] Regarding smoking: *see* S. Cnossen & M. Smart, *Taxation of Tobacco*, in THEORY AND PRACTICE OF EXCISE TAXATION, *supra* note 4, at 20.
[11] Ch. 1, Section III(b): Assessing Impact: Three Kinds of Effects.

from American states with relatively low taxes on tobacco. Estimates suggest that, at its height, black-market traffic in cigarettes constituted 20 percent of the market.

These developments provided a dramatic counter to the potential of excise taxes as a tool in curbing consumption. After several maneuvers the Canadian government decided that it had no other choice and substantially lowered taxes to undercut sales on the black market.[12] As indicated earlier, the evasion of the junk food tax by Danes provides a similar example of the undermining of an intervention because those subject to it have ways to avoid its impact.[13]

There is strong, statistical evidence that increasing alcohol prices (because of taxes) results in a decrease in alcohol consumption.[14] This relationship applies to all types of alcoholic beverages and to all levels of drinkers, from the light to the heavy. At the same time governments (because of the tax) are provided with a revenue source that, at least in theory, is available to address the negative outcomes produced by excessive consumption of the targeted commodity.

In Australia, in the Northern Territory, the application of a five-cent tax on drinks with a higher alcohol content appears to have saved $124 million in health care and policing costs over a four-year period. In contrast, when this tax was abolished, there was an increase in alcohol-related deaths.[15] In 2008, the Australian federal government implemented the "alcopops" tax, which is a tax on ready-to-drink spirit-based alcoholic beverages (RTDs), to reduce consumption among young people. There was a 35 percent decrease in RTD sales.[16]

Evidence indicates that consumers will respond to changes in the price of alcohol similarly to changes in the price of other consumer products.[17] As the price of alcohol rises, consumption levels and, therefore, alcohol-related harm, drops. The manner in which drinkers respond to changes in the price of alcohol varies as there are many possibilities for substitution; for example, some may shift to cheaper drinks. Price changes for alcohol are particularly effective on youth due to their limited incomes.[18]

---

[12] W. A. Bogart, Consequences: The Impact of Law and its Complexity 195–96, 213–14 (2002).

[13] See supra note 6 and accompanying text.

[14] See, e.g., A. Wagenaar, M. Salois & K. Komro, Effects of Beverage Alcohol Price and Tax Levels on Drinking: A Meta-Analysis of 1003 Estimates from 112 Studies, 104(2) Addiction 179 (2009); see, generally, Bogart, supra note 5, at 28–31.

[15] T. Chikritzhs et al., The Public Health, Safety and Economic Benefits of the Northern Territory's Living with Alcohol Programme, 20(22) Drug & Alcohol Rev 167 (June 2001).

[16] T. Chikritzhs et al., The Alcopops Tax: Heading in the Right Direction, 190(6) Med. J. Austl. 294 (2009). See also S. Skov, National Alcohol Policy after Alcopops: What Next?, 190(12) Med J Austl. 662 (2009) (The "alcopops" legislation was defeated in the Australian Senate in March 2009).

[17] World Health Organization, Expert Committee on Problems Related to Alcohol Consumption 26 (Geneva, Switzerland: WHO Technical Report Series No. 944 2007).

[18] Id. at 27.

Those advocating alcohol taxation policies often emphasize the importance of these measures being viewed as part of public health concerns.[19] Increasing taxation on alcohol is not well received by the public, who often view such hikes as merely enlarging government revenues. Dedicating tax revenues or a portion of the revenues to alcohol programs encourages public acceptance even as such taxes reduce consumption and can fund the treatment of alcoholism. Alcohol taxation can also address externality problems. The external costs of alcohol are considerable. They may be borne directly by the individual or by society as a whole in publicly funded medical treatment and research for alcohol-related harm. Levies can help governments recoup those costs.

Yet the argument for the use of higher taxation in discouraging consumption is met with skepticism by some schools of economics.[20] In this view taxation involves an element of paternalism or "society knows best." Moreover, these strategies are not without unintended consequences. Taxes cannot be raised too high or too quickly. A high increase in alcohol taxes may drive the production and sale of alcohol underground into the black market. Alcohol may be illegally produced and traded, and taxes evaded.

It may also be smuggled from countries that have a lower tax policy. There has been a problem of revenue loss in high tax EU (European Union) member states from both legal cross-border shopping and illegal smuggling caused by the nonuniform taxation of alcohol in the EU.[21] These disparities have led to arguments for some level of EU tax coordination among member states. There is also a potential health threat as illegal and cheaply made alcohol may be contaminated and, therefore, even more dangerous and toxic to consume.[22]

Nonetheless, the case for raising taxes on alcohol to lower consumption remains strong. Such arguments are especially powerful in countries such as the United States where, for over two decades, federal and state taxes have not kept pace with inflation. For example, as of 2004, the federal tax on beer needed to be tripled to restore it to its equivalent cost in 1960.[23] Legislators do have an intervention that they can turn to in the struggle to curtail alcohol abuse. Is there the political will to use it more effectively?

---

[19] *Id.*
[20] S. Smith, *Economic Issues in Alcohol Taxation, in* THEORY AND PRACTICE OF EXCISE TAXATION, *supra* note 4, at 56, 67–68.
[21] *Id.* at 76–79.
[22] T. Stockwell, J. Leng & J. Sturge, *Alcohol Pricing and Public Health in Canada: Issue and Opportunities,* CARBC TECHNICAL REPORT 4 (2006).
[23] NATIONAL RESEARCH COUNCIL OF MEDICINE OF THE NATIONAL ACADEMIES, REDUCING UNDERAGE DRINKING: A COLLECTIVE RESPONSIBILITY 240–41 (2004).

III. Junk Food and Beverage Taxes

A) PARTICULAR POLICY ARGUMENTS

We observed at the beginning of this chapter that fiscal policies of governments are rarely neutral. Taxes (and deductions, credits) and subsidies are used to encourage or discourage all manner of activity. This capacity of government to both discourage and encourage various activities has been the focus of advocates of nutritious eating/drinking and of physical activity.

Fiscal policy regarding other forms of consumption such as smoking, use of alcohol, or problem gambling is relatively straightforward. Excise taxes are employed to drive down consumption while creating a revenue stream for governments. Some of those funds may be used for campaigns to curb consumption. But the focus of the policies is comparatively simple: lower the rates of use.

Policies addressing nonnutritious eating and drinking are more complicated. A primary goal is to lower the consumption of nonnutritious snacks and drinks. Another one is to increase the consumption of healthy food and beverages. Because being fit is about combining nutritious eating and drinking with exercise, it is also important to encourage regular physical activity. These several goals—drive down consumption of junk, increase eating and drinking of nutritious foods and drinks, achieve more physical activity—present both complexities and opportunities for health advocates and their use of legal interventions.

These proponents focus on several propositions. First, excise taxes on junk foods, if set at appropriate levels, will decrease consumption.[24] Second, revenue generated from such taxes can be used to subsidize the cost of healthy food and drinks, such as fresh fruit and vegetables. Third, such revenues can also be used to underwrite the cost of encouraging physical activity, such as building bike paths and community recreational centers. Fourth, such underwriting goes a long way to meet arguments that excise taxes on junk foods are regressive: they are much more of a burden on the poor than they are on the affluent. Such burdens can be offset by a considerable measure if the funds generated by taxes are used to make nutritious foods more accessible, especially for those of limited means. Fifth, such subsidies should not be defeated by arguments against government intrusion and manipulation. Governments have been subsidizing the production of corn and soy for decades. These subsidies have been a significant contributing factor to the availability of food and drink of dubious nutritional value at relatively low cost. Thus underwriting the expense of nutritious foods should not be viewed as initiating controversial policies but, rather, modifying existing practices so as to promote the attractive goal of public health.

---

[24] M. Bittman, *Bad Food? Tax It*, N.Y. TIMES, SUNDAY REVIEW, July 24, 2011, at 1, 6.

We will see these arguments play out as we discuss the details of taxes on junk foods. There is a case for their imposition but the evidence, to date, in their favour is not dramatic. As a result, advocates tend to urge a combination of taxes and of other initiatives, particularly subsidies of nutritious food/drink, in order to achieve greater shifts in consumption patterns. Yet underwriting the cost of healthier foods also raises complex and controversial issues.

A particular target of such taxes has been soda (pop) and other sugar-enhanced drinks: sugar-sweetened beverages (SSBs). They have been a focus for several reasons: so much is consumed, and they are aggressively marketed. They are also very popular with children. As we saw in Chapter 4, anti-obesity campaigns almost always get additional clout when such efforts claim to be especially protective of young people.[25]

In aiming their fire at SSBs some advocates engage classical economic analysis regarding "market failures" to justify interventions. Such analysis has relevance for fat taxes, generally, but has been particularly cited by those especially opposed to SSBs. These proponents claim that this analysis provides three reasons for imposing taxes.[26]

First is the problem of imperfect knowledge. Many people do not appreciate the link between SSBs and health consequences. These decisions are further distorted because of the relentless marketing of these drinks. Second are issues of time-inconsistent preferences. Such preferences can lead to choices that result in short-term preferences but long-term harm. The problem can be exacerbated with young people who can place a higher value on immediate satisfaction and can discount future consequences. Third, SSBs impose "externalities." In other words those who consume significant amounts of these drinks do not bear all the costs. SSBs are associated with obesity and health consequences that lead to significant burdens on medical care systems.

In examining fat taxes, in general, and levies on SSBs, in particular, we will also pursue a theme ribboned throughout the book: the actual effectiveness of such taxes. To what extent do they suppress consumption? To what extent is there substitution: consumers buying less of the taxed product, but more of other food and drink of dubious nutritional value? To what extent are the proceeds from these taxes, in fact, used to underwrite the cost of more nutritious food and drinks? To what extent is the target population healthier as the result of any and all such efforts?

---

[25] Chapter 4, Section III: Evidentiary Basis for Interventions.
[26] K. Brownell et al., *The Public Health and Economic Benefits of Taxing Sugar-Sweetened Beverages*, 361(16) New Eng. J Med 1599, 1601–02 (2009).

B) GENERAL ASSESSMENTS

There have been a number of reviews of studies, mostly of wealthier English-speaking countries, of the effects of taxes on such outcomes as diet, weight, and health.[27] Overall, taxes do suppress consumption. Moreover, generally, larger taxes are associated with more significant changes in consumption, body weight, and disease. Nevertheless, one review of empirical evidence of food/drink prices and weight outcomes concluded that the effects, when statistically significant, were generally small, although in some cases they were larger for low-socioeconomic status (SES) populations and for those at risk for overweight or obesity.[28]

At the same time, such evidence has been characterized as "generally of low quality," "not clear," and "sparse and limited."[29] There are a number of reasons for such characterizations. First, there are several ways that food and beverages can be taxed. Such levies are not necessarily aimed at suppression of consumption. Such taxes have generally been imposed in four ways:

- Raising general revenue as in Valued Added Tax (VAT) in the EU or a general service tax (GST) as in Australia.
- Extending VAT to some foods such as those high in fat content and using revenues to fund prevention initiatives.
- Imposing taxes directly on categories of foodstuffs to directly affect behavior with some or all of revenues earmarked for prevention activities.
- Imposing taxes directly on categories of foodstuffs to directly affect behavior, but with no dedication of revenues for prevention, etc.[30]

To date the first approach has been the most common. The goal is to raise revenue generally. Food and drink are included but no particular foods/drinks or nutritional content is targeted. If, instead, an excise tax were to be used (rather than generally applicable sales taxes), particular food/drink or even specific ingredients could be more easily and effectively focused upon. Excise taxes

---

[27] *See, e.g.,* M. Caraher & G. Cowburn, *Taxing Food: Implications for Public Health Nutrition,* 8(8) PUB. HEALTH NUTRITION 1242 (2005); L. Powell & F. Chaloupka, *Food Prices and Obesity: Evidence and Policy Implications for Taxes and Subsidies,* 87(1) MILBANK Q. 229 (2009); A. Thow et al., *The Effect of Fiscal Policy on Diet, Obesity and Chronic Disease: A Systematic Review,* 88(8) BULL. WORLD HEALTH ORG. 609 (2010).

[28] Powell & Chaloupka, *supra* note 27, at 229–30. The assessment was of peer-reviewed English language articles published between 1990 and 2008.

[29] Thow et al., *supra* note 27, at 609 ("low quality") Caraher & Cowburn, *supra* note 27, at 1242: ("not clear") Powell & Chaloupka, *supra* note 27, at 250: ("sparse and limited") *See also,* S. CASH ET AL., FAT TAXES AND HEALTH OUTCOMES: AN INVESTIGATION OF ECONOMIC FACTORS INFLUENCING OBESITY IN CANADA (2007).

[30] Caraher & Cowburn, *supra* note 27, at 1244.

can be imposed quite particularly and directly on producers and then passed on to consumers as part of the overall price.

Second, many of the food taxes have been withdrawn after a short period of time, often because of industry lobbying against them. As a result their overall impacts over the long run are unclear.[31] Third, studies that focused on a single food/drink may have overestimated the impact of taxes by failing to take into account shifts to other foods. In other words, consumption of the targeted food/drink may be decreased but individuals may shift consumption to other foods/drinks of dubious nutritional quality.[32] An example of substitution effects, in a somewhat different context, comes from Canada and the consumption of 1 percent milk. That milk was introduced in 1990, and it quickly gained market share while the consumption of whole milk declined. However, at more or less the same time, total sales of cream and of cheese increased substantially.[33] One source of butter fat had been substituted for another. Fourth, sometimes food/beverage taxes are justified because of the "symbolic" message that is sent to the public about the undesirability of consuming certain products.[34] However, there appears to be little evidence of the effectiveness of such symbolism in altering attitudes and behavior.[35] Fifth, some argue that any such tax should be imposed on calories rather than particular foods/beverages.[36]

A major response in these studies and elsewhere is to pin hopes on greater impact by using a combination of taxes and of subsidies to shift patterns of consumption of food/drink. There are two main reasons for the attraction to subsidies and their pairing with taxes. First, fat taxes can be regressive by imposing a greater burden on the poor.[37] Such burdens may be increased if the poor attempt to shift their diet to healthy but more expensive foods such as fresh fruits and vegetables. Subsidies of nutritious foods could be a partial response to such regressive aspects by being a "carrot" for healthy foods as consumers, including the poor, experience the "stick" of taxes on nonnutritious food/drink.[38]

Second, junk food taxes are viewed as a simplistic response to a complicated situation. At the least, they need to be combined with other strategies such as regulation of advertising and, in particular, subsidies of healthy food/drink.

---

[31] *Id.* at 1242.
[32] Thow et al., *supra* note 27, at 609.
[33] CASH ET AL., *supra* note 29, at 14.
[34] Caraher & Cowburn, *supra* note 27, at 1244.
[35] Thow et al., *supra* note 27, at 612.
[36] A. Okrent & J. Alston, *The Effects of Farm Commodity and Retail Food Policies on Obesity and Economic Welfare in the United States*, 94(3) AM. J. AGRIC. ECON. 611–46; doi: 10.1093/ajae/aar138 (2012).
[37] H. Chouinard et al., *Fat Taxes: Big Money for Small Change*, 10(2) FORUM HEALTH ECON. & POL'Y 1 (2007).
[38] Thow et al., *supra* note 27, at 612.

Caraher and Cowburn, in concluding their review of studies assessing the impact of food taxes, assert: "Food taxes as a stand-alone initiative to counteract obesity are likely to fail... They should be considered alongside other policy initiatives such as restructuring of food subsidies."[39]

Shifting of subsidies to underwrite the cost of nutritious food/drink is a very good idea for lots of reasons. But it will be a transformation not easily accomplished. True, some innovative experiments are occurring. Yet such experiments are few and far between. Efforts to shift subsidies for the production and processing of foods are an even bigger challenge. We return to these issues below.[40]

C) EXPERIMENTS WITH SSBs (SUGAR-SWEETENED BEVERAGES)

1. Why SSBs?

Taxes on sugar-sweetened beverages (SSBs) have become a particular focus for those favoring fat taxes.[41] SSBs are most prominently soda (soft drinks/pop) but also include all beverages that contain added caloric sweeteners, such as sport and fruit drinks. There are several good reasons so much attention is paid to these drinks. These include:

- Young people steadily increasing consumption of SSBs over the last thirty years, including all ages, economic status, sexes, and racial/ethnic backgrounds.[42]
- The preponderance of research indicating that SSB consumption leads to weight gain and higher rates of obesity.[43]
- SSB consumption reducing drinking of milk; important nutrients not ingested.
- SSBs frequently containing high levels of caffeine; they can cause anxiety, poor-quality sleep, and tooth decay.
- Evidence, in controlled experiments, that foregoing SSBs constrains increases in weight.[44]
- The intense marketing of SSBs to young people.[45]

---

[39] Caraher & Cowburn, *supra* note 27, at 1248; Powell & Chaloupka, *supra* note 27, at 250–51.

[40] *Infra*, Section IV: Subsidies.

[41] B. Von Tigerstrom, *Taxing Sugar-Sweetened Beverages for Public Health: Legal and Policy Issues in Canada*, 50(1) ALBERTA L REVIEW 37–64 (2012).

[42] HEALTHY EATING RESEARCH, THE NEGATIVE IMPACT OF SUGAR-SWEETENED BEVERAGES ON CHILDREN'S HEALTH 1 (2009) (all bullet points except the last two).

[43] *See also* INSTITUTE OF MEDICINE, ACCELERATING PROGRESS IN OBESITY PREVENTION: SOLVING THE WEIGHT OF THE NATION 167 *et seq.* (2012).

[44] R. Rabin, *Avoiding Sugared Drinks Limits Weight Gain in Two Studies*, N.Y. TIMES, Sept. 22, 2012, at A16.

[45] K. Brownell & T. Frieden, *Ounces of Prevention—The Public Policy Case for Taxes on Sugared Beverages* 360 NEW ENG. J. MED. 1805, 1805 (2009); M. Bittman, *Soda: A Sin We Sip Instead of Smoke?*, N.Y. TIMES, Feb. 14, 2010, at 1.

What is more, advocates claim the public is ready for increased taxes on SSBs. They suggest that general support for food and beverage taxes increased in the 2000s. Regarding SSBs they cite a 2008 poll of New York State residents in which 52 percent of respondents supported a soda tax; 72 percent did so if the revenue was to be used to prevent obesity.[46] A 2011 poll in Massachusetts revealed that 69 percent would support a sales tax on soda if revenues went to schools or anti-obesity programs focused on children; results were split nearly evenly in terms of support/no support if respondents were not given information about how funds would be used.[47]

Proponents underscore the point arising from this increased percentage: support is highest when the tax is viewed as promoting health (rather than raising revenue), and where the funds are dedicated to prevention programs.[48] Soda consumption does seem to be declining.[49] Such taxes could suppress levels even further and also dampen drinking of other SSBs. Yet how credible are such "dedications" on the part of cash-strapped governments in the midst of fiscal austerity?

2. Fifty Calories a Day?

The title of this subsection comes from the projections for reduction of calories should a penny per ounce tax be imposed on SSBs. We'll come to proposals in that regard momentarily. The current state of taxes and SSBs appears to be as follows. Levies to date, at least in the United States, seem to have had little impact on consumption patterns. However, advocates offer evidence based on economic modeling that suggest that increased taxes would depress consumption and could be even more effective if revenues were to be used for prevention programs. At the same time these models assume no substituting behavior (i.e., that consumers as they drink less of such drinks switch to other high-caloric foods and drinks). Moreover, whether the revenues from such levies would actually be used for health programs is in doubt in these times, when governments are in fiscal crises. With that overview let's turn to some details.

Although many states do tax SSBs, they mostly do so under a generally applicable regime of sales taxes. These taxes, which average 5.2 percent, have had little impact on reducing consumption or on lowering weight.[50] These results have led some to assert that such levies are ineffective in terms of producing health benefits. Those advocating such measures respond that the problem is

---

[46] Brownell et al., *supra* note 26, at 1603–04.
[47] INSTITUTE OF MEDICINE, *supra* note 43, at 181.
[48] *Id.*
[49] S. Strom, *Sipping Less Sugar: As Soda Consumption Declines, Beverage Makers Scramble*, N.Y. TIMES, May 16, 2012, at B1, B4.
[50] HEALTHY EATING RESEARCH, SUGAR-SWEETENED BEVERAGE, TAXES AND PUBLIC HEALTH 1, 2 (2009).

not that the taxes are necessarily ineffective. Rather, they must be higher to produce positive health outcomes.[51]

Proponents suggest a shift from sales to excise taxes would also assist in decreasing consumption. Because sales taxes are imposed as a percentage of the purchase price, they can encourage buying less-expensive brands or larger containers. In addition, because excise taxes are imposed per ounce, they discourage purchases of larger quantities. Further, because excise taxes are usually rolled into the price of a commodity, consumers are alerted to the effect of the levy as they contemplate buying food/drink (rather than paying sales tax at the cash register after that decision has been made).[52]

Economic modeling studies of increased taxes suggest that they could produce substantial results.[53] They claim that a penny-per-ounce levy could reduce SSB consumption by 24 percent. In turn caloric intake would be decreased from 190–200 cal to 145–150 cal per day—a potential loss of 5 lb per year. Consumption rates and caloric intake could be decreased even further for some groups such as young people who, at present, consume even greater amounts of SSBs.[54] Health impacts could be even greater depending on the extent to which revenues from such taxes are dedicated to prevention efforts. They might be greater still, in the United States, if they were combined with a prohibition on the use of food stamps to purchase SSBs. (New York City tried to initiate such bans;[55] such efforts failed for a number of reasons that we discuss later).[56]

But the foregoing predictions are based on economic models. Even ardent supporters acknowledge that concrete impacts can only be ascertained when such taxes pass into law and are put into practice: "the precise effect...cannot be known until...[they are] implemented and studied."[57] There are a number of cautions that should be registered with regard to the robust predictions of these models.[58]

First are the issues regarding the political feasibility of a penny-per-ounce tax. A tax of 1 cent per ounce would raise the cost of a 20-ounce pop by 15–20 percent.[59] Such a hike is bound to be strongly opposed by the beverage industry

---

[51] INSTITUTE OF MEDICINE, *supra* note 43, at 178.
[52] Brownell & Frieden, *supra* note 45, at 1807.
[53] T. Andreyeva, *Estimating the Potential of Taxes on Sugar-Sweetened Beverages to Reduce Consumption and Generate Revenue*, 52(6) PREVENTIVE MED. 413 (2011).
[54] *Id.* at 413.
[55] A. Hartocollis, *City Seeking to Wean Poor from Sodas*, N.Y. TIMES, Oct. 7, 2010, at A1, A28; A. Hartocollis, *Plan to Ban Food Stamps for Sodas Has Hurdles*, N.Y. TIMES, Oct. 8, 2010, at A19.
[56] *Infra* Section IV(c)(3): Soda and the City: Bloomberg's Bans #1 and #2.
[57] Brownell et al., *supra* note 26, at 1604.
[58] Von Tigerstrom, *supra* note 41, at paras. 21–24.
[59] Brownell et al., *supra* note 26, at 1602.

and its confederates.[60] Too heavy handed for a new governance approach they may say.[61] They may also be opposed on philosophical grounds by those who see them as strong measures that hamper choice and that are of questionable benefit.[62] But consumers may also not be supportive either. How likely is it that that level of increase will be supported by individuals even if they could be confident that tax revenues would be used for prevention programs? In these financially strapped times, how sure could consumers be that such increases would, in fact, be used for prevention and other health purposes during a period of relentless demands for resources to respond to the straightened circumstances of many governments?[63]

Second, most estimates of calorie reduction coming from decreased consumption of SSBs assume no substitution of other calorically dense food/drinks for the decreased consumption of SSBs.[64] We saw that substitution is also a concern in gauging the effectiveness of generally applicable fat taxes.[65] There are a few studies suggesting that consumers will substitute healthier beverages for SSBs.[66] Nevertheless, a 2011 paper espousing the economic models, described above, acknowledged that: "Reliable estimates of the...extent of possible substitution and the net impact on caloric intake are not available."[67] The models, just discussed, predict something like a fifty-calorie reduction a day from the suppressed consumption of SSBs. Half a cookie, a small handful of chips etc. could easily amount to fifty calories. Substitution could be the result for many people.

Third, as we have seen, a criticism of fat taxes, generally, is that they are a simplistic solution to a complex problem.[68] They cannot achieve significant change on their own. At the least they must be combined with other interventions: the "regulatory mix" that we have talked about several times. The intervention that these levies may be most closely associated with is subsidies. The hope is subsidies of healthy foods combined with fat taxes (SSBs and

---

[60] A. Hartocollis, *Failure of State Soda Tax Plan Reflects Power of an Antitax Message*, N.Y. TIMES, July 3, 2010, at A12, A13; W. Neuman, *Save the Children Backs Away from Soda Tax Campaigns*, N.Y. TIMES, Dec. 15, 2010, at B1, B4.

[61] J. Solomon, *New Governance, Preemptive Self-Regulation, and the Blurring of Boundaries in Regulatory Theory and Practice*, WISC. L. REV. 591 (2010); Chapter 1, Section V(a): Looking at the State in a Different Way: New Governance.

[62] N. Mankiw, *Can a Soda Tax Save Us from Ourselves?*, N.Y. TIMES, June 6, 2010, BUSINESS WEEK, at 4.

[63] T. Parker-Pope, *Money Is Tight, and Junk Food Beckons*, N.Y. TIMES, Nov. 4, 2008, at D6; J. Brody, *Eating Well on a Downsized Food Budget*, N.Y. TIMES, Mar. 3, 2009, at D7.

[64] See discussion regarding substitution issues in INSTITUTE OF MEDICINE, *supra* note 43, at 179–80.

[65] *Supra* notes 32–33 and accompanying text.

[66] HEALTH EATING RESEARCH, *supra* note 50, at 2.

[67] Andreyeva, *supra* note 53, at 416; *see also* Brownell & Frieden, *supra* note 45, at 1806–07.

[68] *Supra* note 39 and accompanying text.

otherwise) would lead to a "carrots and sticks" approach regarding consumption, encouraging nutritious foods/drinks and discouraging those of dubious quality.

Yet designing and implementing an effective subsidies regime may face even greater complexities and obstacles than junk food taxes. Let's turn to a discussion of some of these underwriting programs and their complications.

IV. Subsidies

A) INTRODUCTION: THE GENERAL AND THE SPECIFIC

Discussion of subsidies focuses on two different kinds of underwriting of food and drink. The first concerns how some crops are supported and how, it is alleged, this underwriting leads to cheap and unhealthy food and beverages. The other kind of subsidies are targeted experiments that provide rewards to low-income individuals, who are on public assistance, if they purchase healthy foods. The goal here is to promote more nutritious diets among individuals who may be prone to obesity and who do not have the economic wherewithal to eat and drink in healthy ways.

The general point about subsidies of certain crops, particularly corn, may have been misdirected. The charge is that such underwriting leads to cheap commodity crops that then lead to plentiful ingredients that then lead to inexpensive, unhealthy foods. Subsidies and overproduction of certain crops may be related but, whatever that relationship, it does not account for the price of most junk food and drinks. The cost of raw commodities is quite small compared with other costs such as processing, packaging, storing, etc. There is little influence on the price paid by the ultimate consumer.

At the same time many healthier crops such as fruits and vegetables cost much more to grow, harvest, and transport. This is not to say that agricultural regulation could not be overhauled to encourage production of healthier foods. Some recommendations are advanced in that regard. But any such reform will be a massive undertaking, opposed by vested interests, and by no means easily achieved.

There are some encouraging pilot projects regarding the subsidizing of healthy foods for low-income people on public assistance, most prominently SNAP (Supplementary Nutrition Assistance Plan—formerly food stamps). But these projects are caught up in debates about whether SNAP recipients should (at the same time or as an alternative strategy to rewards) be banned for buying unhealthy foods with funds that they receive from the program. Even more telling is that incentives pilots' success may be their own undoing. The more the pilot underwrites the cost of healthy food, the more a program costs. Any such success risks colliding with austerity measures of cash-starved governments.

B) SUBSIDIES AND AGRICULTURAL POLICY

1. Subsidies and Obesity

One account of obesity that is advanced, especially by those focused on nutrition, alleges that farm subsidies distort the price of certain commodities by making them much cheaper. These inexpensive foods are then used in a variety of products of dubious nutritional value at price points that promote their consumption. Meanwhile, other wholesome foods, such as fresh fruits and vegetables, do not receive comparable underwriting. They are, therefore, more expensive and less accessible, especially for consumers of modest means.

As a result, farm subsidies, in particular, and agricultural policy, in general, tilt consumption toward junk food/drink and away from nutritious eating/drinking. This account is regularly played out in the media and elsewhere. An ad taken in *The New York Times* by doctors from Mt. Sinai Medical Centre in 2010 is illustrative. Entitled "Why Are We Subsidizing Childhood Obesity?" the ad went on to declare: "It is incongruous and wasteful for health agencies to spend millions of dollars countering obesity while the USDA [United States Department of Agriculture] spends billions in farm subsidies that indirectly promote it."[69]

A particular villain is corn. The claim is that the market is glutted with this crop and its derivatives because of subsidies and policies that have promoted its overproduction. Films such as *King Corn* and books such as the *Omnivore's Dilemma* zero in on this crop as a main culprit in the growth of obesogenic environments.[70] In this account corn is a consistent ingredient in junk food. High-fructose corn syrup (HFCS) sweetens soft drinks. Corn feeds cows, and they become hamburger meat. Corn may be in the oil for the French fries, maybe stabilizing buns. Derivatives of it may even be in the packaging and eating utensils. Corn thus contributes to the wide availability of junk food and drink and is then viewed as a proximate cause of the galloping rates of obesity.

The hugely successful author of several books on food, Michael Pollan opines about such matters:

[C]heap-food farm policy comes at a high price…[F]armers in the United States have managed to produce 500 additional calories per person every day; each of us is, heroically, managing to pack away about 200 of those extra calories per day. Presumably the other 300—most of them in the form of surplus corn—get dumped on overseas markets or turned into ethanol.[71]

---

[69] P. Landrigan et al., *Why Are We Subsidizing Childhood Obesity?*, N.Y. TIMES, Oct. 26, 2010, at A2.

[70] *King Corn* (Mosaic Films 2007) (Mosaic Films. A. Woolf, Director; I. Cheney and C. Ellis, Producers); M. POLLAN, THE OMNIVORE'S DILEMMA: A NATURAL HISTORY OF FOUR MEALS (2006).

[71] M. Pollan, *The Way We Live Now: 10-12-03; The (Agri)Cultural Contradictions of Obesity*, N.Y TIMES, Oct. 12, 2003, *available at* http://www.nytimes.com/2003/10/12/magazine/the-way-we-live-now-10-12-03-the-agri-cultural-contradictions-of-obesity.html?pagewanted=all&src=pm.

The case against this policy seems straightforward: farm subsidies contribute to making certain commodities abundant and, therefore, cheaper, while having the opposite effect for those, such as fruit and vegetables, that are not comparably subsidized. That accusation is so widespread and has been repeated so often it has become "a stylized fact."[72] But, increasingly, that "fact" has been questioned, including by those sympathetic to promoting better nutrition.

Alston and others emphasize that for subsidies to have such effects three things must occur.[73] First, subsidies are needed to make commodities that are an important ingredient of calorically dense foods substantially more available and cheaper. Second, lower commodity prices resulting from subsidies need to result in markedly lower costs to the food industry, and such lower costs need to be passed on to consumers. Third, consumption needs to change substantially as a response to such policy-induced changes in the relative price between calorically dense foods/drinks and more nutritious ones.

However, after examining the evidence, Alston and colleagues concluded that for all three "the magnitude of the impact... is zero or small."[74] Their conclusions led to three basic points:

- Subsidies have had very modest (and mixed) effects on the total availability and prices of farm commodities that are the most important ingredients in calorically dense foods.
- Such small commodity price impacts would imply very small effects on cost of food at retail; even if they were fully passed on to consumers there would be [only] very small increases in prices.
- The very small food prices changes resulting from subsidies could not have had large effects on consumption patterns.[75]

These points can also be grasped by focusing on the relation of commodity prices not only to the consumer but also to the food industry. The cost of a raw commodity is but one of several related to food and drinks. Others include processing, packaging, storing, shipping, and retail markup. The cost of the raw commodity is tiny compared to other expenditures; its impact on the price charged to the consumer is small.[76]

As a more specific illustration of these points, let's return to the much-vilified corn. It has been estimated that farmers are paid only four to five cents from the sale of a box of cornflakes and two to three cents from the sale of a bag of corn chips. High-fructose corn syrup (HFCS), a common caloric sweetener, is just

---

[72] J. Alston et al., *Farm Subsidies and Obesity in the United States: National Evidence and International Comparisons*, FOOD POLICY (May 2008) doi:10.1016/j.foodpol.2008.05.008.

[73] *Id.* at 3.

[74] *Id.*

[75] *Id.*

[76] WHITE PAPER, DO FARM SUBSIDIES CAUSE OBESITY?: DISPELLING COMMON MYTHS ABOUT PUBLIC HEALTH AND THE FARM BILL 8 (2011).

3.5 percent of the total cost of soft drink manufacturing, and the corn content of HFCS is only 1.6 percent of that cost. Overwhelmingly, the retail price of soft drinks is accounted for not by what farmers are paid but by processing and by retail outlets. To the point: only two cents of each consumer dollar spent on soda returns to farmers who grow corn (used in HFCS); ninety-eight cents goes to those who make, market, and sell soft drinks.[77]

A related contention, in terms of these issues, is that a dollar, in the United States, buys many more calories of mass-produced cookies and of potato chips than of carrots.[78] But, again, that gap in purchasing power is not the result of subsidies. Instead, it is largely due to a disparity in the costs of growing and harvesting. Many crops, such as potatoes and corn, used in processing foods of dubious nutritional value cost significantly less to produce on a mass scale than fresh fruit and vegetables.[79]

The former can, mostly, be tilled and harvested by machine. But peaches, strawberries, etc. require substantially more hand labor. True, some of these latter crops have also undergone intensification of production because of breeding, speeding up of crop rotation, and so forth, which do lessen their cost. Nevertheless, they are not nearly as inexpensive as the former. Moreover, for various reasons, there is much more price and yield data for commodity crops than there is for fruits and vegetables. The lack of such information about the latter can make it much more difficult for farmers to obtain loan approval and insurance coverage for these crops.[80] Guthman sums up: "Although the role of subsidies in overproduction is debatable, it is patently false that subsidies make junk food more affordable than fresh fruits and vegetables."[81]

The points just made about the cost of raw commodities and their relation to the price charged to the ultimate consumer are buttressed by international comparisons relating to obesity rates and farm commodity policies. Alston and others have reported on such comparisons. They examined rates of obesity in 2005 and overall farm supports from 1986 to 2001 for several OECD countries.[82]

They did observe that the high costs to consumers of subsidies in countries such as Japan and Korea could have contributed to lower rates of consumption and, therefore, less obesity in those societies. Nevertheless, their conclusion

---

[77] *Id.* at 9.
[78] M. Pollan, *The Way We Live Now: You Are What You Grow*, N.Y. TIMES, Apr. 22, 2007, available at http://www.nytimes.com/2007/04/22/magazine/22wwlnlede.t.html?pagewanted=all&_r=0.
[79] J.GUTHMAN, WEIGHING IN: OBESITY, FOOD JUSTICE, AND THE LIMITS OF CAPITALISM 122–23 (2011).
[80] INSTITUTE OF MEDICINE, *supra* note 43, at 214.
[81] *Id.* at 122.
[82] Farm supports were measured using Producer Support Estimates (PSE). PSE includes all transfers to producers whether through government expenditure or other means. Alston et al., *supra* note 72, at 6.

was that there is no clear connection between support for farmers in a country and its rate of obesity. Some societies that provide relatively large subsidies to farmers, such as Japan, South Korea, and France, have obesity rates that are considerably lower than countries such as the United States and Canada that provide lower subsidies. Obesity rates in Australia and New Zealand, countries that have low rates of subsidies, are higher than France and Japan, and yet lower than the Unites States. The countries of the European Union all have the same farm support policies but their obesity rates vary widely from among the highest (Greece) to the lowest (France).

Others look to how historically overproduction and prices of some crops were managed as a guide to the modification of existing agricultural policies. A paper, prepared by Food and Water Watch, suggests that economic modeling that assumes elimination of subsidies nevertheless indicates a continued overproduction of various crops. Such excess would still occur because farmers are slow to react to alterations in pricing tending to overproduce no matter what they will be paid for their crops.[83]

Historically, things were different. Federal policies, enacted in the 1930s, addressed these market tendencies by promoting leaving certain land idle at certain times to avoid farmers overproducing. In addition, grain buyers and food processors were obliged to pay fixed prices for commodity crops. Because of lobbying, especially by big food companies, such policies were abolished by the mid 1990s. Overproduction and low prices to farmers were frequently the result. Subsidies were then put in place to save farmers, keeping them from going out of business.[84]

Yet, as indicated, because the cost of commodities is so small in terms of the overall price of retail food and drink, subsidies have not had a large impact on rates of consumption. A recent study looked at all forms of subsidies, including trade barriers. It asserted that eliminating all agricultural supports would lead to an *increase* in overall caloric consumption. This conclusion is based on projections indicating that, although the costs of some crops, such as grains, would increase by a small amount, others, such as sugar and dairy products, would fall, become more affordable, and, thus, be consumed in greater amounts.[85]

2. Changing Farm Policies to Promote Healthy Eating and Drinking

Doing away with particular crop subsidies is not part of the complicated answer in trying to shift dietary habits toward more nutritious eating and drinking.

---

[83] WHITE PAPER, *supra* note 76, at 2.
[84] *Id.*
[85] B. Rickard, *How Have Agricultural Policies Influenced Caloric Consumption in the United States?*, Charles H. Dyson School of Applied Economics and Management, Cornell University (Sept. 2011) WP 2011-12, in 22(3) HEALTH ECON. 316–39 (Mar. 2013).

What's more, a rapid ending of such subsidies could diminish the number of farmers who are amenable to increasing the amount of fresh fruits and vegetables. Instead, there needs to be a significant rethinking of agricultural policy in the United States and elsewhere. An enormous undertaking—but if somehow achieved, what might such substantial change look like?

Wallinga, assessing the need for such reconfiguration, suggests there should be: "a long-term commitment to mutually supportive interventions, at multiple levels (local, state, and federal) from farm to plate, to effect change in food availability, relative prices, and marketing, complemented by nutrition education."[86] He recommends some policies,[87] as does Food & Water Watch.[88] They are combined and briefly described here. These suggestions are by no means definitive. Rather, they are presented to illustrate the very substantial issues that must be tackled in terms of any significant change in agricultural policy and health promotion:

- Seek Executive Leadership

In 1969 the White House Conference on Food, Nutrition, and Health was convened. This historic initiative led to the expansion of the food stamp, food labeling, and school lunch programs. Could executive leadership, at present, bring together disparate interests to forge a new comprehensive food policy? Could the efforts of Michelle Obama ultimately prove to be part of what is required?[89]

- Integrate Food and Health Analysis

In the United States several agencies are responsible for various fragments of food policy: U.S. Department of Agriculture, Food and Drug Administration, Environmental Protection Agency, Centers for Disease Control and Prevention, National Institutes of Health, and so on. However, there is no coordinating authority to address the health impacts of the food system. Such an authority could link food production policies with nutrition and health programs.

- Develop Responsible Supply Management Programs

This goal might be achieved by essentially returning to programs that operated before the deregulation that occurred between 1985 and 1996. These programs were described earlier.[90] Advocacy on their behalf can assist in constructing an economically stable family-farming sector that could promote healthy local

---

[86] D. Wallinga, *Agricultural Policy and Childhood Obesity: A Food Systems and Public Health Commentary*, 29 HEALTH AFFAIRS 405 (2010), at 408.
[87] *Id.* at 408–09.
[88] WHITE PAPER, *supra* note 76, at 13–14.
[89] WHITE HOUSE TASK FORCE ON CHILDHOOD OBESITY, REPORT TO THE PRESIDENT, SOLVING THE PROBLEM OF CHILDHOOD OBESITY WITHIN A GENERATION (2010).
[90] *Supra* note 84 and accompanying text.

and regional food systems, increase incomes in rural communities, improve the conditions of work for those who labor in agriculture, enhance environmental protections, etc.[91] Such policies could also undercut the benefits the present deregulated system bestows on food processing, marketing, and retail sectors.

- Support Farmers as Anti-Obesity Partners

If healthy foods are to be more affordable and accessible there needs to be at least as much research, financial, and other incentives to farmers who produce such fruits and vegetables as to those who have grown crops that are an integral part of calorically dense items. Such initiatives could include: recruiting, training, and offering supports for new farmers; promoting shifts by established farmers to growing fruits and vegetables; and permitting fruit and vegetable farmers to participate in any commodity programs of the Farm Bill (the basic federal legislation governing agriculture). The financial infrastructure could be refined to offer a safety net while new farm and marketing systems for crops promoting healthier eating and drinking are developed (for example, loan and credit programs, access to loan restructuring services) and are appropriately available (not focused on just the largest operators).

- Invest in Forward-Looking Research

There should be a research agenda that addresses agricultural and health issues to meet future needs such as: climate uncertainty, availability of water, and pressure to develop croplands. That agenda and its results should shed light on the mix of crops and farming methods that sustainably meet nutrition, health, and other needs. Agencies, such as the National Institutes of Health, could play a greater role in formulating and implementing such an agenda.

- Expand and Codify Healthier Food and Drink Programs

Surplus commodities sometimes are used in the federal child nutrition programs such as the National School Lunch and Breakfast Programs. In these instances such programs may not have conformed to the USDA's own dietary guidelines for healthy eating. Nonetheless, there have been steps taken to raise nutrition standards in these programs and to use any surpluses more appropriately. Such higher standards should be codified in legislation and enforced.

More generally, USDA programs aimed at fighting hunger and improving nutrition should be strengthened, including through any appropriate legislative modifications. Such bolstering of these programs could include:

- Protecting eligibility benefits and program integrity of SNAP and the Women, Infants, and Children Supplemental Nutrition Program so

---

[91] Regarding conditions of work in agriculture *see*: GUTHMAN, *supra* note 79, at 134–37.

that low-income individuals have the resources necessary to afford healthy foods.
- Promoting SNAP incentives to promote purchases of healthy foods and drinks.
- Expanding Electronic Benefit transfer (EBT) availability at farmers markets and other community places.
- Changing government procurement practices.
- Adequately funding the national Healthy Food Financing Initiative to encourage the development of new markets that sell healthy food and drink in under-served low-income communities.
- Expanding the national Fresh Fruit and Vegetable Program in schools.
- Protecting nutrition education programs, such as SNAP-Ed, to provide comprehensive interventions that promote health outcomes in underserved communities.

The Institute of Medicine's *Weight of the Nation* report summarizes this situation: "[A] consensus does appear to be developing around two key points: first, blunt approaches such as eliminating farm subsidies are unlikely to offer a quick fix...and second, there are real opportunities to adjust farm policies...to better support...changing...nutrition needs."[92] Or, as Wallinga eloquently puts it: "We need much more than another Farm Bill. We need a Healthy Food, Healthy Farm Bill."[93] But this is a climate of divisive politics, unqualified free markets, and the influence of powerful forces arrayed against such changes. When will the day of the Healthy Food, Healthy Farm Bill dawn?

C) TARGETED SUBSIDIES THROUGH GOVERNMENT SUPPORT PROGRAMS

1. Poverty and the New Malnutrition

You don't have to be poor to be fat. The percentage of men who are fat is spread across the economic spectrum. For women, there is more concentration of obesity among those who are poor.[94] Those with low incomes are much more likely to rely on government programs, including those that are focused on providing basic requirements for food and drink. The meeting of such needs has come to be referred to as "food security": a term that emphasizes that people have to have not only enough calories but also sufficient nutrients in their diets.[95]

---

[92] INSTITUTE OF MEDICINE, *supra* note 43, at 209.
[93] Wallinga, *supra* note 86, at 409.
[94] C. Ogden et al., *Obesity and Socioeconomic Status in Adults: United States 2005–2008*, NCHS Data Brief, No 50 (Dec. 2010).
[95] USDA, Briefing Rooms, *Food Security in the United States: Definitions of Hunger and Food Security*, available at http://www.ers.usda.gov/topics/food-nutrition-assistance/food-security-in-the-us/measurement.aspx

The focus on obesity, on the one hand, and the need for and lack of food security for the poor, on the other, has led to the "hunger-obesity paradox": individuals can be both fat and ill-fed simultaneously.[96] Or, as some term it: "the new malnutrition." Lack of food security and the hunger-obesity paradox are not exclusive to the poor.[97] It's possible to be affluent, fat, and have a nutritiously challenged diet. It's also possible to be poor, thin, and to lack food security (not enough calories at all? Enough but not disposed to be fat for whatever reason?). But issues of weight, nutrition, and poverty combine to produce particularly negative outcomes.

If our emphasis is on good eating/drinking and physical activity, for everyone, with a de-emphasis on weight, then we should aim for all individuals to be "food secure" regardless of their size. To the extent that food security leads to permanent weight loss or prevents excessive weight gain, so much the better. But the priority is on achieving a nutritious, calorically adequate diet for as many people as possible.

At the same time discussions of food security and the poor should be linked to larger concerns about poverty and health status. Generally speaking, poorer individuals are poorer in terms of their health as well. Food insecurity and its consequences are but one aspect of being poor and its negative effects on a person's well-being. Or, as one commentator has eloquently and provocatively put it: "In an era of stagnant wages, dystopian politics and cultural anomie, eating indulgent if unhealthful food has become a last redoubt of enjoyment for Americans who don't feel they have much control in their lives."[98] To obsess about the weight of low income people is to pave over a larger point: "Deal with income inequalities and the population will be healthier."[99]

2. Ban Candy—Promote Carrots: Can Government Nutrition Programs for the Poor Improve Diets?

Concern for rates of obesity among the poor has led to a consideration of government programs meant to respond to food requirements of those with low incomes. Are there ways that such programs can be shaped in order to respond to obesity among those dependent on public assistance? This is a very good question. However, as with so many other issues in this book, we need to be mindful of the objectives of any such shaping. Is the goal to have people lose weight? To prevent excess weight gain, especially among children? To improve health through better nutrition? To fight stigmatization that can come

---

[96] K. Koh et al., *The Hunger-Obesity Paradox: Obesity in the Homeless*, 89(6) J. URBAN HEALTH 952 doi:10.1007/s11524-012-9708-4 (2012).
[97] B. Keim, *Homeless and Overweight: Obesity is the New Malnutrition*, WIRED SCI., June 4, 2012, available at http://www.wired.com/wiredscience/2012/06/homeless-obesity/.
[98] M. Bruegel, *Classifying Calories*, N.Y. TIMES, Sept. 19, 2012, at A27.
[99] J. Simpson, *Our Obsession with Obesity*, GLOBE & MAIL, June 6, 2012, at A15.

from being obese and on public assistance? We return to these questions about objectives, below.

In the United States, the main government food assistance program is SNAP. There are other targeted programs such as school breakfast and lunch and WIC (Women, Infants, and Children).[100] In 2011 SNAP cost $75 billion (of which $71.8 billion was for benefits).[101] There is a great need for SNAP and related programs. Since the 2008 economic meltdown, demand for government assistance programs has significantly increased. In 2009, in the United States, about 25 percent of households with children reported incidents of food hardship—insufficient money to buy food.[102] In 2011, SNAP assisted almost one in six to put food on the table every month.[103]

At the same time the impact on diets of those participating in SNAP is questionable. SNAP may help individuals have more food (and calories), but what about nutrition? Recipients of SNAP and similar programs have higher rates of obesity than those who are not participants.[104] The fear is that such participants may be getting more than enough calories but also the wrong kinds: calorically dense foods that are comparably inexpensive but unhealthy. That diet leads to the "new malnutrition" referred to earlier.[105]

Two basic strategies for improving nutrition for those on SNAP have emerged: banning junk food and drink and promoting financially the purchase of healthy food such as fresh fruits and vegetables.[106] Discussion of such strategies and ways to implement them are comparatively recent. Efforts to experiment using one or the other tell us much about the current debate about fat and public health.

In terms of prohibition the idea is simple. The central purpose of SNAP is revealed in its title: nutrition assistance. Therefore, funds from this program should not be used to purchase junk food and drink. Any ban would not

---

[100] For a review of some of these other programs and their impact, *see* J. Alston et al., *U.S. Food Policy and Obesity*, in PUBLIC HEALTH-SOCIAL AND BEHAVIORAL HEALTH 165, 170–71 (J. Maddock ed. 2013), *available at* http://www.intechopen.com/books/public-health-social-and-behavioral-health/food-policy-and-obesity.

[101] *United States Farm Bill, 2012: What's at Stake* (Institute for Agriculture and Trade Policy, Mar. 28, 2012), *available at* http://www.iatp.org/documents/whats-at-stake-in-the-2012-farm-bill [hereinafter *U.S. Farm Bill 2012*].

[102] *Food Hardship: A Closer Look at Hunger: Data for the Nation, States, 100 MSAs, and Every Congressional District* (Food Research and Action Center, Jan. 2010), *available at* http://frac.org/pdf/food_hardship_report_2010.pdf. The survey asked this question: "Have there been times in the last twelve months when you did not have enough money to buy food that you or your family needed?"

[103] *U.S. Farm Bill* 2012, *supra* note 101, at 1.

[104] L. Peeples, *Thin Wallet, Thick Waistlines: New USDA Effort Targets Link between Obesity and Food Stamps*, SCIENTIFIC AM., Mar. 2010, *available at* http://www.scientificamerican.com/article.cfm?id=food-stamps-obesity.

[105] Keim, *supra* note 97.

[106] J. Guthrie et al., *Improving Food Choices—Can Food Stamps Do More?*, 5(2) AMBER WAVES 46–52, 48 (2007).

prevent recipients from buying such unhealthy stuff—they would just need to do that with their own resources, not public money.

Proponents of this idea point out that certain prohibitions have applied for some time. For example, a ban on using SNAP funds (and, formerly, food stamps) to purchase cigarettes and alcohol has long been in effect.[107] In addition, the WIC program limits the use of benefits to only certain nutritiously rich foods and drinks.[108] Thus, it is asserted, there is nothing novel, in this context, about banning the use of public funds. The only issue is whether such prohibitions should be extended to food and drink of dubious nutritional value. But, as we shall see in a moment, this simple idea has generated enormous controversy.

Promotions target nutritious foods and drink and encourage their consumption by offering individuals financial rewards to do so. The idea here is to focus on healthy food and drinks, such as fresh fruits and vegetables, and offer incentives to those receiving SNAP benefits to purchase them. Individuals taking advantage of such incentives have greater access to such food and drinks while increasing their overall SNAP benefits.

Of course, there are issues with such incentives. First, the more they are acted upon, the more the cost of any program increases. This is a critical point in this period of government cost cutting, a matter we will return to.[109] Second, the overall impact on diet is unknown. It may be that participants will buy more fruits and vegetables (the target of the incentives). There are a few studies in other countries, such as New Zealand, that indicate that incentives do result in participants increasing their purchasing of targeted foods and drinks.[110] If this is so, what do they do with the extra money that they have because of these subsidies?

Can these underwritings shift participants' overall diet so that they also buy healthy items that may not be part of the incentives program, such as oatmeal and multigrains? Or do they purchase (more) pop and chips? Or booze? The purpose of these questions is not to suggest that those on SNAP necessarily have more suspect consumption habits than others. Most of us need to consume more oats and fewer French fries. The questions are aimed at the need to know critical facts: to what extent will incentives push overall consumption habits in the right direction?

Reconfiguring SNAP to improve diet is only in its initial stages, and its future is uncertain. So far attempts at banning have run afoul of successful

---

[107] A. Lubrano, *The Debate over Food Stamps*, STANDARD-EXAMINER, Sept. 25, 2011, *available at* http://www.standard.net/stories/2011/09/25/debate-over-food-stamps.

[108] Women, Infants and Children (WIC), information page *available at* http://www.fns.usda.gov/wic.

[109] *Infra* Section IV(c)(5): Dollars, Consumption, and Norms.

[110] Peeples, *supra* note 104.

opposition. There's some cautious experimenting with incentives. But, even if successful, expansion of such subsidies will have to deal with the hard fact that they cost more at a time of government austerity, in general, and curtailing of the SNAP budget, in particular.

3. Soda and the City: Bloomberg's Bans #1 and #2

A prominent proponent of bans on use of food stamps to purchase nonnutritious products is Mayor Bloomberg of New York City. In April 2011 his administration took aim at sugar-sweetened beverages, in particular soda.[111] Thus his first attempt at a ban was launched. Some unpleasant facts are on his side.[112] More than 6 percent of SNAP funding is used by beneficiaries to buy sugar-sweetened beverages.[113] Four in ten residents of high-poverty areas of Harlem, Brooklyn, and the South Bronx drink four or more sugary drinks daily. (One in ten in the affluent Upper West Side do so).[114]

His basic argument was the one set out earlier: funds of a program meant to assist nutrition should not be used to buy unhealthy food and drink. In addition, advocates of his proposal highlighted the facts also referred to previously: SNAP already bans certain items, such as tobacco and alcohol, and the WIC program restricts benefits to a limited number of highly nutritious foods and drinks. Because of the high rates of consumption of sugary beverages by the poor, they made an especially promising target.

The Bloomberg proposal ignited a firestorm. There were the predictable libertarian arguments that such a ban would be the thin edge of the wedge with goodness knows what assaults on freedom to quickly follow. A conglomeration of various components of the food industry also weighed in with dire predictions for the future of retail suppliers (even though the same amount of money would be available in the hands of SNAP recipients).[115]

Adding to the hue and cry were anti-hunger advocates. They saw the Bloomberg proposal as a stealth attack on SNAP generally. They worried about the stigma attached to forbidding recipients access to certain foods and drinks. They also pointed out that many other individuals received federal funds (employees, contractors, social security beneficiaries). Would they

---

[111] R. Pear, *Soft Drink Industry Fights Proposed Food Stamp Ban*, N.Y. TIMES, Apr. 30, 2011, at A11; A. Barnhill and K. King, *Evaluating Equity Critiques in Food Policy: The Case of Sugar-Sweetened Beverages* 41:1 J. Law, Medicine & Ethics 30 (2013).

[112] K. Brownell & D. Ludwig, *The Supplemental Nutrition Assistance Program, Soda, and USDA Policy*, 306(12) J. AM. MED. ASS'N 1370, 1370–71 (Sept. 2011).

[113] USDA, Economic Research Service, *What Role Do Food and Beverage Prices Have on Diet and Health Outcomes?*, 10(3) FEATURES (Sept. 2012), available at http://www.ers.usda.gov/media/909975/foodandbeverage.pdf; see also Center for Science in the Public Interest, *Should Taxpayers Subsidize Soda?*, July 15, 2010, available at http://cspinet.org/new/201007151.html.

[114] G. Canada, *NYC's SNAP Sugary Beverage Ban Is the Right Idea*, HUFFINGTON POST, July 15, 2011, available at http://www.huffingtonpost.com/geoffrey-canada/nycs-snap-sugary-beverage_1_b_901480.html.

[115] Pear, *supra* note 111.

be soon told what to eat and drink?[116] In fact something like that requirement has been advocated by the Institute of Medicine in its *Weight of the Nation* Report in terms of federal government-owned, operated, and occupied buildings, worksites, and facilities.[117]

The opponents were successful. In August 2011 the USDA indicated that it would not grant the necessary exemption to allow the Bloomberg proposal to be put into effect.[118] In its refusal to grant an exemption, the USDA indicated that the ban should be "tested on the smallest scale appropriate to minimize any unintended negative effects." Whether this "pilot project" point was part of the real reason USDA withheld its authorization is questionable. This was not the first time the USDA had declined to permit such an exemption. It rejected a similar proposal from Minnesota in 2004.[119]

Other reasons it gave seemed unreasonable. For example, there was a requirement that there be "meaningful results with respect to...effect[s] on obesity and health." This is a very difficult condition to establish given the myriad influences on weight and health of everyone, including participants in SNAP. Imposing such a requirement as a precondition of implementation would defeat almost any intervention that we have discussed at various points in this book.

In the spring of 2012, the stalwart mayor hatched another idea for yet a different sort of ban: prohibit the sale of soda servings in excess of sixteen ounces.[120] Thus, his second ban was launched. This initiative was not limited to SNAP recipients but because it, again, reflected the persistence of Mr. Bloomberg on these issues it deserves mention. His Honor maintained that this initiative would combat obesity. At one level this seemed an odd claim. The ban could be easily evaded by consumers simply buying more containers under the size limit, simultaneously or over a period of time. Moreover, the prohibition applied only to restaurants, street carts, and entertainment and sports venues. Convenience stores, including 7 Eleven and its king-size Big Gulp drinks, were exempt, as were vending machines and some newsstands.[121]

Yet more controversy was stirred by this proposal. The usual cast of characters, and a few others, joined the fray. Public health advocates and officials applauded it.[122] So did members of the diet industry such as Jenny Craig and

---

[116] Lubrano, *supra* note 107.

[117] INSTITUTE OF MEDICINE, *supra* note 43, at 190–201.

[118] Letter J. Shahin, Associate Administrator, Supplemental Nutrition Assistance Program to Elizabeth Berlin, Executive Deputy Commissioner, New York State Office of Temporary and Disability Assistance, Aug. 19, 2011 (on file).

[119] Pear, *supra* note 111.

[120] W. Hu, *Obesity Ills That Won't Budge Fuel a Mayor's Battle on Soda*, N.Y. TIMES, June 12, 2012, at A1, A3; *Fluid Ounces*, NEW YORKER, June 18, 2012, at 26.

[121] M. Grynbaum, *Voting 8 to 0, Health Panel Approves Restrictions on Sale of Large Sugary Drinks*, N.Y. TIMES, Sept. 14, 2012, at A20.

[122] J. Brody, *In Fighting Obesity, Drink Size Matters*, N.Y. TIMES, Oct. 23, 2012, at D7.

Weight Watchers.[123] New Yorkers for Beverage Choices, a group funded by the soft drink industry, opposed it, as did some small-business owners.

Individuals lined up with those who were against the measure. A poll conducted by *The New York Times* found that 60 percent of those interviewed were opposed to this Bloomberg initiative. Those who did not support the proposal thought that the mayor was overreaching and infringing on consumers' freedom of choice: the very points made by the soft drink industry in its battle with His Honor.[124]

The proposal was passed by the City Board of Health. Shortly, thereafter, litigation was launched challenging the Board's authority to enact such a measure. To date that litigation has been successful.[125] Where the Bloomberg ban plan will go, at the date of this writing, remains to be seen. In any event, the mayor's initiatives are an interesting study in "norm cascades." We'll return to that phrase and the New York initiatives in the Conclusion of this section.

4. Promotions Piloted

The USDA point, mentioned just above, about a pilot project was a good one. There are sound reasons to test various interventions through such experiments, including savings of costs, time, and the acknowledgement that interventions to address obesity/health are mostly a matter of trial and error in terms of the effects produced. Efforts using incentives to promote consumption of healthy food and drink have been making more progress than efforts at banning. Such success has occurred for a number of reasons, including the use of pilot projects.

Offering incentives (rewards), underwritten with public money, is an idea that has been around for some time.[126] That idea has experienced a resurgence, in part, because it fits well with notions of the "new governance" and "nudging" that we discussed in Chapter 1.[127] Choice remains with the individual—but certain choices, judged to be good ones, are promoted in concrete ways. Educational campaigns, discussed in Chapter 5, extol healthier choices.[128] Incentives offer tangible support for them. Moreover, in this age of business models, advocates underscore how often rewards are used, in employment

---

[123] J. Peltz, *NYC's Soda Ban Pitch Gets Hefty Endorsement*, TORONTO STAR, Sept. 6, 2012, at L5.

[124] M. Grynbaum & M. Connelly, *60% in City Oppose Soda Ban, Calling It an Overreach by Bloomberg, a Poll Finds*, N.Y. TIMES, Aug. 23, 2012, at A18, A19.

[125] M. Grynbaum, *Soda Industry Sues to Stop City's Restrictions on Sales*, N.Y. TIMES, Oct. 13, 2012, at A19.; M. Grynbaum, *Court Halts Ban On Large Sodas in New York City*, N.Y. TIMES, Mar. 11, 2013, at A1, A17.

[126] BOGART, *supra* note 12, at 63–65.

[127] Chapter 1, Section V(a): *Ideas for the New Governance: Normativity and Its Offspring*.

[128] Chapter 5, Section III(a): *Educating about Nutritious Eating and Drinking*.

contexts, to minimize absenteeism, encourage occupational health and safety, promote productivity and profitability, and so forth.

As a result, experiments with rewards are in progress in several areas. One of these is measures to address traffic tie ups. There are "sticks" being used such as "congestion charges": levies imposed for using high traffic areas at peak times, etc. But "carrots" are also being experimented with: for example, "Capri" (Congestion and Policy Relief Incentives). Sponsored by the U.S. Department of Transportation, "Capri" allows people driving to traffic-clogged places of work to enter a daily lottery with a chance to win up to an extra $50 in their pay check if they shift their commute to off-peak hours.[129] There have also been efforts to use rewards to promote dieting.[130] In Chapter 7 we will discuss another example of a reward to promote children's physical activity, provided through the Canadian tax system.[131]

This interest in rewards to (re)shape behavior has been taken up by those wishing to promote healthier eating. A particular focus is on individuals and families with low incomes. Incentives to eat healthy foods that target the poor can both promote nutrition and increase food budgets for those who have an obvious need. The Institute of Medicine committees have recommended that governments consider incentives, through the tax system and otherwise, to encourage companies that promote healthier food and beverages for children in settings where they typically consume them. Similarly, there could be inducements for small food-store owners in underserved areas to carry food items that are healthier and more affordable.[132]

A number of such programs, specifically focused on low-income individuals and families, are being tried.[133] One of the most prominent is the Healthy Initiatives Pilot (HIP). This experiment began in the fall of 2011 in Hampden County, Massachusetts. There are approximately 50,000 SNAP households in that County of which 7,500 have been randomly selected for the rewards program.[134]

For every dollar participants spend on fruits and vegetables using their SNAP benefit cards, 30 cents is added to the balance on their SNAP Electronic Benefit

---

[129] J. Markoff, *Incentives for Drivers Who Avoid Traffic Jams*, N.Y. TIMES, June 12, 2012, at D1, D4.

[130] H. Sung, *How to Get Dieters to Lose Weight? You Pay Them, Obviously*, GLOBE & MAIL, Jan. 14, 2011, *available at* http://www.theglobeandmail.com/life/fashion-and-beauty/how-to-get-dieters-to-lose-weight-you-pay-them-obviously/article621912/.

[131] Chapter 7, Section V(b)(5): *Vouchers to the Rescue?: The Canadian Children's Fitness Tax Credit*.

[132] INSTITUTE OF MEDICINE, *supra* note 43, at 175 and citing various other IOM reports; *see also* WHITE HOUSE TASK FORCE, *supra* note 89, at 53–54.

[133] Hu, *supra* note 120; Guthrie et al., *supra* note 106.

[134] A. Browne, *Hampden County, Mass. to Conduct First Healthy Incentives Pilot*, USDA BLOG, Aug. 20, 2010, *available at* http://blogs.usda.gov/2010/08/20/hampden-county-mass-to-conduct-first-healthy-incentives-pilot/.

Cards, thus cutting the cost of such foods by 30 percent. The program is to be rigorously evaluated.[135] That assessment will gauge the effects of the incentive on consumption of fruits and vegetables and on the entire diet of participants. The evaluation will also assess impacts on food retailers; the feasibility of HIP, including implementing it nationwide; and other aspects of the pilot.

5. Dollars, Consumption, and Norms

It may come down to dollars. HIP and related pilots may have potential to push low-income people toward a healthier diet. Rigorous evaluations of the experiments such as the assessment planned for HIP are critical in determining their actual effects. The goal is to use the subsidies to buy and consume healthier foods and then to spend the money saved on more healthy foods.

But if successful, such positive outcomes may be the projects' undoing. Cost incentives for HIP could increase the cost of SNAP, for that innovation, by 30 percent. How likely is it in these times of cash-starved governments and neo-liberal tendencies that food programs for poor people will increase? There are good arguments that the resources for SNAP should grow not only to improve the health of low-income people but also the stimulative effects such programs can have on the economy. But those points are mostly being turned aside by the forces who believe the right response to public debt is immediate and long-range cuts. In May 2012 the U.S. Senate Agriculture Committee *cut* $33 billion from SNAP from that year's draft version of the Farm Bill.[136] Into 2013 there was so much debate about its various provisions that the Farm Bill had not been enacted.[137] Should such reductions actually be enacted, it is difficult to see how HIP will survive, after its initial trial period, let alone be expanded.

Prohibitions, such as the ban on using SNAP funds to buy soda advocated by Mayor Bloomberg, could be justifiable in an overall scheme that also offered rewards for purchasing healthy foods. But the actual effects of such bans, if implemented, should be carefully examined.[138] The ban/incentives taken together could be a promotion of norms about good eating and drinking by a program that, as its title indicates, is focused on nutritional assistance. But the bans alone run the risk of being punitive, especially if there are substantial cuts to the SNAP budget.

---

[135] College of Natural Resources, University of California, Berkeley, *Will a 30-Percent Incentive on Fruits and Vegetables Lead to Healthier Eating?*, Aug. 20, 2010, available at http://nature.berkeley.edu/blogs/news/2010/08/abt_will_a_30percent_incentive.php.

[136] A. Ranallo, *Senate Agriculture Committee Falls Short on the Farm Bill*, Institute for Agriculture and Trade Policy, May 3, 2012, *available at* http://www.iatp.org/documents/senate-agriculture-committee-falls-short-on-the-farm-bill.

[137] R. Nixon, *With Farm Bill Stalled, Consumers May Face Soaring Milk Prices*, N.Y. TIMES, Dec. 21, 2012, at A17, A22; R. Nixon, *Senate Passes Farm Bill; House Vote is Less Sure* N.Y. TIMES, June 11, 2013, A10; R. Nixon, *House Defeat of Farm Bill Lays Bare Rift in G.O.P* N.Y. TIMES, June 21 2013, A12, A15.

[138] Alston et al., *supra* note 100, at 176.

Back to Mr. Bloomberg. In many ways his efforts are admirable. When asked about the funds the soda industry was spending in trying to defeat his size ban, His Honor replied: "I just spent roughly $600 million of my own money to try to stop the scourge of tobacco. I'm looking for another cause. How much were they spending again?" [139] The mayor's leadership on these issues takes us back to our discussion of norms in Chapter 1.[140] The hope among his supporters is that he will create "norm cascades" that will lead to a "tipping point" in terms of the much-reviled SSBs that public health officials love to hate.[141] When that shift occurs glasses will be filled with plain water and not Coke.

That change would be welcomed. But in trying to create that shift the mayor and his allies keep focusing on weight, not health. The worry is that this battle will reinforce the message that shedding pounds is the sign of victory. If weight is not reduced, the mayor and consumers have been defeated. It is unlikely that cutting back on soda will lead to permanent weight loss for most large people and, in any event, that cause and effect could be demonstrated given the rest of their diets, physical activity (or inactivity), etc. His Honor's good intentions are not to be doubted. Yet his campaigns run the risk of his being viewed not as a champion of health but, rather, the uber-wealthy scourge of fat people, especially the poor, hectoring those who dare to seek momentary solace in an SSB.[142]

Those interested in SNAP should also surrender the idea that any of these proposals are going to result in permanent weight loss, at least based on the evidence to date. These interventions could possibly play a role, in conjunction with many other factors, in prevention of weight gain. They could be part of healthier eating and drinking. But expecting pounds to be lost and kept off is an elusive goal.[143] The more it is pursued, the more unattainable it may become.

V. Conclusion

Permit but discourage as a theme for regulating consumption is nicely reflected in fiscal policy directed at eating and drinking. Taxes on junk food are meant to dissuade consumers from excess even as they are free to choose to eat and drink unhealthy products. Subsidies, whether in terms of agricultural policy,

---

[139] Grynbaum, *supra* note 121, at A20.

[140] Chapter 1, Section V(b): Ideas for New Governance: Normativity and Its Offspring.

[141] J. Rosen, *The Social Policy: Following the Law because You're Too Embarrassed Not To*, NEW YORKER, Oct. 20, 1997, at 170; M. GLADWELL, THE TIPPING POINT: HOW LITTLE THINGS CAN MAKE A BIG DIFFERENCE (2000).

[142] L. Berlant, *Risky Business: On Obesity, Eating, and the Ambiguity of "Health,"* in AGAINST HEALTH: HOW HEALTH BECAME THE NEW MORALITY 26 (J. Metzl & A. Kirkland eds., 2010); Bruegel, *supra* note 98; G. Bellafante, *In Fight Against Obesity Epidemic, Poverty Is Patient Zero*, N.Y. TIMES, Mar. 17, 2013, at A26.

[143] Von Tigerstrom, *supra* note 41, at para. 24.

in general, or those directed at the poor, are meant to do the opposite of levies: such underwriting is to encourage the consumption of nutritious items.

As an idea, using fiscal policy to "nudge" people toward healthy patterns of eating and drinking makes such sense. The reality may be different. First and foremost, proponents should stop tying the case for such policies to weight loss. We discussed the dismal statistics in Chapter 2 on the inability of most fat people to shed pounds and, in the instances when that occurs, to maintain the loss over time. The case for prevention of excess weight gain, particularly in terms of children, may be stronger. But even with prevention the case is better made by emphasizing improvements in health and not obsessing about weight.

Beyond the weight/health divide the case for taxes is going to be a hard one to establish. To be effective in suppressing consumption these levies will have to be so high as to risk being punitive. Moreover, reasonable levels of public support are tied to revenues from these taxes being used for anti-obesity programs—which are unlikely as cash-starved governments look for any source of money to keep their enfeebled ledgers going. Incessant pushing for these taxes by advocates risks alienating public support for a more general movement for healthier eating and drinking.

Subsidies hold promise. However, such expectations, at a general level, require a comprehensive rethinking of agricultural policy: which crops should receive what kinds of incentives, the actual impacts any such inducements have in bringing about more nutritious consumption, the conditions of work of those who labor in agricultural production, etc. That retooling is a tall order: one facing many challenges, including from those who benefit from the status quo and who are likely to oppose significant changes.

Incentives targeting the poor to encourage them to have better diets should be experimented with in several ways, including pilot projects through SNAP and related programs. Prohibiting purchase of certain nonnutritious products—the opposite of inducements—can be justified; other items such as cigarettes and alcohol are banned. But we need to keep a watchful eye on the actual results. Does forbidding items actually lead to better nutrition for those affected? Or, do they find other ways to consume proscribed items, perhaps, at the same time rebelling against other efforts to improve their diets? At a policy level bans may be justified. But, in the end, will they do more harm than good?

Subsidies—positive reinforcement—is the better route. Experiments should be encouraged. At the same time fiscal reality should be faced. The more successful inducements are, the more they should be used. The more they are used, the more they will, generally, cost. The dollars and cents of improving a nation's diet need to be reckoned with. At the end of the day it is money well spent.

{7}

Encouraging Physical Activity: Children at Play!

I. Introduction

Physical exercise is related to both weight and fitness. That fundamental allows those focused on weight control to emphasize that aspect of an active lifestyle, particularly prevention of obesity. Those focused on fitness can underscore that element of exercise. The common ground may be the recognition and promotion of brisk movement for healthy living in general.

But how to motivate people to get up and go? This is a central question. Individuals in many societies are increasingly becoming less, not more, active. Given the sedentary lives of so many in so many countries it is apparent that there is no straightforward answer. This chapter looks at legal responses that may be available to encourage individuals to adapt more active lifestyles. The message throughout the book is the same one here: there is a role for law, but it is a complicated one. Devising a mix of interventions is one thing. Having them achieve the desired results is yet another. Law's chances of producing sought-after objectives improve when it acts in conjunction with—and influences and is influenced by—relevant norms. If norms shift in the direction of law's goals they are more likely to be achieved; if the law underscores the shift in norms, those changes will be strengthened and have more influence in the larger society. But how to attain such interdependence? Then, too, many of these interventions have a price tag. Will there be the political will and the financial wherewithal to implement them effectively?

The chapter begins with a brief review of a situation that is all too prevalent: the inactive ways of too many in too many societies. It then surveys the field of choice in terms of legal responses to promote physical activity.

Next it discusses in detail various efforts to promote physical activity among children. We focus here on children for the same reasons that we made them central to our other detailed examinations of interventions: restrictions of advertising and marketing and use of fiscal policies. The best way to address a health problem is to avoid it: prevention. Whether the emphasis is on weight control, on fitness, or on both, avoiding the development of negative conditions is frequently a key consideration. Thus the focus is on kids to keep them fit and active right from the start and to develop good habits for a lifetime.

We examine a number of strategies: preschool, formal education programs, community efforts, the built environment, and the tax system to create incentives for physical activity. We discuss the theory and policy behind these interventions. We look at assessments of those that have been implemented. At the end of the day, our greatest curiosity concerns their effectiveness. Here, again, we ask what we mean by effectiveness: Shedding pounds? Prevention of weight gain? Achieving fitness? Healthier eating/drinking? Protection from stigma? Then, too, there is a critical reality that must be faced: however effectiveness may be measured, most of the recommended interventions come with a price tag. If we want our children to be more physically active, public resources must be allocated to the cause.

II. The Sedentary We: Lifestyles of The Physically Inactive

Michelle Obama's "Let's Move" campaign is a rallying cry calling all to physical activity.[1] For good reason: there are major benefits from sports, exercise, and other forms of recreation. What is more, starting young helps to produce these benefits right from the beginning and to form habits that can last a lifetime. A survey has found that 90 percent of Americans who participate in an outdoor activity began to do so between the ages of five and eighteen.[2] Young people who grow up being physically active are more likely to be so as adults.[3] Exercise helps control weight, at least for some; build muscle; achieve healthy cardiovascular, hormonal, and immune systems; and promote strong bone and joint development. Physical activity can also strengthen mental health, relieving depression and increasing self-esteem. It may help to prevent dementia in older adults.[4] There is also research that suggests that exercise is correlated with improved academic performance.[5]

---

[1] Let's Move, *America's Move to Raise a Healthier Generation of Kids*, available at http://www.letsmove.gov/.

[2] Outdoor Industry Foundation, *Exploring the Active Lifestyle: An Outdoor Industry Foundation Consumer Outreach Report* (Jan. 2004), available at http://www.outdoorfoundation.org/pdf/ResearchActiveLifestyleExecutive.pdf.

[3] U.S. Department of Health and Human Services, Office of Disease Prevention and Health Promotion, *Physical Activity Guidelines for Americans* (2008), available at http://www.health.gov/paguidelines/pdf/paguide.pdf.

[4] *Fitness May Prevent Dementia*, N.Y. TIMES, Feb. 12, 2013, at D4.

[5] WHITE HOUSE TASK FORCE ON CHILDHOOD OBESITY, REPORT TO THE PRESIDENT, SOLVING THE PROBLEM OF CHILDHOOD OBESITY WITHIN A GENERATION 65–66 (May 2010).

The *Physical Activity Guidelines for Americans* recommends that children and adolescents should be physically active for at least sixty minutes every day participating in age-appropriate, enjoyable, diverse group and individual sports and recreation.[6] Such activity should include moderate-to-vigorous aerobic exercises and muscle and bone strengthening. Ideally vigorous movement should be woven into a child's day: walking or biking to and from school, physical education classes, and active games during recess and after school in parks and playgrounds.[7]

Yet such prescriptions for youthful frolicking are far from the reality for too many children. In 2010 it was reported that fewer than one in five high school students meet the recommendations of sixty minutes of daily physical activity. As children get older the situation deteriorates: Older adolescents are less likely to be physically active than youngsters; girls are even less active than boys, with African-American and Hispanic teenage girls least active of all.[8] Children with various disabilities experience a range of challenges to engaging in sports and recreation. These youths have a rate of inactivity that is 4.5 times higher than other children.[9]

As with the child so, too, the adult. The hard, toned body ready to spurt into action at a moment's notice is an illusion for most American adults.[10] In surveys, over a period of time only about a third of men and women reported enough activity to meet public health guidelines. Even worse: about 30 percent were sedentary. These individuals reported essentially no leisure time activity. The remainder (about 45 percent) reported some activity, but not at a sufficient level to maintain wellness. Yet, even comparatively small levels of activity can make a difference to fitness if not to weight.[11] Significant health benefits can be achieved by as little as thirty minutes of moderate physical activity accumulated throughout the day.[12]

There are many social and environmental factors that inhibit active lifestyles. Just some of these are: urban spaces centered on the car, limited access to low- or no-cost facilities (playgrounds, parks, trails), and concerns for safety in various neighborhoods and other city spaces.[13] Technology and its promotion

---

[6] *Physical Activity Guidelines, supra* note 3.
[7] WHITE HOUSE TASK FORCE, *supra* note 5, at 66.
[8] *Id.*
[9] *Id.* at 67.
[10] F. Bruni, *The Ripped and the Righteous*, N.Y. TIMES, WEEK IN REVIEW, Jan. 30, 2011, at 1, 3.
[11] R. Rabin, *How Much Exercise Prevents Weight Gain?*, N.Y. TIMES, Apr. 6, 2010, at D6; G. Reynolds, *Weighing the Evidence on Exercise*, N.Y. TIMES MAG., Apr. 18, 2010, at 36.
[12] L. FRANK ET AL., HEALTH AND COMMUNITY DESIGN: THE IMPACT OF THE BUILT ENVIRONMENT ON PHYSICAL ACTIVITY 4, 48, 50 (2003).
[13] WHITE HOUSE TASK FORCE, *supra* note 5, at 66; FRANK ET AL., *supra* note 12, at 57.

of sedentary ways is also a huge factor. In 2010 it was reported that adolescents in America spend more than seven hours a day watching television, DVDs, or movies, or using a computer, cell phone or other mobile device.[14] Those youths with disabilities are even more susceptible to technology and its capacity to physically pacify. They are twice as likely to watch television for more than four hours a day than other adolescents.[15]

Various barriers and technology, just described, clearly have a dampening effect on physical activity. The individual's state of mind is important as well: young people who believe that they have the skills to participate are more likely to be active.[16] Then there are norms, those techniques of social control that have fascinated us throughout this book.[17] Peer influence pushes toward, or away from, exercise depending on the attitudes of the relevant group: "social norms are powerful in determining people's actions."[18] Adolescents who feel supported by others who are physically active are more likely to participate in structured and unstructured activities.[19]

Research indicates that coordinated, multi-component programs are necessary to significantly change norms and, ultimately, behavior so that more individuals are more physically active. Massive transformation will need to take place: "changes at all levels, including individual [modifications]; choices, attitudes, and behaviours about physical activity; the structure of school days; teaching approaches; the physical environments of communities; and policy decisions that govern our way of life."[20] A tall order, and what are the chances of success? What role can and should law play in promoting norms to achieve these goals?

---

[14] WHITE HOUSE TASK FORCE, *supra* note 5, at 66. Differences in media use in relation to race and ethnicity are even more pronounced, and they hold up after controlling for other demographic factors such as age and parent education, or whether the child is from a single- or two-parent family. For example, Hispanic and Black youth average about thirteen hours of media exposure daily (13:00 hours for Hispanics and 12:59 hours for Blacks), compared to just over 8½ hours (8:36 hours) among Whites. Watching TV on new platforms has become fairly routine among young people. Almost half (48 percent) of all eight- to eighteen-year-olds say they have watched TV online, and 30 percent report having watched TV on a cell phone, iPod, or other MP3 player: *See* A Kaiser Family Foundation Study, *Generation M2: Media in the Lives of 8- to 18-Year-Olds* (Jan. 2010), *available at* http://www.kff.org/entmedia/upload/8010.pdf.

[15] WHITE HOUSE TASK FORCE, *supra* note 5, at 67.

[16] S. Trost et al., *Correlates of Objectively Measured Physical Activity in Preadolescent Youth*, 17(2) AM. J. OF PREVENTIVE MED. 120–26 (1999).

[17] Chapter 1, Section V: Some Ideas about Law Shaping Behavior.

[18] WHITE HOUSE TASK FORCE, *supra* note 5, at 66.

[19] *Id.* at 66 and n.253, authorities cited.

[20] *Id.* at 67–68.

III. Promoting Active Lifestyles: The Range of Interventions

There are a number of ways that law could be used to promote physical activity. The following is a list of some of the major ones:

Education (supported by legislation)

– Mount major campaigns to promote exercise.
– Require daily opportunities for physical education and sports in schools.

Health care and Training

– Require health care training programs, whether public or private, to teach methods of counseling patients about activity and health, including the care of infants and young children.

Advertising

– Prohibit misleading health claims in advertising for exercise programs and equipment.

Insurance

– Regulate life and health insurance premiums to provide incentives for participation in approved activity programs.

Taxes and Fiscal Laws

– Provide incentives for employers to encourage staff to be physically active including: providing exercise facilities, allowing extra time at lunch for an exercise break, and subsidizing gym memberships.
– Permit individuals to deduct the cost of or be given a credit for approved gym and sports facilities memberships.
– Remove any sales tax on sporting equipment such as bicycles, skates, rock climbing gear, etc.

Urban Development and Transportation

– Require communities and builders to develop parks and other venues for exercise, sports, and recreational programs.
– Modify zoning requirements to encourage creation of sidewalks, pedestrian malls, and bicycle paths and adoption of architectural designs for buildings that promote walking and use of streets.
– Develop programs to discourage use of cars and encourage walking; for example "car-free days" and surcharges on use of cars in dense urban cores.

Litigation

– Create liability for damage caused to health and for other consequences on the part of those who fail to carry out specific obligations to provide opportunities for physical activity.

As our discussion in Chapter 4 indicated, we will not try to tackle all of these interventions.[21] However, several of these aspects will be addressed when we turn, below, to our discussion of physical activity for children. Many of these interventions are mostly about "nudges": promoting good choices while leaving decisions up to the individual.[22] Coercion by the state is mostly avoided. Such legal strategies should also buttress shifts in norms. Ultimately we need people to embrace physical exercise not as a necessary, unavoidable evil but as part of a full and enjoyable lifestyle.

IV. While They're Young: Law's Role from The Start

What we experience from the first few years of life greatly influences who we are in later years. Infant development proceeds rapidly. What happens to children at the start is "built into their bodies," affecting neural, metabolic, and behavioral systems in ways that can influence well-being throughout the life span. Early development provides a period in which healthy dietary and activity patterns can be established that can provide a foundation for all the other years.[23] However, infants who gain weight rapidly in the first year of life are 1.17 to 5.70 times more likely to become obese compared with those who do not experience such gains during the same period.[24]

If bad habits are set during that early time, they can be undone only with difficulty. Survey data in the United States indicate that the youngest children have diets that are too high in energy and added sugar, fat, and salt, and that include too few fruits, vegetables, and complex carbohydrates. With respect to activity patterns, too many young children have lifestyles that include too much screen time, not enough sleep, and too little active play.

In all of this, caregivers are tremendously influential. Children learn from the lifestyles in which they are raised. Environments can differ significantly in the opportunities provided for active play but also for television viewing—for

---

[21] Chapter 4, Section V: What's Being Assessed; Section VI: Noted but Not Examined.

[22] Chapter 1, Section V(a): Ideas for the New Governance: Normativity and Its Offspring.

[23] COMMITTEE ON OBESITY PREVENTION POLICIES FOR YOUNG CHILDREN, INSTITUTE OF MEDICINE OF THE NATIONAL ACADEMIES, EARLY CHILDHOOD OBESITY PREVENTION POLICIES 19–22 (2011); for a note of caution about the influence of the formative years see: G. Kolata, *Many Weight Loss Ideas Are Myth, Not Science Study Finds,* N.Y. TIMES, Jan. 31, 2013, at A13.

[24] COMMITTEE ON OBESITY PREVENTION, supra note 23 at 43.

consumption of fruits and vegetables but also for French fries. In sum: "[A]dults have a powerful impact on children's developing patterns of eating and activity; they structure their children's environments through the choices they make, both within the family and through the child care arrangements they select for out-of-home care."[25]

Yet, despite what is known about the importance of the early years to patterns of living in the later ones, infancy and early childhood were usually not a focus of obesity prevention efforts until recently. There are several reasons for this lack of attention:[26]

- The difficulty of designing studies that satisfy Institutional Review Board criteria for conducting research on young children
- Both federal and private funding has targeted school-age children
- Most policy and environmental interventions are expensive with impact difficult to observe over a short period
- Younger children are more difficult to recruit for participation
- Childhood obesity prevention policy is a relatively new area for research funding

In the last five years or so there have been important initiatives to bring more attention to these beginning years to see what can reasonably be done to provide children with a healthy, active start in life. Let's look at some of these efforts.

V. Playgrounds, Schoolyards, Games, and Sports

A) GENERAL CONSIDERATIONS: THE BUILT ENVIRONMENT

There are a number of fundamental issues that planning, zoning, and transportation laws need to address, more or less at the same time, such as pollution and traffic density. In addition, there are direct connections between the way communities are built because of such laws and the amount that individuals exercise. Such implications are among those pursued by the "smart growth"/ "new urbanism" movement.[27]

That movement also examines the way that urban and other spaces can influence nutrition. For example, there is the problem of poor city neighborhoods as "food deserts" where there is little access to fresh fruits and vegetables and other nutritious food and drink. Constructive responses to those issues examine the way zoning laws, tax deductions, incentives, and other legal strategies might be employed to encourage merchants and others, such as community

---

[25] *Id.* at 21.
[26] *Id.* at 24–25.
[27] FRANK ET AL., *supra* note 12, at 190–94.

and religious groups, to provide access to nutritious food and drink in such areas.[28] Here we want to focus on the built environment and its potential for encouraging physical activity.

Before the coming of the automobile many cities in western Europe and North America were designed to permit such basic activities as school, work, shopping and, going to religious services to be engaged in on foot. Neighborhoods developed with mixed land use, and connected streets, with populations of medium to high density. In Canada and the United States, streets were often laid out in a grid pattern so as to create high levels of connectivity permitting pedestrians direct routes to various destinations.[29]

Ironically, the various developments that eventually led to the urban sprawl that characterizes so many Canadian and American cities were, initially, promoted by some noble, if erroneous ideas. Many nineteenth-century reformers, led by such luminaries as Fredrick Law Olmsted, the designer of New York's Central Park, were influenced by the theory of "miasma." This idea held that infectious diseases were caused by vile gases in the air, which, when inhaled, led to afflictions such as tuberculosis. Cities, with their dense cores, particularly the poorer ones, were thought to be prime sources of miasma.

The solution was to have urban spaces spread out so that boulevards, parks, sunshine, and fresh air could disperse such toxins and prevent the dreadful consequences that ensued from exposure to them. Such misguided ideas buttressed notions that the more spread out a city was, the better it was, including for the health of the inhabitants.[30] Yet that dispersal contributed to sprawl. It also harmed well-being by discouraging day-to-day physical activity such as walking and cycling: a prime example of the phenomena of unintended consequences discussed in Chapter 1.[31]

With the coming of widespread travel by car, suburbs, particularly in Canada and the United States, began to develop even more. Different uses of land were separated, through zoning laws, so that houses, schools, stores, places of worship, etc. were often separated by distances that discouraged walking. Low-traffic residential streets often fed into multilane, high speed, noisy roads that also inhibited use by pedestrians.

Meanwhile, as the suburbs developed, the cores of cities often deteriorated. This decline occurred for several reasons, including the loss of many affluent families and high-paying jobs to the suburbs. The state of urban parks shed light on such issues. In the last two decades or so, in the United States there has

---

[28] WHITE HOUSE TASK FORCE, *supra* note 5, at IV: "Access to Healthy, Affordable Food"; COMMITTEE ON OBESITY PREVENTION, *supra* note 23, at 27.

[29] J. Sallis & K. Glanz, *The Role of Built Environments in Physical Activity, Eating, and Obesity in Childhood*, 16 FUTURE CHILDREN 89, 92–93 (2006).

[30] FRANK ET AL., *supra* note 12, at 2, and Chapter 2: Public Health and Urban Form in America.

[31] Chapter 1, Section III(b): Assessing Impact: Three Kinds of Effects.

been a 25 percent reduction in the amount of time that children play in parks and a 50 percent reduction in spontaneous outdoor activities by kids.[32] Related activities, such as bicycling and walking to school, have also declined.[33] There are a number of reasons for this abandoning of simple day-to-day exercise. In terms of parks, some may be far away, be dangerous, or simply not exist. Parks and playgrounds may be required in development proposals, but planning authorities often do not consider their adequacy or accessibility.

A different conception of planning and relevant regulation could lead to different results. In Europe, parks, playing fields, and other amenities to encourage exercise are frequently required as part of the community infrastructure. Medium-to-high density usage of urban cores has long been encouraged.[34] For example, in the Netherlands, national standards exist for the inclusion of parks and similar amenities in residential developments, and there is a requirement that all developers must meet such standards. Often local governments directly oversee the construction of such parks and amenities to ensure such standards are complied with.[35]

Provision of adequate parks and other opportunities for outdoor exercise will not, by itself, ensure that individuals are physically active. There are a number of factors that must be addressed simultaneously in order to combat sedentary ways in society. But adequate parks should be viewed as a critical element to help people be more active.

More dramatically, the fundamentals of zoning and usage laws could be rethought and reshaped. In America, organizations such as the Congress for the New Urbanism and Smart Growth America are promoting such reforms.[36] Similarly the "complete streets" idea urges that streets be made suitable for multiple usages: cars, but also pedestrians and cyclists.[37] Governments, within their mandates, could offer tax deductions and other incentives to private actors to provide more parks and recreational facilities, especially in economically stressed neighborhoods.[38] There is evidence that streets frequented by pedestrians help neighborhoods prosper economically.[39] Urban planners such

---

[32] J.Kushner, Healthy Cities: The Intersection of Urban Planning Law and Health 155 (2007).

[33] Centers for Disease Control and Prevention, *Barriers to Children Walking and Biking to School—United States, 1999*, 51(32) Morbidity and Mortality Weekly Report 701–04 (Aug. 16, 2002).

[34] Kushner, *supra* note 32, at 174–76.

[35] *Id.*

[36] Congress for the New Urbanism, *New Urbanism: It Just Performs Better*, 1997–2011, *available at* http://www.cnu.org; Smart Growth America: *Making Neighborhoods Great Together*, 2010, *available at* http://www.smartgrowthamerica.org.

[37] See National Complete Streets Coalition, *available at* http://www.smartgrowthamerica.org/complete-streets.

[38] Sallis & Glanz, *supra* note 29, at 92.

[39] D. Israelson, *Why Walkable Cities Are a Step Ahead*, Globe & Mail, Dec. 7, 2012, at B10.

as Speck urge us to embrace the "walkable city" for all the economic, social, environmental, and physical benefits that such metropolises can produce.[40]

Changing attitudes toward such provisions in order to make them legally required will be no easy task. Some states in America prohibit developers paying for off-site facilities.[41] However, that struggle, as hard as it may be, may itself bring benefits in terms of shifting norms about the fundamental changes that must occur in many aspects of our individual and communal lives in order to have people become more physically active.

All sorts of factors could be relevant. The phenomenon of self-selection may be present: otherwise active individuals may choose to be in locations that accommodate such individuals; the locations, themselves, do not cause people living there to be physically engaged.[42] Self-selection, to the extent it is applicable, also underscores the importance of shifting norms: once a critical mass of individuals gain the urge to exercise, their behavior will promote all sorts of legal and societal changes to encourage physical activity. Yet such shifting of norms and changing of behavior face huge challenges. Consider the threat of violence. There is evidence that individuals who characterize their neighborhood as "not at all safe" are three times more likely to be inactive during leisure than those who believe that the area where they live is "extremely safe."[43]

The foregoing underlines the need for rigorous evaluation of various attempts to alter the built environment to promote physical exercise. Some such efforts are underway. One is PAPRN (Physical Activity Policy Research Network). Its mission is to "identify physical activity policies and their determinants, describe the process of their implementation, and determine their outcomes."[44] Its assessments give pause regarding the extent to which good proposals are implemented. Consider walking trails: between 2000 and 2008 there was a flurry of legislative proposals in this regard. A study found that the effectiveness of such trails to boost activity was not straightforward; it depended on such factors as connectivity, accessibility, maintenance, funding, and liability. It also found that of the 475 bills (not dependent on federal funds), only 29 percent were ever enacted.[45] Many good ideas; too few put into successful practice.

---

[40] J. SPECK, WALKABLE CITY: HOW DOWNTOWN CAN SAVE AMERICA, ONE STEP AT A TIME (2012).
[41] KUSHNER, *supra* note 32, at 174–75.
[42] Sallis & Glanz, *supra* note 29, at 90.
[43] WHITE HOUSE TASK FORCE, *supra* note 5, at 80.
[44] INSTITUTE OF MEDICINE, MEASURING PROGRESS IN OBESITY PREVENTION: WORKSHOP REPORT 80 (2012).
[45] *Id.* at 81 citing A. Eyler et al., *An Analysis of State Legislation on Community Trails*, 7 (Suppl. Mar.) J. PHYSICAL ACTIVITY & HEALTH 540–47 (2010).

B) ACTIVITY AND CHILDREN

1. Introduction

The relationship kids have with their parents is central to their well-being and, except in unusual circumstances such as neglect, is not the business of the state. But governments can establish conditions under which good habits can be formed—where norms solidify in the direction of healthy routines. Consider one example for the earliest days of infancy. There can be several benefits to breastfeeding. Reduced risk of childhood obesity may be one of them.[46] At the same time it is hard to imagine governments requiring mothers to feed their babies by this method. Nevertheless, breastfeeding can be encouraged by the state in several ways, ranging from education to laws requiring that employers provide time and places to facilitate mothers doing so.[47]

Professional child care providers can also be involved with the day-to-day lives of preschool children. Responsible agencies can use their regulatory powers to require certain conditions be met that are conducive to children in the care of these professional providers being physically active. We'll say more later about using those legal oversight powers to promote active children.[48] Some states in the United States have already implemented some of these or similar recommendations.[49]

Expert panels examining the issues and relying on the available evidence have frequently recommended that increased physical activity be targeted as one strategy for reducing the prevalence of obesity among children. What appears to be clear is that young children need substantial amounts of exercise to develop fundamental motor patterns that support skilled and efficient movement.[50] Physical activity can also assist cognitive and social development.[51] Thus there are sound reasons to encourage lots of movement in infants and toddlers, whatever the impact on weight control.

Once children are in school, the presence of the state looms large—clearly in public institutions, but private education is regulated in all sorts of ways as well. Schools are not only a major source of academic learning, but are also essential for acquiring various habits that can carry through for a lifetime. Education can be not only about reading, writing and arithmetic but also about socialization, what to eat/drink, and all manner of physical activity from highly

---

[46] COMMITTEE ON OBESITY PREVENTION, *supra* note 23, at 86–98, *but compare* J. Wolf, *Against Breastfeeding (Sometimes)*, *in* AGAINST HEALTH: HOW HEALTH BECAME THE NEW MORALITY 83 (J. Metzl & A. Kirkland eds., 2010).

[47] COMMITTEE ON CHILDHOOD OBESITY PREVENTION ACTIONS FOR LOCAL GOVERNMENTS, LOCAL GOVERNMENT ACTIONS TO PREVENT CHILDHOOD OBESITY 61 (Washington, DC: Institute of Medicine and National Research Council 2009).

[48] Infra Section V(b)(3): Professional Childcare Providers.

[49] COMMITTEE ON OBESITY PREVENTION, *supra* note 23, at 30 and 71.

[50] *Id.* at 63.

[51] *Id.* at 67.

organized sports to playing tag. There is a need for collective action on the part of parents (or guardians), professional childcare providers, early childhood educators, community organizations, schools, colleges, universities, and national health organizations to promote active, healthy children.

In the early years, pre- and school, there are also many issues concerning the development of eating and drinking habits. For example, schools and what they permit to be available as food and beverages raise significant issues about children and nutrition.[52] But, here, as with the rest of the chapter, we focus on questions regarding the encouragement of physical exercise.

2. The First Years and Parenting

Parents (or guardians) have the most influence over the lives of very young children. A sphere of autonomy in the rearing of children is seen to be an essential part of parenting. The state should compromise that independence only in very clear cases. Young children, even those who have some time with professional childcare providers, still spend the majority of days and evenings with parents. It is for parents to determine how infants and toddlers will be nurtured, including in terms of diet and activities.

At the same time parents can be encouraged to instill good eating and drinking habits, and to promote physical activity. Governments, through a variety of health and education programs, can support these healthy practices. Our discussion of the regulation of marketing, especially to children (discussed in Chapter 5), and subsidization of nutritious foods, especially for low-income families (discussed in Chapter 6), are two such examples.[53] The rearing of children remains the responsibility of parents; individual mothers and fathers decide many issues concerning their kids' development. When government intervenes it should respect the autonomy of parents and guardians as it promotes healthy choices for families.

We will come to a number of recommendations for professional settings outside the home (childcare providers, schools, etc.) regarding the promotion of physical activity for children. Many of them may require regulatory oversight; some will be mandatory. Such legal supervision is clearly not the way to go for parenting. But many of these recommendations could be useful for parents in their day-to-day nurturing of their kids.[54] Parents can be aided in taking advantage of appropriate recommendations by health and childcare professionals from whom they seek advice and care. Messages about the promotion

---

[52] M. Story et al., *Schools and Obesity Prevention: Creating School Environments and Policies to Promote Healthy Eating and Physical Activity*, 87 MILBANK Q. 71, 73–82 (2009); WHITE HOUSE TASK FORCE, *supra* note 5, at 37: III. "Healthy Food in Schools."

[53] Chapter 5, Section IV: Marketing: The Special Case of Children; Chapter 6, Section IV(c): Target Subsidies through Government Support Programs..

[54] COMMITTEE ON OBESITY PREVENTION, *supra* note 23, at 75–76.

of physical activity need to be clear and consistent across these settings: hospitals and midwives taking care of neonates, pediatricians' offices, childcare centers, early school programs, etc.

3. Professional Childcare Providers

If a young child is cared for outside the home, he or she is often placed with professional care providers that operate under various legal regulations. Such are the circumstances for a significant number of children. In the United States, more than 63 percent of mothers with young children are working outside the home. About 80 percent of preschool children whose mothers are employed are in some kind of nonparental childcare setting for an average of about forty hours a week. Most of these kids are in nonfamily arrangements such as childcare centers, preschools, and Head Start.[55]

Those concerned with promoting physical activity in infants and toddlers recommend that a number of actions be taken, including that regulatory authority be used to require conditions that are conducive to age-appropriate exercise for kids in care of facilities. Their suggestions need to be addressed. The opportunities for physical activity in many of these settings appear to be woefully inadequate. Several studies have concluded that children in many childcare centers engaged in moderate-to-vigorous physical activity in less than 3 percent of the observation periods of the investigation and were sedentary over 80 percent of that time.[56] One study examined childcare regulators in the various states based on ten model regulations formulated by relevant experts. No state had all ten model regulations. States had an average of only 3.7 of such regulations for childcare centers, and 2.9 for family childcare homes. They had few regulations pertaining to physical activity and screen time.[57]

The following are potential actions that the Institute of Medicine of the National Academies recommends that appropriate regulatory agencies should require of childcare providers.

For infants, potential actions include

- providing daily opportunities for infants to move freely under adult supervision to explore their indoor and outdoor environments;
- engaging with infants on the ground each day to optimize adult–infant interactions;

and

- providing daily "tummy time" (time in the prone position) for infants less than 6 months of age.

---

[55] N. Larson et al., *What Role Can Child-Care Settings Play in Obesity Prevention? A Review of the Evidence and Call for Research Efforts*, 111(9) J. AM. DIETETIC ASS'N 1343, 1343–44 (2011).
[56] *Id.* at 1345.
[57] WHITE HOUSE TASK FORCE, *supra* note 5, at 20.

For toddlers and preschool children, potential actions include

- providing opportunities for light, moderate, and vigorous physical activity for at least fifteen minutes per hour while children are in care;
- providing daily outdoor time for physical activity when possible;
- providing a combination of developmentally appropriate structured and unstructured physical activity experiences;
- joining children in physical activity;
- integrating physical activity into activities designed to promote children's cognitive and social development;
- providing an outdoor environment with a variety of portable play equipment, a secure perimeter, some shade, natural elements, an open grassy area, varying surfaces and terrain, and adequate space per child;
- providing an indoor environment with a variety of portable play equipment and adequate space per child;
- providing opportunities for children with disabilities to be physically active, including equipment that meets the current standards for accessible design under the Americans with Disabilities Act;
- avoiding punishing children for being physically active; and
- avoiding withholding physical activity as punishment.[58]

The foregoing are simply examples. There are several dimensions to professional caregivers promoting children's activity. Kids can be even more active outdoors. More attention needs to be paid to what children are doing when they are on playgrounds and the conditions of those facilities.[59]

Regulatory powers should be used, as appropriate, to ensure encouragement of various kinds of appropriate physical activity. Of course, care must be taken that in invoking such authority, the burden placed on care providers is not such as to stymie their providing accessible services. Moreover, regulation should be focused on policies that are demonstrated to be effective in promoting physical activity. That said, a 2011 study found that most states lack strong regulations for childcare settings that address nutritious eating/drinking and physical activity.[60] The lack of physical activity in childcare centers, discussed earlier, also suggests that government intervention is required.[61] Children frolicking while in loving care is such a beautiful image. Sadly, it is, too often, not a reality.

---

[58] COMMITTEE ON OBESITY PREVENTION, *supra* note 23, at 61.
[59] *Id.* at 66.
[60] Larson et al., *supra* note 55, at 1343.
[61] *Supra* note 56 and accompanying text.

4. School-Age Kids

i. In Class

[one] General Discussion

A basic finding needs to drive promotion of exercise and related programs for school-age children: physical education, activities, and sports in schools can all be associated with better fitness. Physical education classes will increase children's activity if these sessions include substantial amounts of moderate and vigorous exercise for stipulated periods of time in environments where kids feel supported.[62] In addition, there is evidence that up to an hour of daily physical activity can be added to school curriculum by taking time from other subjects without hurting students' academic achievements. Conversely, removing time for physical education and adding it to academic subjects does not improve students' performance in those subjects. A reason for the foregoing is that physical activity is related to students' learning efficiency. Other benefits of physical activity in conjunction with extracurricular activities include: lower dropout rate, better classroom behavior, and enhanced self-esteem.[63]

Several prominent organizations have tried to encourage physical activity in schools by articulating standards and providing research and funding. For example, the National Association for Sport and Physical Education (NASPE) has published standards for schools that support a comprehensive activity program that emphasizes daily time requirements, curriculum benchmarks, and qualified educators with appropriate equipment. Further, the Centers for Disease Control, among other activities in this area, funds education and health agencies in twenty-three states to support coordinated school health programs.[64]

Yet, despite these initiatives there is insufficient commitment at the U.S. federal and most state levels to physical education in schools. There is essentially no such law at the federal level. At the state level there has been some legislative activity. However, many bills have not been enacted. Of those bills that have been passed, only a few have addressed elements of physical education identified by research as critical to children's well-being. Story and others, after a recent review of schools and physical activity in the United States, observed: "Policy and legislative initiatives at the national, state, and local levels are needed to develop and support healthful food and physical activity behaviors that will promote energy balance and a healthy body weight."[65]

[two] U.S. Federal and State Law

At the U.S. federal level there is very little regulation requiring physical education to be provided to students in American schools. A recent development

---

[62] INSTITUTE OF MEDICINE, *supra* note 44, at 80.
[63] Story et al., *supra* note 52, at 82–83 and the sources therein cited.
[64] *Id.*
[65] *Id.* at 94.

is the School Wellness Policies (SWP) for districts with federally funded meal programs.[66] These SWPs address aspects of physical activity in schools. SWPs have potential to stimulate exercise regimes, but the extent to which they have been implemented and their effectiveness has not yet been evaluated.[67]

There are some grants available under the *No Child Left Behind Act* (NCLB) to improve physical education programs, though their impact has not been evaluated.[68] However, it may be that NCLB has had the overall effect of creating disincentives for physical education in schools. This is because the list of core academic subject grades for achievement under NCLB does not include physical education. In addition, NCLB's goal of "highly qualified teachers" does not include those who teach physical education. These unintended consequences of the NCLB have been noted as an example of legal policy gone awry.[69]

At the state level there have been some good initiatives, but much more can be done, particularly regarding basic opportunities for physical activity. There is frequently a gap between what is supposed to occur and what actually happens in individual schools. As of 2007 at least half of the states had some sort of policy relating to physical activity, instructors' qualifications in schools, etc.[70] For example, most states now require that instructors in physical education have at least undergraduate training in that regard.[71] Some states are addressing not only the quantity of time but also its quality.[72]

However, what actually happens in particular schools can be another matter. As of 2009 at least thirty-three states had some requirement for physical education at some level of schools (forty-two states had such a requirement for high schools). Yet only 4 percent of elementary, 8 percent of middle/junior, and 2 percent of high schools provided for daily physical education.[73] Only six states required (thirteen recommended) that elementary schools give students regularly scheduled recess. Only five states had adopted policies that prohibit denying recess as a punishment for poor behavior.[74] Only seven states had adopted policies supporting walking or biking to and from school.[75]

Or, to look at the situation in a somewhat different way: from 2001 to 2007, about eight hundred bills relating to physical activity in schools were introduced

---

[66] *Id.* at 89, citing Section 204 of Public Law 108-265, June 30, 2004, Child Nutrition and WIC Reauthorization Act of 2004.

[67] Story et al., *supra* note 52, at 93.

[68] Public Law 107-110, January 8, 2002, 115 STAT. 1425, cited as the "No Child Left Behind Act."

[69] Chapter 1, Section III(b): Assessing Impact: Three Kinds of Effects.

[70] Story et al., *supra* note 52, at 85.

[71] *Id.* at 87.

[72] *Id.* at 86.

[73] *Id.* at 85.

[74] *Id.* at 86.

[75] *Id.*

into state legislatures. About 20 percent were enacted, a rate consistent with the fate of other health-related bills. However, very few of the laws stipulated components of physical education that research has indicated are important in order to improve well-being, including: time allotted, activity level, teacher certification, and the environment in which classes are held. What is more, little funding was provided to assess the effects of the legislation on children's activity levels, health, and other relevant considerations.[76]

In 2009, Story and others reviewed schools' efforts to promote physical activity. They concluded that progress was being made in terms of promoting exercise as part of children's education. However, much more needed to be done: "Policy and legislative initiatives at the national, state, and local levels are needed to develop and support healthful food and physical activity behaviors that will promote energy balance and a healthy body weight. The states should establish policies that increase the amount of time children spend in physical education and improve the quality of this physical education."[77]

[three] Measuring BMI?

We discussed BMIs in Chapter 2 and the controversy surrounding this measurement of body weight. Traditional approaches to obesity use cutoff points to indicate that a person is overweight (greater than 25 BMI), obese (greater than 30), or morbidly so (great than 40). These indicators serve as a straightforward way to determine if an individual has excessive weight (and how much) and to track the number of those with such issues in the general population and various subgroups.

But there has been lots of criticism of this measure. First, by focusing on body mass, this assessment does not differentiate between fat and muscle. The latter weighs more than the former. Many athletic individuals can have BMIs in excess of 25 (or even 30) and not be overweight by any sensible definition. Second, like any sharp point of demarcation, the cutoffs have an element of arbitrariness to them. The boundaries for who is overweight and obese were suddenly shifted downward in the late 1980s. It is as if overnight vast numbers of people were considered overweight and obese, who days before were not so, as measured by BMIs. Third, these cutoff points do not necessarily signal danger to health. Recall the famous Centers for Disease Control study and follow-ups discussed in Chapter 2.[78] At the end of the day the association of deaths and high BMI (and in any event over 35) was much lower than originally

---

[76] INSTITUTE OF MEDICINE, *supra* note 44, at 80–81 citing A. Eyler et al., *Examination of Trends and Evidence–Based Elements in State Physical Education Legislation*, 80 J. SCH. HEALTH 326 (2010).

[77] Story et al., *supra* note 52, at 94.

[78] Chapter 2, Section IV(c): The Physical Health Problems Related to Obesity Are Misrepresented.

asserted. At the same time it was demonstrated that slightly overweight individuals had lower mortality rates and underweight people had higher ones.

Finally, there is the overarching criticism of focusing on weight rather than healthy eating/drinking and exercise. BMI reduces a complex array of factors concerning pounds and health to a single number that may not signify much that is useful concerning either. At the same time, because BMI assigns a single number, the competitive instincts of individuals can tempt them to compare themselves based on that score. Those with lower numbers can claim superior status without regard to how the number is derived (muscle versus fat) and the actual health of any particular individuals (including those with lower BMIs).

Yet for all the controversy surrounding BMIs, schools in the United States are using them as a means to address obesity issues among children. What is more, some respected authorities, such as the Institute of Medicine of the National Academies, the White House Task Force on Childhood Obesity, and some prominent individual researchers, such as Story, suggest the possibility of regular measuring of children's BMI.[79] The firm hope is that such assessment strategies will help to prevent obesity. Many proponents of measuring children's BMIs are also great advocates for nutritious eating/drinking and enhanced physical exercise programs in schools and elsewhere.

Proponents of such assessments point to some sobering statistics that relate parental BMI and propensity of kids to become obese. Mothers' and fathers' BMI is the strongest predictor of obesity in young adulthood. In children aged one to five having an obese mother increases the risks of their becoming obese in their twenties by 3.6 percent; having an obese father increases the odds by 2.9 percent. If both parents are obese, the odds of a child becoming obese at one to two years are increased by 13.6 percent; for those aged three to five, the odds are increased by 15.3 percent.[80]

It is important in discussing schools' use of BMI measurement to distinguish between two kinds of strategies that are being employed: surveillance (alone), or a combination of surveillance and screening. The latter is much more controversial than the former. Surveillance programs collect prevalence data on weight. Such data can be utilized to monitor trends in obesity over time. That monitoring can help in planning and in the delivery of services, and in determining their effectiveness. In contrast screening programs are meant to identify students at risk for obesity and to give that confidential information to parents. Such programs are not unique. Some schools also screen for such things as vision and hearing.

---

[79] INSTITUTE OF MEDICINE, PREVENTING CHILDHOOD OBESITY: HEALTH IN THE BALANCE (2005); WHITE HOUSE TASK FORCE, *supra* note 5, at 35–36 (endorses measurements by child's pediatrician); Story et al., *supra* note 52, at 87–89.

[80] COMMITTEE ON OBESITY PREVENTION, *supra* note 23, at 44.

Advocates claim that "BMI screening and reporting programs can help increase public and professional understanding of children's weight issues and can be a useful vehicle for engaging with children and families about healthy lifestyles and weight problems."[81] At the same time it is acknowledged that there has been little examination of these programs' actual effectiveness.[82] As of 2003, twelve states had passed legislation either enabling or mandating schools to engage in BMI assessments.[83] Arkansas has required BMI assessments since 2003. In that state parents can opt out by filing a written refusal to participate. Nevertheless, participation runs between 90 and 95 percent. Apparently the BMI data show that the obesity rate for children in this state has not increased since 2003.[84] A different slant is taken by the White House Task Force on Childhood Obesity. It endorses assessments of BMI not by schools, but by a child's pediatrician—a strategy that might protect privacy and create more opportunity for counseling of both kids and parents.[85]

Focus groups that have been conducted have found that parents were generally supportive of BMI screening. But they wanted the children's privacy to be maintained and results to be reported in a neutral manner that avoided weight labeling. Another study found that most parents did read letters reporting the BMI assessment results and that most parents and children were comfortable with the information that was conveyed, though parents of overweight children were more likely to report discomfort.[86]

Skepticism involves all the criticisms of BMI laid out at the beginning of this subsection. In addition, as advocates acknowledge, there has been little assessment of the programs' "effectiveness." And what would effectiveness mean? That BMI scores are lowered? That there is evidence that such screening contributed to children eating/drinking better and being more physically active? The lingering worry is that, over time, such screening will lead to even more stigmatization of fat children as information about scores leaks out and kids are ranked. The scores, themselves, will say little about children's health, eating/drinking patterns, or activity levels. Measuring BMI may promote censorious norms toward the obese, particularly fat kids: by no means the intended result but a negative outcome just the same.

The scores, alone, will be the focus; an array of complex individual and societal issues will be ignored. Even some anti-obesity advocates have worries about the possible effects of measuring BMIs: "the information can do more harm

---

[81] Story et al., *supra* note 52, at 88.
[82] *Id.*
[83] *Id.*
[84] *Id.*
[85] WHITE HOUSE TASK FORCE, *supra* note 5, at 35–36.
[86] Story et al., *supra* note 52, at 89.

than good if individuals draw the wrong conclusions—for example, developing anorexic behavior because of concern about modest excess weight."[87]

ii. Out of Class

Children spend a great deal of time in school: thus the previous section and its focus on exercise opportunities. However, they are away from formal education even more, especially when weekends and vacations are taken into account. Therefore, occasions for activity in the larger community are important to consider in the overall accounting of opportunities for exercise.

Those studies that have examined children and activity outside of school confirm what many might consider obvious: the more opportunities for exercise, the more they are engaged. Sallis and Glanz, assessing the available evidence, conclude: "[C]hildren and adolescents with access to recreational facilities and programs, usually near their homes, are more active than those without such access."[88] What constitutes "access" for such activity can vary significantly. For example, a study in Australia concluded that the way people perceive their neighborhood environment can affect the extent to which children walk and cycle. Heavy traffic, and a lack of public transportation, street-crossing aids, and nearby recreational facilities were all linked to lower activity levels of kids in that neighborhood.[89] Conversely, more children walk to school when there are safe sidewalks. For example, the Marin County, California Safe Routes to Schools program promoted more activity combined with changes to the built environment (more sidewalks and improved street crossings). An evaluation found a 64 percent increase in walking and a 114 percent increase in cycling to school.[90]

But there are enormous challenges to making the built environment conducive to physical activity. Despite the promising California experiment just mentioned, walking/cycling commuting rates range from just 5 to 14 percent.[91] Many suburbs have been designed to facilitate extensive use of the car: they are often simply "unwalkable."[92] The affluence of the community also comes into play. Studies in the United States have found poorer neighborhoods, generally, have fewer parks, sports fields, fitness clubs, and trails. They also tend to have fewer free rather than pay-for-use facilities, possibly because of lower community tax bases and related spending policies.[93] The potential of built

---

[87] INSTITUTE OF MEDICINE, *supra* note 44, at 48.
[88] Sallis & Glanz, *supra* note 29, at 91.
[89] *Id.* at 93, citing A. Timperio et al., *Perceptions about the Local Neighborhood and Walking and Cycling among Children*, 38 PREVENTIVE MED. 39–47 (2004).
[90] *Id.* at 94, citing M. Boarnet et al., *Evaluation of the California Safe Routes to School Legislation: Urban Form Changes and Children's Active Transportation to School*, 28 AM. J. PREVENTIVE MED. 134 (2005).
[91] *Id.* at 93.
[92] *Id.*
[93] *Id.* at 91.

environments to facilitate exercise, on the one hand, and the many barriers to such activity that exist, on the other, have led to intense interest in the changes that should occur to promote recreation as part of community surroundings.

In 2009 the Institute of Medicine (IOM) and the National Research Council released a report, *Local Government Actions to Prevent Childhood Obesity*.[94] Clearly written and based on the best evidence available, the report contains a series of recommendations for actions at the local level to promote healthy eating and physical activity. Of critical importance it emphasizes "health equity" in addressing relevant issues: "[L]ooking at communities and their members' health status through the lens of health equity can help policy makers understand the health impacts of such factors as racism, poverty, residential segregation, poor housing, lack of access to quality education, and limited access to health care."[95]

Or, as Guthman puts it in discussing related issues: "[T]he very conditions and amenities that make certain places sites of 'the good life' make them unobtainable to most...[E]lite suburbs...came into being in escape from the 'dangerous classes' of the city."[96] Other commentators cast similar concerns in terms of civil rights issues: "Communities of color and low-income communities suffer disproportionately from environmental degradation; they lack public goods, such as parks and school playing fields; they lack information about the impact of decisions on their lives; and they are systematically denied full and fair public participation in the decision-making process."[97]

The larger concerns raised by the IOM Report's invoking of "health equity" and the analysis of Guthman and others are crucial. Grappling with them is important in forging an approach focused on health, not weight. We will return to them and related ideas in the Conclusion to the book.

The IOM Report makes a series of recommendations to promote physical activity. They are practical and could encourage everyone to be more physically active, especially children. Moreover, the report frequently provides concrete examples of how particular local governments can implement specific strategies. For example, one recommendation regarding the built environment is to *"Encourage walking and bicycling for transportation and recreation through improvement in the built environment."*

The Report then lists several "action steps" related to this recommendation. One such step is: "Plan, build, and maintain a network of sidewalks and street crossings that creates a safe and comfortable walking environment and

---

[94] COMMITTEE ON CHILDHOOD OBESITY, *supra* note 47.
[95] *Id.* at 46.
[96] J. GUTHMAN, WEIGHING IN: OBESITY, FOOD JUSTICE, AND THE LIMITS OF CAPITALISM 88 (2011); *see generally*, Ch. 4: Does Your Neighborhood Make You Fat?
[97] INSTITUTE OF MEDICINE, LEGAL STRATEGIES IN CHILDHOOD OBESITY PREVENTION: WORKSHOP SUMMARY 49 (2011).

that connects to schools, parks, and other destinations." It then lists concrete illustrations of how some local governments have implemented that particular "action step":

- Establish a sidewalk maintenance program to ensure that existing sidewalks are kept in a good state of repair. [retrofit][98]
- Develop a program to fill gaps in the sidewalk network, especially on routes near schools, transit stops, and retail. [retrofit]
- Establish an intersection/pedestrian crossing retrofit program to make it easier for pedestrians to cross streets safely. [retrofit]
- Revise subdivision ordinances or other codes to require sidewalks and safe pedestrian crossings in all new developments. [new]
- Revise city/county codes to require short, well-connected blocks or a minimum number of intersections to provide direct connections between destinations. [new]

The foregoing indicates the level of detail in the Report as it exhorts local governments to action to achieve healthy eating/drinking and physical activity in the day-to-day lives of children. It and related efforts are admirable. What impact could they have? And what are the prospects that these recommendations will be implemented?

We know that roads, sidewalks, and related infrastructure can be configured to achieve positive results. Rates of pedestrian and cycling accidents are much higher in the United States than in Western Europe. There are several reasons for this difference. However, in most countries, mandated cycling and pedestrian lanes and laws that make drivers, rather than cyclists and walkers, liable are an important reason for such lower rates.[99] Some ten years ago it was reported that 39–48 percent of trips for Germans and 19–24 percent for the Dutch were on foot, as compared with 6 percent for Americans.[100] The work reporting on these results pointed to two factors that we have referred to many times in this chapter: "cultural values" (norms) and "the built environment."[101] In the recent past there have been some bright spots of local activity, such as those already mentioned and Atlanta's commitment to a network of mixed-use walking and cycling paths.[102]

---

[98] COMMITTEE ON CHILDHOOD OBESITY, *supra* note 47, at 76: Retrofit: Modification of infrastructure and facilities in existing areas of the community rather than the provision of infrastructure and facilities in new areas of development.

[99] Sallis & Glanz, *supra* note 29, at 94, citing J. Pucher & L. Dijkstra, *Promoting Safe Walking and Cycling to Improve Public Health: Lessons from the Netherlands and Germany*, 93 AM. J. PUB. HEALTH 1509 (2003).

[100] FRANK ET AL., *supra* note 12, at 91.

[101] *Id.*

[102] Sallis & Glanz, *supra* note 29, at 92.

Yet, despite evidence and valiant efforts to promote benefits and instill receptive attitudes, there is insufficient movement in the United States to design and build communities with health and safety considerations in mind. The progress that has been made in some cities—for example, the increase in biking lanes in New York—is too often hesitant and subject to political whims.[103] Then there are financial considerations. Local governments in many states are in dire shape.[104] When cities declare bankruptcy and municipal employees' remuneration is reduced to minimum wage (to cite two examples of desperate circumstances), reconfiguring the built environment may seem like an unaffordable luxury.[105] There may be lots of evidence that, over the long haul, such changes could produce several substantial benefits. But can that case be made in the scramble to find enough dollars to keep urban governments afloat?

5. Vouchers to the Rescue?: The Canadian Children's Fitness Tax Credit

i. New Governance and Vouchers

We talked in Chapter 1 about new governance.[106] This approach to regulation de-emphasizes the centrality of the state, administrative agencies, and command and control legislation. Instead, there is emphasis on various "tools" and their potential to achieve diverse regulatory goals. Such tools are deployed as a result of negotiated agreements reflecting public–private partnerships and so forth. New governance and its seeming potential to use the state in a more effective way have been embraced in many areas, including the regulation of consumption.

One tool that is a favorite of new governance are vouchers.[107] The idea here is both simple and ingenious. The simple part is that they are a subsidy to qualified persons that provides funds to purchase specified goods and services.[108] The ingenious part is that they are meant to empower consumers, allowing them to participate in various markets for goods and services. Individuals can be subsidized so as to have greater access to education, medical care, housing, and so forth with a much reduced role for bureaucracy, especially compared with the situation where governments attempt to deliver goods and services directly to target populations. Or, to put it another way, vouchers are "consumer-side

---

[103] M. Flegenheimer, *Anxiety over Future of Bike Lanes*, N.Y. TIMES, Feb. 13, 2013, at A22.; More *generally, see* C. Waters, The Rebirth of Cycling Law?, Dec. 2012 (unpublished manuscript) (on file with author).

[104] N. Popper, *Rate Scandal Stirs Scramble for Damages*, N.Y. TIMES, July 11, 2012, at B1, B5.

[105] M. Cooper & M. Walsh, *Unions Fight Scranton Mayor after He Cuts Pay to Minimum Wage*, N.Y. TIMES, July 11, 2012, at A14; M. Wollan, *Years of Unraveling, Then Bankruptcy for a City*, N.Y. TIMES, July 19, 2012, at A1, A15.

[106] Chapter 1, Section V: Some Ideas about Law Shaping Behavior.

[107] R. DANIELS & M.TREBILCOCK, RETHINKING THE WELFARE STATE: GOVERNMENT BY VOUCHER (2005).

[108] C. Steuerle & E. Twombly, *Vouchers*, in THE TOOLS OF GOVERNMENT: A GUIDE TO THE NEW GOVERNANCE 445, 446 L. Salamon & O. Elliott, eds., (2002).

subsidies" permitting individuals to purchase what they need from a variety of suppliers competing to meet these demands.[109] We looked at a form of vouchers in Chapter 6 when we discussed the various projects to subsidize the purchase of healthy foods by SNAP recipients.[110]

Recently vouchers have been associated with many conservative ideas regarding privatization, ending of government dominance in a variety of areas, and the enlargement of the market for provision of goods and service, including to those of limited means. One area where such ideas and vouchers have come together is in terms of schools in the United States.

Yet vouchers, themselves, are not emblazoned with any particular ideology. The SNAP pilots demonstrate that they can have quite progressive goals: ones that, if widely implemented, could increase governmental expenditures. In Canada all citizens receive a voucher so as to access universal health care while choosing the services of individual doctors and other health care providers.[111] In some Canadian provinces legal assistance to those of limited income largely operates through a system of such subsidies.[112]

Vouchers often become controversial because of the context in which they are proposed to be used. Their potential to employ public funds to give more choice to individuals and to bolster competitive markets may appeal to various constituencies with differing political viewpoints in diverse contexts. Such attractiveness (or lack thereof) may be largely dependent on the specifics of how vouchers are intended to be employed. Or, as Steuerle and others put it: "[W]hile a voucher...may produce significant efficiency and equity gains under the right conditions...it has also acquired...ideological baggage as a consequence of often intense political arguments."[113]

ii. Vouchers as the Solution?: HLVs

Given the resurgence in interest in vouchers, on the one hand, and the search for legal intervention to combat obesity, on the other, it is little surprise that those determined to combat excess weight, yet dissatisfied with the record of more traditional interventions, would turn their interest to this tool espoused by new governance. Such is the case for Seeman and Luciani and their advocacy of Healthy Living Vouchers (HLVs).

We discussed some of the ideas of Seeman and Luciani in Chapter 2, including their protesting of discrimination against fat people.[114] Seeman and Luciani

---

[109] *Id.*

[110] Chapter 6, Section IV(e): Targeted Subsidies through Government Support Programs.

[111] Canada Health Act, 1985 RSC, c. C-6; see *also* Government of Canada, Health Canada, Canada Health Act, Apr. 19, 2010, *available at* http://www.hc-sc.gc.ca/hcs-sss/medi-assur/cha-lcs/index-eng.php.

[112] Legal Aid Ontario (LAO), 2012, *available at* http://www.legalaid.on.ca/en/.

[113] Steuerle & Twombly, *supra* note 108, at 462.

[114] Chapter 2, Section IV(e)(3)(i): Fight Stigma—Battle Weight.

are unqualified in their denunciation of stigma directed at fat people. That said, in their estimation, obesity is the problem; weight loss is the solution. They rail against the traditional public health model and its various, failed attempts to address obesity through weight loss and prevention of excess weight gain.

That model disappoints because of its misdirected focus: too little attention is given to the needs of individuals and personally tailored solutions.[115] Those who promote the traditional public health model are system planners who are determined to configure public attitudes to support overall collective goals. The needs of individuals are paved over in pursuit of some common good.[116] In terms of obesity this ignoring of specific, personal needs has resulted in a "maze of policy incoherence."[117]

Their critique takes issue with numerous government policies, including educational efforts,[118] taxes on soda,[119] physical activity requirements in schools,[120] financial incentives,[121] and banning of junk food in some educational institutions.[122] They are not against some government programs (such as making fresh fruits available to schoolchildren).[123] Nevertheless, they underscore an all-too-valid point: such interventions have not "made an appreciable dent."[124] Their solution is Healthy Living Vouchers (HLVs).[125] We need to "stop subsidizing the current producer of anti-obesity sloganeering—the state, through its public health messaging and healthy eating campaigns—and to start subsidizing individuals so that they have more choice over how to curb their own obesity."[126] Seeman and Luciani take their cue from school vouchers in the United States. They praise their effectiveness while giving little weight to the criticisms of responsible critics.[127] They suggest that HLVs should have three characteristics:

- Universal eligibility (all individuals sixteen and over; thin or obese);
- Sufficiently funded to provide real purchasing power; and
- Elimination of monopolistic barriers over weight management solutions[128]

---

[115] N.SEEMAN & P.LUCIANI, XXL: OBESITY AND THE LIMITS OF SHAME 64 (2011).
[116] Id. at 62.
[117] Id. at 64.
[118] Id. at 100–01.
[119] Id. at 99.
[120] Id. at 67.
[121] Id. at 84.
[122] Id. at 67.
[123] Id. at 105.
[124] Id. at 105.
[125] M. Ridley, *Free-Market Solutions for Overweight Americans*, WALL ST. J. Apr. 2, 2011, available at http://online.wsj.com/article/SB10001424052748704471904576230692570676256.html.
[126] SEEMAN & LUCIANI, *supra* note 115, at 112.
[127] Id. at 106–08. J. GROSS STEIN, THE CULT OF EFFICIENCY, ch. III: "Efficiency and Choice: Pubic Education and Public Health Care" (2001).
[128] SEEMAN & LUCIANI, *supra* note 115, at 123.

At the same time Seeman and Luciani emphasize flexibility in the design of HLVs. For example, they allow that some governments would want to limit their availability to low-income individuals.[129] They claim that availability to individuals regardless of weight will reduce stigma because fat people will not be targeted.[130]

The core idea is to provide financial wherewithal to allow people to consult with their "primary care provider" (a doctor?) with a view to "committing in writing...to follow through on an individualized weight management plan."[131] The spending of funds available from HLVs would, in turn, "increase competition among a wide assortment of healthy living service providers, from specialized gyms to grocery chains to technology companies to home retrofitting businesses."[132] Seeman and Luciani provide details on such issues as how the very considerable costs of HLVs would be financed, patient commitment to individual plans worked out with the primary care provider, prevention of abuse, etc.[133] The foregoing describes the essence of their proposal, one that is unambiguous in its goal: "The *participatory and accountable journey* to a weight loss option is what matters."[134]

HLVs are an imaginative response to intractable issues. Given the track record of weight loss programs and efforts to promote healthier lifestyles, we should encourage responses that propose novel ways to define and tackle such problems. Yet those are several concerns raised by the Seeman and Luciani proposal.[135]

First, the suggestion that HLVs be available to everyone, whatever their weight and health status, seems to be a significant and unnecessary expense—one that could threaten health budgets generally.[136] The use of HLVs should be more targeted, with particular efforts regarding prevention, at people who are at substantial risk for health and weight issues. HLVs for individuals who do not have weight or eating/exercise issues and who give no indication that they will have such issues do not require the financial and other support coming from these vouchers.

Second, the undue emphasis on individual responses and solutions is a limit on effectiveness. Yes, people must accept responsibility for their health. But decades of research indicate that individuals' decisions take place in a larger social, political, and economic context that shapes their decision-making processes. The traditional public health response to obesity may be misdirected in

---

[129] *Id.* at 125.
[130] *Id.*
[131] *Id.*
[132] *Id.* at 128–29.
[133] *Id.* at 129–37.
[134] *Id.* at 126 (emphasis in the original).
[135] G. Marchildon, *Self-Destructiveness and the State*, LITERARY REV. CAN. 3 (June 2011).
[136] *Id.*

some ways, but not in its insistence that the larger context plays a role in people's health and, therefore, must be taken into account in formulating and implementing any response. That larger context includes financial wherewithal to buy healthy food and drink and an environment conducive to physical activity.

Third, the focus on weight loss flies in the face of the evidence regarding the inability of people to lose weight and to maintain that loss. It is also at odds with the view that the emphasis should be on healthy eating/drinking and physical activity, not on weight. Seeman and Luciani protest the stigma visited on fat people by society. Yet their obsession with shedding pounds through HLVs, in the face of all evidence to the contrary, could lead to even more oppression of fat people.

If a government wants to take up their recommendations or variations, it should proceed cautiously. At several places Seeman and Luciani describe pilot projects for HLVs.[137] Limited, well-designed experiments with these vouchers could be a way to test their efficacy. Exclusive emphasis on weight loss (or prevention) should not be the goal; far better to underscore healthy eating/drinking and active lifestyles.

iii. CFTC

[one] A Voucher to Get Kids Moving

One way to implement vouchers is through the tax system. Imposing lower rates on certain income, creating deductions or credits, etc., encourage taxpayers to engage in targeted activities by subsidizing their doing so: saving for retirement, investing in the stock market, accessing education, and so forth.

Enter the Canadian Children's Fitness Tax Credit (CFTC). The idea is simple: children need to be more active. Governments have a role to play in encouraging kids to exercise more. A voucher will promote involvement in sports and recreation, provide choice to parents and their children, and encourage positive competition on the part of service providers as they seek to persuade the beneficiaries of the subsidy to spend their dollars with them, while preserving the spirit of volunteerism that is critical to many sports and recreation programs. The proposal for the CFTC was examined by an expert panel and given its blessing.[138]

The essentials of the CFTC are:

- Qualifying programs must:

  o Be continuous—programs must last at least eight weeks with at least one session a week or, in the case of camps, run for five consecutive days.
  o Be supervised.

---

[137] SEEMAN & LUCIANI, *supra* note 115, at 125, 130, and 132.
[138] K. LEITCH, REPORT OF THE EXPERT PANEL FOR THE CHILDREN'S FITNESS TAX CREDIT (2006).

- o Be suitable—for children.
- o Include a significant amount of physical activity contributing to cardio-respiratory endurance and to at least one of: muscular strength, muscular endurance, flexibility, or balance.

• Eligible fees must be paid for:

- o A child who is under 16 at the beginning of the income tax year.
- o A child with disabilities who is under 18 at the beginning of the income tax year and who must also be eligible for the disability tax credit.
- o The cost of registration or membership in an eligible program of physical fitness activity. Related costs such as accommodation, travel, or food do not qualify for the income tax credit.
- o Registration or membership of at least $100 in the physical activity program.
- o In the year the physical activity takes place.[139]

In addition, some of the provinces, invoking their taxing powers, have given additional fitness credits aligned with the CFTC in order to generate even more savings for parents of participating children in those provinces.[140]

[two]Impact

As an idea the CFTC has much to recommend it. Its effects regarding activity levels of Canadian kids are another matter. There are significant shortcomings in terms of the actual outcomes related to it based on: who uses it, the extent to which physical activity is increased for those who do use it, the complexity of the legislative scheme for claiming the credit and the appropriate trade-offs between the CFTC, and direct spending by governments to promote children's physical activity.

A study was done in 2009 (two years after the CFTC was implemented) of the effects of the tax credit.[141] By that point 54.5 percent of parents stated that their child (age two to eighteen) was in organized physical activity, and 55.5 percent were aware of the CFTC. However, parents in the low-income

---

[139] *See* Income Tax Act, 1985 RSC, c. 1 (5th Supp.), ss. 118.03(1)(2)(2.1)(3), 118.031(1)(2)(3)(4).

[140] The Income Tax Act, 2012, CCSM c110, s. 46, Government of Manitoba, *available at* http://web2.gov.mb.ca/laws/statutes/ccsm/i010e.php; Canada Health Act, 1985 RSC, c. C-6; *see also* Government of Canada, Health Canada, Canada Health Act, Apr. 19, 2010, *available at* http://www.hc-sc.gc.ca/hcs-sss/medi-assur/cha-lcs/index-eng.php; Children's Activity Tax Credit Act, SO 2010, c 21, Province of Ontario, *available at* http://www.e-laws.gov.on.ca/html/source/statutes/english/2010/elaws_src_s10021_e.htm; Income Tax Act, RSBC 1996, chapter 215, s. 4.34, Province of British Columbia, *available at* http://www.bclaws.ca/EPLibraries/bclaws_new/document/LOC/freeside/--%201%20--/00_Income%20Tax%20Act%20RSBC%201996%20c.%20215/00_Act/96215_01.xml#section4.

[141] J. Spence et al., *Uptake and Effectiveness of the Children's Fitness Tax Credit in Canada: The Rich Get Richer*, 10 BMC Pub Health 356 (June 2010).

quartile were significantly less aware and less likely to claim the CFTC than other income groups.

The proportion of individuals in quartiles three and four who claimed the credit was double the proportion of those in (the lowest) quartile one.[142] Many of those with low incomes cannot take advantage of this provision, even if they are aware of it, because it is a nonrefundable credit available only to those who pay tax. In 2009 some eight million Canadians filed nontaxable returns.[143] Further, among parents who did claim the CFTC only 15.6 percent believed it had increased their child's participation in physical activity programs.[144] The tax credit has also been criticized as complicated (as these provisions, by their nature, usually are).[145]

All these results have led critics of the credit to suggest other means for promoting physical activity, particularly among children in low-income families. They suggest funding activity programs directly with a targeted subsidy for poor families. They point to a few sports initiatives that provide registration fees geared to income and free equipment to children in need.[146]

[three] More of a Good Thing

The criticisms of the CFTC are valid. The question is how, if at all, should it be altered? The question is apt, especially as the Canadian federal government has suggested that it might increase the amount of the credit and expand its coverage to adults.[147]

A very attractive aspect of the CFTC is that its focus is physical activity: putting the emphasis where it belongs—on health not weight. Even with limitations interventions with that message should be encouraged. They signal that our norms should be about active living (and nutritious eating/drinking) and not weight and censorious attitudes toward the obese. Moreover, architects of the CFTC never suggested that it was *the* solution;[148] rather, it is one of several interventions to promote active lifestyles. There are financial implications

---

[142] *Id.* at 3.

[143] In 2009, Canadians filed nearly 24.5 million tax returns: *see* J. Golombek, *How Much do Canadians Make?*, FIN. POST, Mar. 26, 2011, *available at* http://www.financialpost.com/personal-finance/taxes/much+Canadians+make/4497362/story.html. Of the 24.5 million, 3.7 million Canadians, aged sixteen and older, filed tax income returns online: see Statistics Canada, Income tax...by the Numbers, 2011, *available at* http://www42.statcan.gc.ca/smr08/2011/smr08_154_2011-eng.htm.

[144] Spence, *supra* note 141, at 356.

[145] K. Milligan, *Fitness a Worthy Goal—But Not with Gimmicky Tax Credit*, GLOBE & MAIL, Apr. 3, 2011, *available at* http://www.theglobeandmail.com/report-on-business/economy/economy-lab/fitness-a-worthy-goal---but-not-with-gimmicky-tax-credit/article546894/.

[146] T. Saunders, *Canada's Children's Fitness Tax Credit—The Rich Get Richer?* PLOS BLOG, Apr. 8, 2011, *available at* http://blogs.plos.org/obesitypanacea/2011/04/08/canadas-childrens-fitness-tax-credit-the-rich-get-richer/.

[147] *Id.*

[148] LEITCH, *supra* note 138, Letter of Transmittal, Oct. 26, 2006 (no page number).

but advocates could suggest that there should be both the CFTC and the sports programs, described earlier, that gear registration to income and that provide equipment to children in need.

What is more, a number of things might be done to improve the effectiveness of the CFTC. First, more education about the existence of the tax credit could assist more qualified people to claim it. Second, if it were larger, it could have more effect and promote more physical activity even among those already inclined to play sports, etc. Third, it could be modified so that it is available even to those who file a tax return but who do not have taxable income.

VI. Conclusion

Story and others urge action to respond to the needs of the youngest members of society: "[W]e need a coordinated and systematic plan and the political will to place a priority on children's health and well-being."[149] We do indeed. But how to achieve that plan and, even more so, that political will?

The former, a plan, has many resources to draw upon, including the several initiatives cited in the chapter. There are specific differences to be resolved: measuring and reporting BMI would be one example.[150] More, generally we need to move to broad agreement that what is critical, as Story and others state, is kids' "health and well-being." To the extent the components of the plan actually prevent (or address) obesity so much the better. But "health and well-being" should be the focus. What, more precisely, health and well-being means in any particular context may be a matter for fair debate but, in such discussion, issues of weight should be secondary.

The elements of the plan will need to be continuously assessed. The focus should be on interventions that actually help to improve health and well-being—not pounds lost or gained but the several other indicators that a child is thriving, such as actual amounts of physical activity before and after school and on the weekends: in schoolyards, backyards, parks, and other community settings. Such activity should be combined with a healthy diet at school and at home.

Again, the effect of the "mix" also needs to be evaluated.[151] Progress may be made not so much because of any one element but as a result of the outcomes produced by several components and their cumulative influence. To the extent that this is the case there needs to be something of a leap of faith: that several components, working together, will produce positive results exceeding anything that each of them might bring about on their own. The "mix" may be critical.

---

[149] Story et al., *supra* note 52, at 95.
[150] *Supra* Section V(b)(4)(i)[three]: Measuring BMI?
[151] Chapter 1, Section II: The Regulatory Mix.

Or, as one commentator has put it: "Advising individuals to be more physically active without considering social norms for activity, resources, and opportunities for engaging in physical activity, and environmental constraints such as crime, traffic, and unpleasant surroundings, is unlikely to produce behavior change."[152]

The latter, political will, is an even greater challenge. Societies, the United States in particular, have to come face-to-face with a fact: health and well-being of children comes with a price tag. Let's sign up for elimination of waste and government heavy-handedness. Let's recognize that just throwing money at a problem doesn't necessarily produce solutions; matters may even get worse. Let's acknowledge these are very austere times for the public purse.[153] All that said, many of these interventions will need resources for their implementation, maintenance, and evaluation. Children are the greatest potential that we have. Spending even very scarce resources on their betterment will yield a much better future for them and for the societies for which they will soon be responsible. But will the dollars be forthcoming?

---

[152] COMMITTEE ON CHILDHOOD OBESITY, *supra* note 47, at 46, quoting L. McNeill et al., *Social Environment and Physical Activity: A Review of Concepts and Evidence*, 63(4) SOCIAL SCI. & MED. 1011–22, 1012 (2006).

[153] M. Walsh & M. Cooper, *For States, Gloomy Forecast even if Economy Rebounds*, N.Y. TIMES, July 18, 2012, at A1, A3; Editorial, *The Rush to Abandon the Poor*, N.Y. TIMES, July 18, 2012, at A22.

Conclusion: Not Fat But Health—and Health Equity

"[A] condition that can be changed at will."

Catherine Hakim, quoted in Chapter 3[1]

"[L]ooking at communities and their members' health status through the lens of health equity can help policy makers understand the health impacts of such factors as racism, poverty, residential segregation, poor housing, lack of access to quality education, and limited access to health care."

Institute of Medicine (IOM), *Local Government Actions to Prevent Childhood Obesity*, quoted in Chapter 7[2]

The foregoing are two very different reactions to obesity. In short order they reflect the wide range of views about fat in contemporary societies discussed in this book. The parting note of the book is to leave Hakim behind and push forward by emphasizing health and viewing the world and fat through the "lens of health equity."

Hakim espouses an extreme but not uncommon view as she excoriates "fatties."[3] If they really want to, obese people can shed pounds. If they fail to do so they need to bear whatever consequences follow whether in terms of physical or mental health or the stigma that is visited upon them by a society repulsed by their slovenly ways. The thin, especially women, should flaunt their bodies for whatever advantages and pleasures come their way. Her views are as mean as they are wrong.

The IOM Report has a very different point of departure. The situation of fat people, especially children, should be examined in the larger context in which they live. That analysis should focus on "health equity": "the fair distribution

---

[1] C. Hakim, Honey Money: The Power of Erotic Capital 131 (2011), quoted in Chapter 3, Section V: Resisting the Prejudice of Looks: Justifications for Invoking Law.
[2] Committee on Childhood Obesity Prevention Actions for Local Governments, Local Government Actions to Prevent Childhood Obesity 46 (2009).
[3] Hakim, *supra* note 1, at 130.

of health determinants, outcomes, and resources within and between segments of the population, regardless of social standing."[4] Or, as a leading Canadian journalist has concisely put it in writing of our obsession with obesity, especially the weight of poor people: "Deal with income inequalities and the population will be healthier."[5]

Health equity does take note of the fact that low-income children often eat fewer fruits and vegetables and are frequently inadequately active. But, critically, this perspective goes on to ask why the lives of poor kids are this way. It examines such aspects as the distribution of supermarkets, the availability of transportation, the safety of neighborhoods, access to parks, and opportunities for recreation. It looks to the larger context of residential segregation, high rates of unemployment, and absence of social capital.[6]

Health equity, certainly the perspective animating this book, is also anxious about issues of "food security" (sufficient calories, sufficient nutrients) and "the hunger-obesity paradox" (individuals can be both fat and ill-fed).[7] It takes seriously the analysis of Guthman and others and the questions they ask about food justice and the urban environments in which so many Americans live: " [T]he very conditions and amenities that make certain places sites of 'the good life' make them unobtainable to most ... [E]lite suburbs ... came into being in escape from the 'dangerous classes' of the city."[8] Health equity, in this corner, also does not definitely conclude that obesity is always simply a matter of "calories in/calories out" gone wrong. It urges examination of other possible causes in some instances—for example the questions raised by the White House Task Force on Childhood Obesity and by others on the impact of endocrine disrupting chemicals (EDCs) on the health of individuals and on their weight.[9]

The concept's insistence on "the fair distribution of health determinants, outcomes, and resources" should also embrace protecting the obese from stigma and the many acts of discrimination they now face.[10] Such stigma and discrimination affects fat people's mental and even physical health and denies

---

[4] COMMITTEE ON CHILDHOOD OBESITY, *supra* note 2, at 46 citing Centers for Disease Control and Prevention, (2007) Unpublished Health Equity Working Group Atlanta, GA: CDC.

[5] J. Simpson, *Our Obsession with Obesity*, GLOBE & MAIL, June 6, 2012, at A15, quoted in Chapter 6, Section IV(c)(1): Poverty and the New Malnutrition.

[6] COMMITTEE ON CHILDHOOD OBESITY, *supra* note 2, at 46.

[7] Chapter 6, Section IV(c)(1): Poverty and the New Malnutrition

[8] J. GUTHMAN, WEIGHING IN: OBESITY, FOOD JUSTICE, AND THE LIMITS OF CAPITALISM 88 (2011) quoted in Chapter 7, Section V(b)(4)(ii): Out of Class; *see generally*, Chapter 4: "Does Your Neighborhood Make You Fat?"; *see also* INSTITUTE OF MEDICINE, LEGAL STRATEGIES IN CHILDHOOD OBESITY PREVENTION: WORKSHOP SUMMARY 49 (2011), also quoted in Chapter 7, Section V(b)(4)(ii): Out of Class.

[9] WHITE HOUSE TASK FORCE ON CHILDHOOD OBESITY REPORT TO THE PRESIDENT, SOLVING THE PROBLEM OF CHILDHOOD OBESITY WITHIN A GENERATION 17 (2010).

[10] Chapter 3: Appearance Bias-Fat Rights.

to them education, employment, and other opportunities integral to their well-being. There are strong arguments that such protection should be grounded in legal provisions. The work of Hamermesh, Kirkland, Rhode and others lead the way in that regard.[11]

Being poor and being fat do not always go hand in hand. An appreciable portion of the population, especially men, are obese, but they are also relatively affluent.[12] These individuals may not need the benefits of a health equity perspective as much as those who are poor and fat. Still, one can be better off, obese, and still feel the sting of prejudice from the workplace to the schoolyard. Those who are affluent and fat can still benefit from protections from discrimination. What's more, even those of relatively high income and their children can enjoy built environments designed to be conducive to physical activity.[13] Lower-income neighborhoods have particular needs in this regard, but they are present alongside overarching requirements for all urban spaces to be conducive to safe, active lifestyles as part of "the fair distribution of health determinants, outcomes, and resources"

It remains the case that in 2011, SNAP (Supplementary Nutrition Assistance Plan) helped something like one in six Americans eat on a regular basis.[14] That's one important indicator that there are a substantial number of individuals in the United States who may not be unambiguously poor, but who are clearly challenged economically. They are struggling to enjoy "the fair distribution of health determinants, outcomes, and resources." A lot of these men, women, and children are fat. They could benefit enormously from a health equity approach to the many issues they encounter.

The overarching emphasis should be on health not weight. The claims of health equity should not hinge on "defeating" obesity. Health equity succeeds when individuals enjoy the fair distribution of the elements of well-being regardless of their weight for all the reasons recounted in these pages. Invoking obesity and its supposed consequences to obtain support for otherwise worthy goals raises the prospect of harming the very individuals intended to be helped. It also obscures the fact that many adults and children who are not fat struggle with "racism, poverty, residential segregation, poor housing, lack of access to quality education, and limited access to health care."[15]

---

[11] D. HAMERMESH, BEAUTY PAYS: WHY ATTRACTIVE PEOPLE ARE MORE SUCCESSFUL 48 (2011); A. KIRKLAND, FAT RIGHTS: DILEMMAS OF DIFFERENCE AND PERSONHOOD (2008); D.RHODE, THE BEAUTY BIAS: THE INJUSTICE OF APPEARANCE IN LIFE AND LAW 26 (2010). Hamermesh, Kirkland, and Rhode are discussed, at length, in Chapter 3.
[12] Chapter 6, Section IV(c)(1): Poverty and the New Malnutrition.
[13] Chapter 7, Section V(a): General Considerations: The Built Environment.
[14] Chapter 6, Section IV(c)(1): Poverty and the New Malnutrition.
[15] COMMITTEE ON CHILDHOOD OBESITY, *supra* note 2, at 46.

As just one example of the health/not weight emphasis let's return to the IOM Report quoted at the beginning. It focuses on prevention of childhood obesity, and it does make specific recommendations in that regard. Its overarching approach, articulated at the beginning of the Report, emphasizes the health/not weight perspective ("actions that can be taken to promote healthful eating and physical activity"[16]):

- Improve coordination among agencies ... [to] address determinants of health
- Engage with communities ... to improve health and health equity
- Increase availability of healthy affordable food
- Create a built environment that encourages [physical activity]
- Consider cultural barriers to purchasing healthier foods and physical activity
- Work with community partners to ... build upon cultural assets[17]

The list is not definitive, and the Report does not suggest that it is. There can be room for lots of discussion regarding appropriate strategies. The point here is that "obese," "weight," and "BMI" nowhere appear in the list. In contrast there are many references to "health," "determinants of health," and "healthy." Achieving the well-being of children is the paramount objective.

We discussed the ideas of Anna Kirkland in Chapters 2 and 3.[18] She is eloquent in warning us of the dangers of "using fat panic as a cover (or accepting its assistance) to drum up support for reforms that would otherwise not be so popular."[19] She suggests that if we shift "from concern about fatness, we could make a very rich array of observations about human misery that would not be so overinclusive (because many fat people are not miserable, unhealthy, and eating to escape it all) and underinclusive (because conditions of suffering may have little to do with fat)."[20]

America and other societies would be better to deal with the complicated relationship of health, income, and other life chances directly.[21] They should face the very unpleasant fact that equal opportunity has become much more a myth than a reality.[22] A place to start to address these issues, in this context,

---

[16] *Id.* at 47.

[17] *Id.*

[18] A. Kirkland, *The Environmental Account of Obesity: A Case for Feminist Skepticism*, 36(2) SIGNS 463–86 (2011), discussed in Chapter 2, Section V: The Heavy Hand of the State; KIRKLAND, *supra* note 11 discussed in Chapter 3: Appearance Bias-Fat Rights.

[19] Kirkland, *supra* note 18, at 481.

[20] *Id.* at 480.

[21] J. HACKER & P. PIERSON, WINNER TAKE ALL POLITICS : HOW WASHINGTON MADE THE RICH RICHER AND TURNED ITS BACK ON THE MIDDLE CLASS (2010); J. Simpson, *Income Inequality: Deep, Complex, and Growing*, GLOBE & MAIL, Dec. 9, 2011, at A21; A. Hacker, *We're More Unequal than You Think*, N.Y. REV. BOOKS, Feb. 23, 2012, LIX:3, at 34.

[22] J. Stiglitz, *Equal Opportunity, Our National Myth*, N.Y. TIMES, Feb. 17, 2013, SR, at 9; G. Collins, *The State of the 4-Year-Olds*, N.Y. TIMES, Feb. 14, 2013, at A25; for a differing view

is to use the insights of health equity to improve the well-being of the population generally—especially children. That perspective brings us back to the various interventions that we have discussed, whether in terms of marketing, fiscal policy, or strategies to promote physical activity. Turn to them to improve health—leave weight largely to the side. Evaluate their impact not by counting calories and obsessing with weight loss but by assessing improvements to well-being of the population, especially children.

Finally, a word about the ideas presented at the beginning of this book. In Chapter 1 we discussed the Institute of Medicine's Report on the role of law in grappling with health issues.[23] We quoted the Report's assertion that: "law specifically and public policy more generally, are among the most powerful tools to improve population health."[24] We discussed the "regulatory mix" and the many ways legal interventions can be used to deal with various issues.[25] When it comes to addressing fat based on the considerations of health equity (just discussed), let's hope that the Report's claims about the power of law are on solid footing. Nonetheless, the rest of Chapter 1 suggests a number of reasons the Report could be unduly optimistic. The outcomes produced by any set of laws can be complicated and can defy the predictions of advocates and detractors alike.[26] The Danes and their junk food tax, imposed and then quickly repealed, have come to learn about the complex impact of law only too well.[27] Borderless cyberspace may blunt various jurisdictions' regulatory efforts to curtail the aggressive marketing of Big Food to children.[28] Incentives to promote physical activity provided through the tax system may be merely decorative without adequate financial clout.[29]

Chapter 1 does suggest that the effectiveness of law, perhaps particularly regarding consumption and related issues, can be improved by taking account of the intricate relationship between law and norms: normativity. The suppression of smoking is the classic example of the codependence of intensifying regulation and of shifting norms: from smoking as a glamorous, sophisticated pleasure enjoyed by so many to cigarettes as a filthy, expensive addiction of far fewer.[30] Discussions of normativity in terms of obesity bring us back to the central point: focus on health not weight. Use legal interventions to promote

---

of Canada see; K. Yakabuski, *Inequality, Yes, but Canada's in a Sweet Spot*, GLOBE & MAIL, Mar. 18, 2013, at A11.

[23] INSTITUTE OF MEDICINE, FOR THE PUBLIC'S HEALTH: REVITALIZING LAW AND POLICY TO MEET NEW CHALLENGES (2011).

[24] *Id.* at 18.

[25] Chapter 1, Section II: The Regulatory Mix.

[26] Chapter 1, Section III: How Effective Is Regulation?.

[27] Chapter 6, Section II: Taxes and Consumption.

[28] Chapter 5, Section IV(b)(3): The Challenges of the Internet and Digital Media.

[29] Chapter 7, Section V(b)(5): Vouchers to the Rescue?: The Canadian Children's Fitness Tax Credit.

[30] Chapter 1, Section IV: Consumption Encounters Law: *Permit but Discourage*.

people being more active, eating more fruits and vegetables, and accepting bodies of all shapes and sizes. Use adequate public resources, as appropriate, to achieve these goals—and put children first.

Can these changes occur? Yes—but not easily and not quickly. A great deal of effort, debate, and trial and error will be necessary. Time (and probably a long time) will tell. Whatever the outcomes, aiming for these changes is better than obsessing about calories, invoking extreme measures in the name of elusive weight loss, and beating up on the "fatties."

{ INDEX }

Active lifestyles. *See* Physical activity
Adolescent levels of physical activity, 180–181
Advergames, 142–143
Advertising. *See* Marketing
Agencies responsible for food policy, 165
Age-related regulation, 27. *See also* Children
Agricultural subsidies. *See* Subsidies
Agriculture Department, U.S., 165, 166, 172, 173
Alcohol
    age-related regulation of, 27
    danger of cheaper alcohol being contaminated, 151
    history of prohibition, 13–14
    label warnings, 118
    negative consequences of prohibition, 4, 13, 18
    panic in U.S. about, 51
    parallels to junk food, 118
    partial success of prohibition, 4, 18
    public education campaigns, 52, 124
    ready-to-drink spirit-based alcoholic beverages (RTDs), 150
    taxes, 148, 150–151
Allergan, 110, 111
Alston, J., 162, 163
Americans with Disabilities Act, 87
Anorexia, 47
Antibiotics as cause of obesity, 37
Antidiscrimination protection, xvi, xvii, xxi, 27. *See also* Appearance bias
Aphramor, L., 48
Appearance bias, 70–94
    attorney's fees and compensatory damages, 86
    attractiveness and cosmetic interventions, 71, 74–77, 79
    complexities of banning weight discrimination, 87–89
    dispute resolution process, 86
    dress and grooming codes, 75–77
    impact of laws against bias, 90–93
    joined with human rights issues, 71–73, 80
    laws against bias, 82, 85–86, 211
    overview, 70–71
    prohibiting prejudice against looks, 85–87
    reasonable accommodation, 86, 88
    scope of "appearance," 86
    sexualizing women, 75, 77–78
    young children, 92–93
Appetite suppressants, 107
Arizona ban on nutrition requirements for meals sold with toys, 136
Arkansas requiring BMI assessments, 196
Australia
    alcohol tax, 150
    children's activity level and built environment, 197
    general service tax (GST), 154
    legislation for protection from appearance bias, 86
    obesity rate, 164
    schools' measurement of children's weight, 53

Bacon, L., 48
Bariatric surgery, 109–112
The Beauty Bias (Rhode), 43, 61, 74, 108
Beauty Pays (Hamermesh), 81
Behavioral change
    after bariatric surgery, 111–112
    lawsuits' effect, 115
    normativity and, 22–23, 51, 100
    regulation and, 4, 5–6, 12, 19–28
    subsides to induce. *See* Subsidies
Bergold, Roy, 136
Best available evidence, 104
Big Food. *See* Food-and-drink industry
Black market, 151
Bloomberg, Michael, 171, 172, 176
Body Mass Index (BMI)
    children and, xx, 194–197
    critics of importance of, 44–46, 194, 207
    depression in women and, 40
    earning power of women and, 55
    mortality rates and, 47
    parameters of, 35
    schools measuring, xx, 194–197
Body Project, 91
Bogart, W. A., 3
"Borgata Babes" and employment requirements for women, 78, 80
Boston public advertising campaign, 54
Breastfeeding, 188
Britain. *See* England

Brownell, Kelly, 49
Bruni, F., 120
Built environment, xvii, xx, 12, 39, 57, 182, 184–187, 197–199, 211
Bullying, 55

California Safe Routes to Schools program, 197
Calories
　food and beverage industry and, 38–39
　labeling for. *See* Labeling for calories and nutrition
　menu disclosure of, 126–128, 131
　taxation on, 155
Canada. *See also* Quebec
　built environment, 185
　Children's Fitness Tax Credit, xx, 204–207
　obesity rate, 36, 44–46, 164
　substitution effects and 1 percent milk, 155
　suburban sprawl, 185
　tobacco regulation and taxes, 15, 18, 100, 149–150
"Capri" (Congestion and Policy Relief Incentives), 174
Caraher, M., 156
Carmona, Richard, 55
Cates, C., 113–114
Centers for Disease Control and Prevention, 38, 45, 47, 165, 186, 192, 194, 210
Central Park (NYC), 185
Centre for Science in the Public Interest, 136
Cereals, 114
Chemicals as cause of obesity, 37, 41
Childcare providers, professional, 188, 190–191
Children
　attractiveness as desirable, 74
　bariatric procedures, 110–111
　Canadian Children's Fitness Tax Credit, xx, 204–207
　caregivers as role models, 183–184
　fetal and infant development associated with obesity, 99, 183, 188
　first years and parenting, 189–190
　hospitalization costs of overweight children, 43
　IOM report. *See* Institute of Medicine (IOM) reports
　marketing aimed at, xiv, 119, 122–123, 131–144
　　advergames, 142–143
　　Internet and, 132, 142–143, 213
　　legislative initiatives on, 135–140
　　Quebec law on, xix, xx, 27, 106, 119, 137–140
　　regulation of, 133–140
　　self-regulation of, 133–135

　measuring BMI, 194–197
　obesity prevention and. *See* Prevention of obesity
　physical activity of, 180, 188–207
　primary focus on programs targeting, 99–100
　professional childcare providers, 188, 190–191
　removal of obese children from home, 92–93
　school-age kids, 192–200. *See also* Schools
　tobacco use and, 27
　weight of, 36
　White House Task Force. *See* White House Task Force on Childhood Obesity
Children's Advertising Review Unit (CARU), 134
Children's Fitness Tax Credit (CFTC, Canada), xx, 200–207
Children's Food and Beverage Advertising Initiative (CFBAI), 134, 143
Children's Healthcare of Atlanta, 31, 32, 56, 57, 69
Choice. *See also* Healthy lifestyle choices; Individual responsibility
　consumers' preferences, 121
　ease of selection as factor in, 128
　importance in America, 33
　incentives and, 173–174
　normativity and, 24–26
Choice architects, 24–26, 128
Christakis, N., 39
Christie, Chris, 56
Cigarettes. *See* Tobacco
Civil rights, 71, 84. *See also* Human rights law
Cohen, L., 120, 121
Commonsense Consumption Act (proposed), 112
Congress for the New Urbanism, 186
Consequences of obesity, 42–43. *See also* Costs to society
A Consumers' Republic (Cohen), 120
Consumption. *See* Excessive appetites; Regulating consumption
Corn, 161, 162–163
Cosmetics industry and interventions, 75–76
Costs to society, 42–43, 87, 101, 203. *See also* Public resources to promote health
Cowburn, G., 156
Cultivating Conscience (Stout), 23–24
Cultural values. *See also* Normativity
　obsession with weight, 53–58
　walking, 198–199
Cyberspace. *See* Internet

Danish junk food levy, xx, 147, 148, 150, 213
Daycare providers, professional, 188, 190–192

Index

Department of ___. *See name of specific department*
Dependence, 120, 121, 123
Depression, 40, 42, 179
Deterrence, effectiveness of, 8
Diet, xv. *See also* Nutrition; Weight loss industry
  food-and-drink industry's view of, 62, 64–65
Diet pills, 106–108
Digital media. *See* Internet
Discrimination, xv, 43, 55, 71–73, 82–84, 210. *See also* Appearance bias; Employment discrimination; Stigma and shame
Doctors' treatment of heavier patients, 55, 58
Dress and grooming codes, 77, 78, 80, 82. *See also* Appearance bias
Drugs, illicit use
  decriminalization reflecting social views, 51–52
  historical views of, 51
  legal intervention, 17–18, 27
  stigma and, 56–57
  war on drugs, effectiveness of, 18, 28
Drugs, prescription, 103, 106–108

Earning power of women and weight issues, 55, 75, 86
"Eatertainment," 123
Eating disorders, 47, 91
Educational campaigns
  active lifestyles, 118–119, 182
  alcohol, 52
  effectiveness of, 144, 202
  nutrition, 105, 118–119, 123–126, 202
  tobacco, 124
Effectiveness of regulation, 6–10
  causation issues, 9
  compliance with law, 7–8. *See also* Legal intervention
  Internet challenges, 10. *See also* Internet
  normativity. *See* Normativity
  unintended consequences, 9–10. *See also* Unintended consequences
Electronic Benefit Transfer (EBT), 167
Employment discrimination, 70, 75, 78–81, 94
Endocrine disrupting chemicals (EDCs), 37, 41, 98–99, 210
England
  advertising aimed at children, 137
  caloric labeling, 126
  cosmetic interventions, 75–76
  gambling in, 50–51
  removal of obese children from home, 92–93
  traffic light system for foods' nutritional content, 129
  view of obesity, 53

Environment and obesity, 38–39, 63–69, 180. *See also* Built environment
Ethnicity and obesity, 38
European Union (EU)
  alcohol taxes, 151
  obesity rate, 164
  Value Added Tax (VAT), 154
  video depiction of obese, 53
Excessive appetites, 120–121, 123, 148
Excise taxes, 147–148, 152, 154–155, 158. *See also* Taxes
Exercise. *See* Physical activity
Explanations of causes of weight gain, 35–41

False advertising, 132
Farm Bill, 166, 167, 175
Farm subsidies. *See* Subsidies
Farmers as anti-obesity partners, 166
Farrell, A., 43
Fat Politics (Oliver), 43
Fat Rights (Kirkland), 43, 61, 68, 90
"Fat rights," 73, 87
Fat Seltzer Reduce, 108
Fat Shame (Farrell), 43
Fat taxes. *See* Taxes
FDA. *See* Food and Drug Administration
Federal Communications Commission (FCC), 143
Federal Trade Commission (FTC), 108, 132, 135, 138, 143
Feminists, 76, 83, 91
Fen-phen, 107
Finland, advertising aimed at children, 137
Fiscal interventions, xvii, xix–xx, 146–176
  junk food and beverage taxes, 152–160, 176
  overview, 146–147
  subsidies, xix–xx, 160–176. *See also* Subsidies
  sugar-sweetened beverages, 156–160. *See also* Sugar-sweetened beverages (SSBs)
  taxes, xix, 135–136, 147–151. *See also* Taxes
Fitness, xv, 178. *See also* Physical activity
Flegal, K., 47
Florida ban on nutrition requirements for meals sold with toys, 136
Food and drink
  advertising. *See* Marketing
  calories disclosure. *See* Calories
  as causes of obesity, 38–39
  children and. *See* Children
  expansion and codification of healthier food and drink programs, 166–167
  sugar-sweetened beverages. *See* Sugar-sweetened beverages (SSBs)

Food and drink industry
  criticism of, 64, 67–68, 122–123
  Internet advertising by, xix, 142–143
  labeling for calories and nutrition, xviii, 123–130
  litigation against, causation issues, 115
  lobbying and lawsuits, xvi, 64, 164
  marketing and advertising by. *See* Marketing
  obesity and, 34
  opposition to government intervention, xvi, 63, 64
  regulation of, 91
  self-regulation. *See* Self-regulation
Food and Drug Administration (FDA). *See also* Drugs, prescription
  bariatric procedures, 110
  food policy, 165
Food and Water Watch, 164, 165
Food Politics (Nestle), 38, 68, 122
Food pyramid, 125
Food security, 167–168, 210
Food stamps. *See also* SNAP (Supplementary Nutrition Assistance Program)
  purchase of sugar-sweetened beverages with, 158, 171–173
Ford, Richard, 55
For the Public's Health. See Institute of Medicine (IOM) reports
Fowler, J., 39
Framingham Heart Study, 39
France
  obesity rate, 164
  warnings in food advertising, 118
Free speech, 117, 138
French language television. *See* Quebec regulation on advertising to children
Friedman, Lawrence, 73
Front of package (FOP) labeling, xviii, 119, 128–130
Fruit drinks. *See* Sugar-sweetened beverages (SSBs)
Fruit Loops, 114
FTC. *See* Federal Trade Commission

Gambling
  English views on, 50–51
  Internet and, 17, 142
  legal interventions, 15–16
  litigation against casinos, 114
  partial success in curtailing problem gambling, 18
  precautionary principle, 103
  recreational vs. problem gamblers, 52
Gastric banding, 110
Gastric bypass surgery, 110

Gastric imbrications, 110
Genes as cause of obesity, 36–37, 195
Georgia billboard campaign on child obesity, 31, 32, 56, 57, 69
Glanz, K., 197
Global Commission on Drug Policy, 18
Grefe, Lyn, 70
Grooming. *See* Appearance bias; Dress and grooming codes
Guthman, J., 37, 43, 163, 198, 210
Guttmacher, Alan, 56

Habitual Inebriates Act (England), 13
Hakim, Catherine, 76–77, 83, 209
Haltom, W., 115
Hamermesh, D., 79, 81, 84–85, 94, 211
Happy Meals (McDonald's), 135–136
Health
  illnesses associated with excess weight, xiv–xv, 12, 37, 42, 47
  improved health as goal, xxi
  obesity issues for, 42, 46–47
  training on active lifestyles and, 182
Health at Every Size (HAES), 44, 61–63, 68, 101
Health equity, xxi, 209–211, 213
Health Impact Assessment (HIA), 11
"Healthism," 68–69
Healthy Food Financing Initiative, 167
Healthy Initiatives Pilot (HIP), 174–175
Healthy lifestyle choices, xiv–xv, 91, 99. *See also* Nutrition; Physical activity
  costs of, 163
  expansion and codification of healthier food and drink programs, 166–167
  subsidies to promote, 152, 164–176
  use of tax revenues to encourage, 152
Healthy Living Vouchers (HLVs), 59, 66, 67, 201–204
Heart disease, 42
Helmet laws, 32–33
Heyman, G., 121
High-fructose corn syrup (HFCS), 161, 162–163
Highway Safety Act (1966), 32
Himalayan Diet Breakthrough, 108
Hirsch, Dr. Jules, 108
Honey Money (Hakim), 76
Hooters Restaurant, 77–78
Hospitalization costs of overweight children, 43
Human rights law, 71–73, 80, 87, 93–94, 100. *See also* Discrimination
Humiliation. *See* Stigma and shame
Hunger-obesity paradox, 167–168, 210

Index

Idiosyncrasies, 24
Individual responsibility, 9, 64, 66, 118, 202
Inner city neighborhoods, 174, 184. *See also* Poverty and the poor
Institute of Medicine (IOM) reports
   on childcare providers and activities, 190–191
   Food Marketing to Children and Youth, 126, 133
   on FOPs, 128–130, 144
   on incentives, 174
   Local Government Actions to Prevent Childhood Obesity, 198, 209
   Preventing Childhood Obesity, 104, 195, 212
   For the Public's Health, 6, 10–12, 65, 103–104, 213
   Weight of the Nation, 125, 144–145, 167, 172
Insurance premiums and active lifestyle, 182
Interagency Working Group on Food Marketed to Children, 135
Internet
   gambling and, 17, 142
   marketing via, xix, 10, 119, 132, 140–144, 213
   YouTube videos mocking fat people, 54
Interventions, 97–116
   bariatric surgery, 109–112
   drugs, 106–108
   evidentiary basis for, 102–105
   goals of, 98–100, 207
   ineffectiveness of, 202
   litigation, 112–116, 136, 183
   overview, 97–98
   perspectives on assessment, 101–102
   precautionary principle, 103–104
   presumptions about, 60–61
   types of, xvii, 3–4
   weight loss-diet industry, 108–109

Japan
   consumer subsidies, 163–164
   regulation of weight, 54
Jazzercise, 79, 89
Jenny Craig, 109, 172
Journal of the American Medical Association, 93
Junk foods, 38, 118, 119, 122
   SNAP recipients and ban on, 169–171
   taxes, 152–160, 176

Kennedy-Nixon debate, 74
Kessler, D., 22
King Corn (film), 161
Kirkland, Anna, 43, 45, 61, 67, 68, 71, 81, 88–89, 90–91, 94, 211, 212

Korea, consumer subsidies, 163–164
Kristof, N., 37

Labeling for calories and nutrition, xviii, 123–131
   educating about nutrition, 105, 123–126
   effectiveness of, 144
   front of package labeling, xviii, 119, 128–130
   menus, caloric disclosure on, 126–128, 131
Lauder, Estee, 75
Legal intervention
   alcohol use. *See* Alcohol
   drug use, 17–18, 27
   gambling, 15–16
   harm caused by, 18–19
   incidence of excess and, 18
   obesity, 5, 10–12, 63–69, 211
   tobacco use, 14–15, 27
"Let's Move" campaign, 179
"License to do," 148. *See also* Taxes
Lifestyles. *See* Physical activity; Sedentary lifestyles
Lincoln University, 54
Litigation, 112–116, 136, 183
Lobbying, 64, 164
"Lookism," 76–77
Luciani, P., 58–59, 66, 67, 201–204

Maggie Goes on a Diet, 109
Marin County, California Safe Routes to Schools program, 197
Marketing
   to children, 131–144. *See also* Children
   on Internet, xix, 10, 119, 132, 140–144
   interventions, xvii–xviii, 117
   misleading advertising, 92, 114, 182
   new governance of, xviii–xix
   power of advertising, 117, 119–123
   truth in calories on menus and package labeling. *See* Labeling for calories and nutrition
McCann, M., 115
McDonald's, 135–136
McIntosh, W., 113–114
Mello, M., 134
Mental health issues, 40, 42, 179
Menu disclosure of calories, 126–128, 131
Metabolism as cause of obesity, 37
Miasma, 185
Michigan
   ban on physical characteristics discrimination, 84
   school bus driver applicant in, 88–89
Milk, substitution effects and, 155

Minnesota proposal to restrict use of welfare benefits for food purchases, 172
Misleading advertising. *See* Marketing
Mlodinow, L., 75
Monetary incentives. *See also* Fiscal interventions; Subsidies; Taxes
  to limit consumption, 57
  for weight loss industry, 34
Moral panics, 50–51, 90
Motorcycle helmet laws, 32–33
Mt. Sinai Medical Centre, 161
Municipal governments and built environment, 198–200

National Association for Sport and Physical Education (NASPE), 192
National Cancer Institute, 47
National Institutes of Health (NIH, U.S.), 45, 48, 165, 166
National School Lunch and Breakfast Programs, 166
National Weight Control Registry, 48–49
Nestle, Marion, 38, 64, 65, 68, 122–123, 131
Netherlands, built environment, 186
New governance
  critics of, 26–27
  delegation of rulemaking and rule enforcement, 20
  difference from command and control, 20–21, 133
  incentives and, 173
  marketing and, xviii–xix
  normativity and, 21–28. *See also* Normativity
  as paradigm shift, 20–21
  regulating consumption, 4, 19–28
  vouchers as tool of, 200–201
Newspaper reporting on litigation against fast-food industry, 115
New urbanism, 184
New York City
  ban on food stamp use to purchase sugar-sweetened beverages, 158, 171–172
  bike lanes, 200
  Central Park, 185
  menu disclosure of calories, 126–127
  soda serving size restrictions, 172–173
New Yorkers for Beverage Choices, 173
New York State survey on soda tax, 157
New York Times
  ad by Mt. Sinai Medical Centre doctors (2010), 161
  survey on Bloomberg initiative to limit soda serving size (2012), 173

New Zealand
  obesity rate, 164
  welfare benefits and incentives to purchase healthy food, 170
No Child Left Behind Act (NCLB), 193
Normativity, xvii, 4–5, 7, 21–28, 100
  changing values and, 56
  choice architects and, 24–26
  defined, 21
  educational campaigns and, 123
  effectiveness of, 28, 178
  shaping behavior and, 22–23, 51, 100, 213–214
  smoking rates and, 100
  taxes and, 148
  urban planning for physical activity and, 186–187
Norm cascades, 173, 176
Norway, advertising aimed at children, 137
Nudge (Thaler & Sunstein), 24–25, 26
"Nudge," 23, 24–25, 33–34, 127–128, 173, 177, 183
Nutrition
  as goal of healthy eating, 101–102
  labeling for. *See* Labeling for calories and nutrition
  nutritious eating, what constitutes, 122
  SNAP and, 169–171
  weight loss programs and, 109
Nutrition fact panels (NFPs), 129

Obama, Michelle, 165, 179
Obesity
  built environment and. *See* Built environment
  chemicals and, 37–38, 41
  compared to other consumption problems, 57. *See also* Alcohol; Drugs, illicit use; Tobacco
  consequences of, 42–43
  costs to society, 42–43
  defined, xiii
  depression and, 40, 42
  environment and, 38–39, 180
  farmers as anti-obesity partners, 166
  "fat" vs. "obese," xiii, 59
  genes, metabolism, and antibiotics and, 36–37, 195
  government intervention. *See* Legal intervention
  health problems of, 34, 42, 46–47
  hunger-obesity paradox, 210
  illnesses associated with, xiv–xv, 12, 37, 42, 47
  media stories about, xiii–xiv

Index 221

overview of issues, 31–32
physical aspects of, 42
prevention. *See* Prevention of obesity
as problem, 32–35
psychological aspects of, 42
as public health issue, 35–43
race and ethnicity and, 38
rates of, 36, 44–46
social contagion and, 39
socioeconomic status and, 41.
  See also Poverty and the poor
stigma and shame, 49–58.
  See also Stigma and shame
subsidies and, 161–171
technology and, 40
weight loss. *See* Weight loss
Obesogens, 37, 41, 67, 93, 161
Ohio, removal of obese children from home, 92–93
Oliver, E., 43, 45
Olmsted, Fredrick Law, 185
Omnivore's Dilemma (Pollan), 161
"One size fits all" slogan, xiv
Ontario vs. Quebec marketing, 139–140
Opium and "the yellow peril," 51
Ordinances banning physical characteristics discrimination, 84–85
Orford, J., 120
Overindulgence, 52

Panics, 50–51, 90
PAPRN (Physical Activity Policy Research Network), 187
Parents
  early child development and, 189–190
  as role models, 183
Parker-Pope, Tara, 31, 32, 48, 49
Paternalism, 151
Patient Protection and Affordable Care Act, 26, 126
Peer influence on adolescent levels of physical activity, 181
Pepsi, 65
Permit but Discourage: Regulating Excessive Consumption (Bogart), 3
Permit but discourage principle, 4, 13–19, 27, 51, 146, 176
Personal choice. *See* Choice; Individual responsibility
Personal Responsibility in Food Consumption Act (proposed), 112
Pharmaceutical companies, xiv, 106–108
Phentermine, 107
Physical activity, xx, 178–207
  benefits of, 99, 178–79

Canadian Children's Fitness Tax Credit (CFTC), xx, 204–207
children, 180, 188–207
  parents' role in early child development, 189–190
  professional childcare providers, 188, 190–191
  promotion of active lifestyles, 64, 152, 182–183
  school-age kids, xx, 192–200
  sedentary lifestyles, 40, 46, 57, 64, 90, 119, 179–181
Physical Activity Guidelines for Americans, 180
Physical health. *See* Health
Planned obsolescence, 121
Plausible rival hypotheses, 9
Plural equality, 73
Political candidates' appearance, 74–75
Pollan, Michael, 161
Pondimin, 107
Potter, D., 120
Poverty and the poor, 41–42, 67
  health equity and, 209–211
  subsidies to improve diet of the poor, 167–177, 177
  taxes and, 148, 152
Precautionary principle, 103–104
Prevention of obesity, 61, 99, 101, 102, 177, 184
Privileged status of the thin, 55, 68
Productivity costs, 42
Professional childcare providers, 188, 190–192
Prohibition (alcohol), 4, 13–14
Provine, D., 17
Psychological aspects. *See* Mental health issues
Public assistance for low-income persons. *See* SNAP (Supplementary Nutrition Assistance Program); Women, Infants, and Children Supplemental Nutrition Program (WIC)
Public health issue, obesity as, 35–43
  educational campaigns and, 125
  explanations of causes of weight gain, 35–41
  misdirected efforts associated with, 66, 202, 203–204
  weight loss as solution, 98
Public opinion. *See also* Normativity
  on gambling, 16
  on government size, 20
  panic and negative views, 50–52
  presumptions about interventions, 60–61
  urban planning for physical activity and, 186–187
Public resources to promote health, xv, 208, 212, 214. *See also* Subsidies; Taxes

Qsymia (Qnexa), 107–108
Quebec regulation on advertising to children, xix, xx, 27, 106, 119, 137–138
  impact of ban, 143–144

Race
  appearance bias and, 78
  obesity and, 38, 67
Racism and drug enforcement, 17, 18, 51
Ready-to-drink spirit-based alcoholic beverages (RTDs), 150
Recreational drugs. *See* Drugs, illicit use
Redux (drug), 107
Regulating consumption, 3–28
  consumption vs. law, 13–19
  effectiveness of regulation, 6–10
  Internet's effect on, 17
  legal regulation, 5, 10–12
  lessons from alcohol prohibition. *See* Alcohol
  lessons from drug abuse. *See* Drugs, illicit use
  lessons from gambling. *See* Gambling
  lessons from tobacco. *See* Tobacco
  new governance, 4, 19–28. *See also* New governance
  overview, 3–5
  regulatory mix, xv–xvi, xvii, 5–6, 13, 16, 28, 105, 116, 159, 207, 213
  shaping behavior, 4, 5–6, 12, 19–28
Religious practices and appearance bias, 78
Research agenda, 166
Rhode, Deborah, 43, 61, 74–77, 82–84, 85–87, 91, 92, 94, 108, 109, 211
Rice Crispies, 114
Rival hypotheses, 9

Saguy, A., 43
Salamon, L., 20
Sales taxes, 157–158. *See also* Taxes
Sallis, J., 197
San Francisco ordinance on nutrition required for meals sold with toys, 136
Santa Clara ordinance on nutrition required for meals sold with toys, 136
Santa Cruz ban on physical characteristics discrimination, 84
Schools
  Fruit and Vegetable Program, 167
  National School Lunch and Breakfast Programs, 166
  No Child Left Behind Act (NCLB), 193
  physical activity and, xx, 188–189, 192–200
  removal of soft drink vending machines and transfat foods, 114
  reporting on students' BMI, xx, 194–197
  SNAP-Ed program, 167
  vouchers, 201, 202
School Wellness Policies (SWPs), 193
Sedentary lifestyles, 40, 46, 57, 64, 179–181
Seeman, N., 58–59, 66, 67, 201–204
Self-acceptance, 61, 91
Self-control, lack of, 54
Self-regulation, 27, 91, 117, 133–135, 143
Self-selection, 187
Sexualizing women in order to sell products, services, etc., 77–78
Sexual orientation and school dress requirements, 78, 80
Siluette Patch, 108
Sleeve gastrectomy, 110
Small food-stores in underserved areas, 174
"Smart Choices" food program, 114
Smart Growth America, 186
Smart growth/new urbanism, 184
Smoking. *See* Tobacco
SNAP (Supplementary Nutrition Assistance Program), xx, 147, 160, 166–167, 169–171, 174–176, 211
SNAP-Ed program, 167
Social contagion, 39
Societal messages on obesity, xiv, 59–61
Society for the Study of Inebriety, 13
Socioeconomic status, 41
Soda. *See* Sugar-sweetened beverages (SSBs)
Sotomayer, Sonia, 79, 80
South Carolina, removal of obese children from home, 92–93
South Korea, consumer subsidies, 163–164
Speck, J., 187
Sport drinks. *See* Sugar-sweetened beverages (SSBs)
Statistics on weight, 36, 44–46, 164. *See also* Body Mass Index (BMI)
Status quo bias, 24
Stereotypes of fat people, 58. *See also* Stigma and shame
Stigma and shame, 49–63
  bullying, 55
  cultural obsession with weight, 53–58
  Health at Every Size (HAES) movement, 44, 61–63
  panics, good norms, and overindulgence, 50–52
  responses to, 43–44, 58–63
  social attitudes as problem, 59–61, 201–202, 210
  weight loss as solution to, 58–59, 202
Story, M., 192, 194, 195, 207
Stout, L., 23–24

Index

Subsidies, xix–xx, 105, 146, 160–176
    agricultural policy and, 152, 161–167, 176–177
    government support programs and targeted subsidies, 167–176
    to improve diet of the poor, 167–171, 177
    obesity and, 161–164, 202
    pairing with taxation, 155–156, 159
    promotion pilots, 160, 168–175
    retooling needed, 177
    soda bans, 171–173
Substitution effects, 155
Suburban sprawl, 185
Sugar-sweetened beverages (SSBs), 146, 153, 156–160, 171–173
Suicide, 40, 112
Sunstein, C., 23, 24–25, 26–27, 33
Super Size Me (documentary film), 135
Sweden, advertising aimed at children, 137
Symbolism of excise taxes, 155

Taxes
    alcohol, 148, 150–151
    Canadian Children's Fitness Tax Credit (CFTC), xx, 204–207
    cigarettes, 15, 149–150
    deduction not allowed for advertising aimed at children, 135–136
    deductions to encourage physical activity, 182
    effectiveness of, 154–156
    as fiscal interventions, xix, 146, 147–151
    junk foods and beverages, 152–160, 176
    pairing with subsidies, 155–156, 159–160
    sugar-sweetened beverages (SSBs), 156–160
    use of tax revenues to subsidize healthy food and drinks and encourage physical activity, 152
Teacher performance, 56
Technology, 40, 180–181
Television
    advertising on. *See* Children; Marketing
    shows on obesity and weight loss, 54
    viewing levels of children, 180–181, 183
Texas hospital's refusal to hire person with BMI over 35, 70, 94
Thaler, R., 23, 24–25, 33
Thinness and good health, 47
Tobacco
    advertising, regulation of, 117–118, 149
    age-related regulation of, 27
    decline in users, 15, 18, 100, 124
    harm from efforts to regulate, 18
    historic changes in attitudes toward, 51, 52
    legal intervention, 14–15, 27
    litigation against cigarette manufacturers, 112, 113
    regulatory mix, 15, 149
    stigma and, 56
    taxes, 15, 149–150
Tort litigation, 113
Toys, 135–136
Transportation Department, U.S., 174

Undue hardship, 86, 88, 89
Unequal under Law: Race in the War on Drugs (Provine), 17
Unintended consequences, 9–10, 15, 149, 151, 185
Urbana, Illinois, ban on physical characteristics discrimination, 84
U.S. Chamber of Commerce, 135
U.S. Dieting Guidelines, 45
USDA. *See* Agriculture Department, U.S.

Veblen, T., 119
Vending machines
    caloric content disclosures, 126
    removal of soft drink vending machines from schools, 114
Vouchers
    Healthy Living Vouchers (HLVs), 59, 66, 67, 201–204
    as new governance tool, 200–201
    school vouchers, 201, 202

Waistline as meaningful indicator, 44–45
Wallinga, D., 165, 167
Wansink, B., 22, 125
Warnings
    about alcohol consumption, 118
    about nonnutritious eating and drinking, 118
    about smoking, 149
Weighing In (Guthman), 43
Weight gain, explanations of causes of, 35–41
Weight loss
    campaigns aimed at, drawbacks of, 99, 204
    healthy lifestyle more important than, 91
    regaining after, 48–49, 112
    as solution to stigma, 58–59, 202
    SSB campaigns unlikely to result in, 176
Weight loss industry, xiv
    expenditures on, 42–43
    interventions, 108–109
    monetary incentives for, 34, 60
Weight Watchers, 109, 172–173
Welfare programs. *See* SNAP (Supplementary Nutrition Assistance Program); Women, Infants, and Children Supplemental Nutrition Program (WIC)

What's Wrong with Fat? (Saguy), 43
White House Conference on Food, Nutrition, and Health (1969), 165
White House Task Force on Childhood Obesity, 37, 41, 101, 195, 196, 210
Women
  activism on behalf of appearance issues, 91
  appearance and attractiveness, 75–76
  "Borgata Babes" and employment requirements, 78
  as broadcasters, 83–84
  depression linked to weight issues, 40
  earning power and weight issues, 55, 75, 86
  gastric bypass surgery, 111
  sexualizing in order to sell products, services, etc., 77–78
Women, Infants, and Children Supplemental Nutrition Program (WIC), 166–167, 169, 170
World Health Organization (WHO), 36, 45

XXL: Obesity and the Limits of Shame (Seeman & Luciani), 58–59

YouTube videos mocking fat people, 54

Printed in the USA/Agawam, MA
January 20, 2014